Nakón-i'a wo!
Beginning Nakoda

ARMAND McARTHUR & WILMA KENNEDY | COMPILED AND EDITED BY **VINCENT COLLETTE**

© 2019 Pheasant Rump Nakoda Nation and Vincent Collette

All rights reserved. No part of this work covered by the copyrights hereon may be reproduced or used in any form or by any means — graphic, electronic, or mechanical — without the prior written permission of the publisher. Any request for photocopying, recording, taping or placement in information storage and retrieval systems of any sort shall be directed in writing to Access Copyright.

COVER AND TEXT DESIGN: Duncan Campbell, University of Regina Press
INTERIOR LAYOUT: John van der Woude, JVDW Designs
PROOFREADER: Donna Grant
COVER ART: "Gentle Breeze" by Daryl Growing Thunder

Library and Archives Canada Cataloguing in Publication

Title: Nakón-i'a wo! = Beginning Nakoda / Armand McArthur & Wilma Kennedy ; compiled and edited by Vincent Collette.
Other titles: Beginning Nakoda
Names: McArthur, Armand, author. | Kennedy, Wilma, author. | Collette, Vincent, 1976- editor.
Description: Includes bibliographical references and index.
Identifiers: Canadiana (print) 20190142073 | Canadiana (ebook) 20190142324 | ISBN 9780889776777 (hardcover) | ISBN 9780889776623 (coil bound) | ISBN 9780889776630 (PDF) | ISBN 9780889776647 (HTML)
Subjects: LCSH: Assiniboine dialect—Study and teaching—Foreign speakers. | LCSH: Assiniboine dialect—Textbooks for foreign speakers—English. | LCSH: Assiniboine dialect—Vocabulary.
Classification: LCC PM1024.Z9 A876 2019 | DDC 497/.52—dc23

We acknowledge the support of the Canada Council for the Arts for our publishing program. We acknowledge the financial support of the Government of Canada. / Nous reconnaissons l'appui financier du gouvernement du Canada. This publication was made possible through Creative Saskatchewan's Book Publishing Production Grant Program.

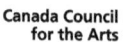   

We dedicate this book to all Nakoda language learners and young mothers who will teach the language to future generations.

CONTENTS

Introduction 1

CHAPTER 1
Objectives, Dialogues, and Vocabulary 3
Thanking, Farewell, and Self-Introduction 5
Nakoda Alphabet and Sound System 5
Syllables and Accent 7
Parts of Speech 8
Note on Spelling 11
Chapter 1 Exercises 12

CHAPTER 2
Objectives, Dialogues, and Vocabulary 13
Word Order in Nakoda 15
Demonstratives 16
Class 1: Regular Stem Verbs 17
Dual *ų-* "we two" 20
Sounds: Uvulars *ǧ* and *ȟ* 20
Chapter 2 Exercises 21

CHAPTER 3
Objectives, Dialogues, and Vocabulary 24
Interrogative Sentences 26
Imperative Particles *wo* and *bo* 27
Class 2: Y-Stem Verbs 28
Potential/Future Marker *-kta* 30
Sounds: Glottal Stop ['] 31
Chapter 3 Exercises 31

CHAPTER 4
Objectives, Dialogues, and Vocabulary 34
Cardinal Numbers 36
Ordinal Numbers 38
Mathematical Operations 38
Age and Time 39
Distance and Height 40
Chapter 4 Exercises 42

CHAPTER 5
Objectives, Dialogues, and Vocabulary 45
Kinship Nouns 47
Reference to Time: Past, Present,
    and Future/Potential 48
Class 3: Nasal Conjugation Verbs
    (or N-Conjugation) 49
Plural of Subjects 51
Chapter 5 Exercises 54

CHAPTER 6
Objectives, Dialogues, and Vocabulary 57
Negation 59
Active and Stative Verbs 59
Stative Verbs: Colours 63
How to Say "To Be" in Nakoda 64
Sounds: Nasal Spread 66
Chapter 6 Exercises 67

CHAPTER 7

Objectives, Dialogues, and Vocabulary   70
Declarative Male Enclitic *no*   72
"Let's" Constructions   72
Conjunction Markers: *įš* "and, also, him/her/it/they too"; *hį́kna* "and"; *eštá* "or"   73
Spatial Adverbs and Postpositions   74
Chapter 7 Exercises   76

CHAPTER 8

Objectives, Dialogues, and Vocabulary   79
Asking Questions with *Where*, *When*, and *Who*   81
Verbs of Departing, Going, and Arriving   82
Active Verbs: Intransitive and Transitive   84
Inflections of Transitive Verbs (Third Person Object)   85
Sounds: Ejective Consonants   88
Chapter 8 Exercises   89

CHAPTER 9

Objectives, Dialogues, and Vocabulary   91
More Verbs Expressing States and Bodily Functions   93
Ownership and Possession   94
Part/Whole Relations   98
Noun Quantifiers *edáhą* "some" and *dóna* "some, many"   99
Chapter 9 Exercises   99

CHAPTER 10

Objectives, Dialogues, and Vocabulary   102
Complex Noun Formation   104
Noun Incorporation   106
Independent Pronouns for Focus and Contrast   107
Intensifiers *-ȟ* and *-ȟtįyą*   108
Chapter 10 Exercises   109

CHAPTER 11

Objectives, Dialogues, and Vocabulary   112
Adverbs of Time/Space and Manner   115
Formation of Irregular Verbs   117
Inflections of Transitive Verbs (Third Person Subject)   119
Chapter 11 Exercises   123

CHAPTER 12

Objectives, Dialogues, and Vocabulary   126
Tribes and Tribal Affiliation   128
Transitive Verb Inflections: *-ci-* "I on You" and *-maya-* "You on Me"   129
Aspectual Markers   131
Chapter 12 Exercises   133

CHAPTER 13

Objectives, Dialogues, and Vocabulary   136
Linkers: *cén, nécen, žécen, ecén*   139
Complex Sentences with the Conditionals *štén* "if, when" and *hą́da(hą)* "whenever"   141
Inflections of Transitive Verbs: *-wįca-* (Third Person Plural Object)   143
Chapter 13 Exercises   145

CHAPTER 14

Objectives, Dialogues, and Vocabulary   149
Gicí "with someone"; *óm* "with them"   152
Reciprocal *-gici-/-ci-* "action done to one another"   152
Modality Particles   154
Specific, Unspecific Objects   155
Interjections   156
Chapter 14 Exercises   157

CHAPTER 15

Objectives and Dialogues   160
Instrumentals   161
Indefinite Prefix *wa-*   163
Locatives *a-, o-, į-*   164
Nominalizing Ablaut and Zero
    Nominalization   167
Chapter 15 Exercises   170

CHAPTER 16

Objectives, Dialogues, and Vocabulary   173
Reduplication   175
Compounding   176
Causatives *-ya* and *-kiya*   178
Aspectual Auxiliary Verbs   181
Modality Verbs   182
Chapter 16 Exercises   185

CHAPTER 17

Objectives, Dialogues, and Vocabulary   189
Reflexive *-ic'i-/-ik-* "to act upon oneself"   190
Possessive *-gi-/-k-* "to act on one's own"   192
Dative *-gi-* "to act to, for, of somebody else"   194
Benefactive *-giji-* "to act for the benefit
    of somebody else"   196
Chapter 17 Exercises   199

CHAPTER 18

Objectives   203
Dialectal Differences   203
Chapter 18 Exercises   204
Text 1. *Né wótijağa gáğa mitúgaši*   204
Text 2. *Wašpáyąbi*   206
Text 3. *Mniwája agásampadahą ųhíbi-c'ehą*   208
Text 4. *Įkusana hįk šųkcúk'ana*   210
Text 5. *Wacégiyabi*   214

References   215

APPENDICES

Appendix 1: Kinship Table   217
Appendix 2: Glossary of Grammatical Terms   220
Appendix 3: Verb Classes   222

Nakoda/English Lexicon   225

INTRODUCTION

The Nakoda language (Nakón-i'abi, also formerly known as Assiniboine) is a gift of the Creator and is at the very core of Nakoda cultural identity. Nakoda is, through prayers and songs, the means by which important cultural values and spiritual knowledge are transmitted from generation to generation. Even though it was spoken for hundreds of years, Nakoda is now seriously endangered due to the trauma of residential schools and intermarriage with non-Nakoda, which halted its transmission in the 1950s to '70s. Consequently, only a handful of elderly speakers living in Saskatchewan and Montana know the language today, and most have nobody to talk with since the remaining speakers are relatively isolated from one another.

Despite the odds, many middle-aged Nakoda—some of whom are semi-fluent speakers or rememberers—strongly feel the need to learn and pass down the Nakoda language to their children and grandchildren but lack concrete teaching/learning tools to do so. One can always rely on published or unpublished works of varying quality, apps or verb books, but this material does not touch upon word and sentence formation, two crucial aspects for meaningful communication. What is needed, then, is a user-friendly book that explains word-formation processes and how to use them in sentences. The main goal of *Nakón-i'a wo! Beginning Nakoda* is to compensate for this lack of educational material and to breathe life into a language that will otherwise soon disappear.

The main informants for this work were Elders Armand McArthur, Wilma Kennedy, and Pete Bigstone. During the first part of the fieldwork, Dr. Collette worked with Armand McArthur (Pheasant Rump First Nation, Saskatchewan) and Pete Bigstone (Ocean Man First Nation, Saskatchewan) to collect the basic vocabulary and sentence structures; then, in the second part of the fieldwork, extensive lexical and grammatical documentation was undertaken with Elder Wilma Kennedy, who is one of the last fully fluent speakers in Carry The Kettle First Nation (Saskatchewan). We also had the opportunity to access Elder Leona Kroeskamp's Nakoda teaching material. Mrs. Kroeskamp taught Nakoda at First Nations University for many years, and we have reproduced, with her permission, some of her material in this book. We gratefully acknowledge here both her lifelong teaching and documenting efforts as well as her desire to pass on the language to future generations.

Finally, we have benefitted from the input of some of the Nakoda students who took NAK-100 and NAK-101 Conversational Nakoda I and II during the 2017–2018 school year at First Nation's University of Canada.

Even though it is modest in size and evidently incomplete, *Nakón-i'a wo! Beginning Nakoda* is nevertheless a first step in documenting and, hopefully, revitalizing Nakoda language and culture for future generations.

Nakón-i'abi oǧúǧa!
Wake up the Nakoda language!

Vincent Collette and
Elder Armand McArthur
Regina, April 5, 2018

CHAPTER 1

Objectives

VOCABULARY

- Basic kinship nouns and greetings
- Weather verbs

ALPHABET AND SOUNDS

- Nakoda alphabet and sound system
- Syllables and accent
- Parts of speech
- Note on spelling

Dialogues

1. Háu, Alicia emágiyabi. Dóken eníjiyabi?   *Hello, my name is Alicia. What is your name?*
   Carlos emágiyabi.   *My name is Carlos.*

2. Hą micįkši, tągán osní he?   *Hello, my son, is it cold outside?*
   Hą adé, tągán wáhįhą.   *Yes, father, it is snowing outside.*

3. Hą iná, mağážu he?   *Hello, mother, is it raining?*
   Hą micų́kši, mağážu.   *Yes, my daughter, it is raining.*

4. Hą adé, mağážu he?   *Hello, father, is it raining?*
   Hiyá, waná tągán nína maštá.   *No, now it is very hot outside.*

5. Hą adé, ąba né maštá he?
   Hiyá micį́kši, waná tadéyąba.

   Hello, father, is it a hot day today?
   No, my son, now it is a very windy day.

6. Adé, pinámayaya. Aké wącímnagįkta.
   Hą micų́kši, aké wącímnagįkte no!
   Wašté!

   Father, thank you. I will see you again.
   Yes, my daughter, I will see you again!
   Good!

Vocabulary

KINSHIP NOUNS

Adé	*Father!*	micį́kši	*my son*
Iná	*Mother!*	micų́kši	*my daughter*

GREETINGS, INTERJECTIONS

ejíya ~ egíya	*she/he calls him/her*	he	*question*
hą	*yes, hello*	hiyá	*no*
háu	*hello*	pinámayaya	*I thank you*[*]

WEATHER VERBS

ą́ba wašté	*it is a nice day*	osní	*it is cold*
mağážu	*it rains*	tadéyąba	*it is a windy day*
maštá	*it is a hot day*	wáhįhą	*it snows*

ADVERBS, VERBS

ą́ba	*it is a day; day*	tągán	*outside*
ą́ba né ~ ąba nén	*today*	timáhen	*inside*
dóken	*how*	waná	*already, now*
nína	*very / a lot*	wašté	*it is good*

---

[*] Literally *pinámayaya* means "you please me," but it has been extended to mean "I thank you," thus "you pleased me, and I am grateful for it."

Thanking, Farewell, and Self-Introduction

To introduce oneself, the verb *emą́giyabi* "they call me thus" is used (from *egíya* "she/he calls him/her"). The person markers *-mą-* "me," *-ni-* "you," and *-bi* "they" will be explained later. The first task here is to learn these expressions by heart and to practise your pronunciation of the Nakoda sounds.

Háu, dóken ya'ų́ (he)?	*Hello, how are you?*
Wašté!	*Good!*
Ą́ba wašté!	*It is a nice day!*
Hą́!	*Indeed!*
Peter emą́giyabi.	*I am called Peter.*
Rick eníjiyabi he?	*Are you called Rick?*
Hiyá, Jim emą́giyabi.	*No, I am called Jim.*

In Nakoda, thanking and farewell expressions are conveyed with the verbs *pinámayaya* "I thank you" and *wącímnaga* "I see you." The internal structure of these verbs will be dealt with later. For now, it is important that you learn the proper male and female versions of some basic expressions. Greetings and introductory sentences are geared for practical conversation, and this is why they are introduced in Chapter 1.

Pinámayaya!	*I thank you.* (female speaker)
Pinámayaye no!	*I thank you.* (male speaker)
Aké wącímnagįkta!	*I will see you again.* (female speaker)
Aké wącímnagįkte no!	*I will see you again.* (male speaker)
Hą́!	*Yes, alright!*

Nakoda Alphabet and Sound System

In these Nakoda language lessons the Fort Belknap spelling is used. Some of the sounds will require a lot of pronunciation practice since they do not occur in English. We have included the pronunciation of Nakoda sounds in the International Phonetic Alphabet (IPA). The task here is to imitate the Nakoda sounds produced by the instructor.

VOWELS

Nakoda Alphabet	English equivalent	Nakoda example	IPA
A a	at, hat	aké – again	[a]
Ą ą	man (nearest equivalent)	cą́ – wood	[ã]
E e	bet	nén – here	[ɛ] or [e]
I i	beat	nína – very	[i]
Į į	mink	mįknúš'aga - I am pregnant	[ĩ]
O o	open	ómna – he smells it	[o] or [ɔ]
U u	two	súda – it is hard	[u] or [ʊ]
Ų ų	noon	hų́gu – his/her mother	[ũ]

Nakoda has eight vowels: five orals and three nasals. When producing oral vowels *a*, *e*, *i*, *o*, and *u*, the airstream coming from the lungs goes directly through the mouth, as in AAAAAH. However, nasal vowels *ą*, *į*, and *ų* are produced by letting air escape through the nose and mouth at the same time. The closest English equivalent of nasal vowels occurs in the words *man*, *mink*, and *monk*. Since the oral vowel *i* is flanked with two nasal consonants *m* and *n*, they are slightly nasalized. Nasal vowels are indicated by a small hook underneath like: *ą*, *į*, and *ų*. The vowels *e* and *o* are never nasalized in Nakoda.

CONSONANTS

Nakoda Alphabet	English equivalent	Nakoda example	IPA
B b	bat, tab	basnóhą – she/he pushes it	used for [b] and [p]
C c	chill	cába – beaver	[tʃʰ]
C' c'	*not found in English	cic'ú – I give it to you	[tʃʔ]
D d	damp	dágu – what, thing	used for [t] and [d]
G g	gum	gúwa – Come!	used for [g] and [k]
Ǧ ǧ	*not found in English	ǧí – it is yellow	[ɣ]
H h	happy	hiyá – no	[h]
Ȟ ȟ	*not found in English	ȟóda – it is grey	[x]
J j	jam	júsina – it is small	[dʒ]
K k	keep	kuwá – he chases him	[kʰ]
K' k'	*not found in English	k'ú – he gives it to him	[kʔ]
M m	mine	mína – knife	[m]
N n	night	nųwą́ – she/he swims	[n]
P p	Peter	pahá – hair	[pʰ]

Nakoda Alphabet	English equivalent	Nakoda example	IPA
P' p'	*not found in English	cup'ó – *it is foggy*	[pʔ]
S s	sit	sihá – *foot*	[s]
Š š	shadow	šų́ga – *dog*	[ʃ]
T t	team	tanó – *meat*	[tʰ]
T' t'	*not found in English	t'á – *to die*	[tʔ]
W w	water	wá – *snow*	[w]
Y y	yes	yatką́ – *he drinks*	[j]
Z z	zipper	zizíbena – *thin cloth*	[z]
Ž ž	measure	ožúna – *it is full*	[ʒ]
'	button	wa'ówabi – *paper*	[ʔ]

Syllables and Accent

Words in English and Nakoda can be divided into syllables. Every syllable consists of one vowel (obligatory) and a preceding and/or following consonant (optional). Syllables are separated by a hyphen in the following English examples:

    no   as-pen   ca-li-ber   se-pa-ra-tion
    1   1 2   1 2 3   1 2 3 4

When a word has more than one syllable, one of them is produced with more force or amplitude, as in "**as**-pen." We call this syllable the "stressed" syllable. It is the one that carries the accent. In Nakoda, stress is indicated by a diacritic sign put on top, like *ú* as in *súda*, which is pronounced "**sou**-da." For English speakers learning Nakoda, it is difficult to guess which vowel will be stressed. A rule of thumb is that the vowel of the second syllable will carry the stress; however, there are some counterexamples.

SECOND SYLLABLE ACCENT

tok**á**na	*grey fox*	ško**š**k**ó**bena	*banana*
mat**ó**	*bear*	hąc**ó**gądu	*midnight*
hąg**é**	*half*	pah**á**	*hair*

FIRST SYLLABLE ACCENT

n**é**ža	*she/he urinates*	h**á**ba	*moccasin*
šk**ó**bena	*it is slightly crooked*	h**á**dahą	*when, whenever*
m**á**za	*iron*	šk**á**da	*she/he plays*

With words that consist of only one syllable, the vowel will automatically carry the stress. For the sake of consistency, the accents are written everywhere, even on monosyllabic words, to distinguish them from particles.

t**ó**	*it is blue, green*	t**á**	*moose, ruminant*
šk**ą́**	*she/he moves, feels thus*	**ú**	*she/he goes*

Finally, in English the position of the stress in a word can make a difference in meaning between two words, as in the case of the verb "per-**mit**" (she/he gives permission) versus the noun "**per**-mit" (official document granting someone with an authorization to do something). These two words have different stress patterns and mean different things. Nakoda, too, has meaningful stress, and this is why it is always indicated in the spelling with an accent (´). Here are a few examples:

tog**á**	*before, ahead of time; chief*	oh**ą́**	*she/he wears footwear; she/he cooks by boiling*
t**ó**ga	*enemy*	**ó**hą	*in the middle, in it*

Parts of Speech

Nakoda has eight types of words (or parts of speech): nouns, verbs, adverbs, demonstratives, pronouns, particles, postpositions, and interjections. It also has a fairly large series of enclitics.

NOUNS

Nouns describe a person, place, thing, or idea.

búza	*cat*
cąpásusuna	*pepper*
įhámnabi	*dream, vision*

VERBS

Verbs express an action, a state of being, a condition, an event, or a natural phenomenon.

kuwá	*she/he chases him/her/it*
yazą́	*she/he is sick*
osní	*it is cold weather*

Technically, Nakoda does not have a separate class of adjectives like English does (e.g., *nice, big, small*). To express the colour or the size of something, a stative verb is used.

sijá	*she/he/it is bad*
wasnóhya	*she/he is wise*
sába	*she/he/it is black*

ADVERBS

Adverbs modify a verb (e.g., arriving *late* or *early*) or indicate a location in time or space (e.g., *now, there*).

wanágaš	*long ago*
gakí	*over there, yonder*
nén	*here*
wakáya	*in a holy manner*

DEMONSTRATIVES

Demonstratives indicate the location and the distance of an entity in relation to the speaker's point of view (e.g., *this* man, *that* house *over there*).

né	*this*
žé	*that*
gá	*that over there*

PRONOUNS

Pronouns replace a noun (e.g., *Paul* is sick > *He* is sick; *The plant* is green > *It* is green); some pronouns are used to form interrogative sentences.

íš	*he, it, they too; also*
duwé	*who*
miyé	*myself*

PARTICLES

Particles are small words that are not inflected for tense or person. In Nakoda, particles express modality, commands, and interrogations.

jé	*always, habitually*
no	*declarative* (male speaker only)
wo	*command to single person* (male speaker only)
he	*question, interrogation*

INTERJECTIONS

Intejections are small words that indicate the mood, feeling or attitude of the speaker. Some of them constitute a sentence by themselves. In this book we have put an exclamation mark with most interjections.

há	*yes, hello*
Hį́į́!	*Oh my!* (women's expression of surprise)
Waktá!	*Beware!*

POSTPOSITIONS

In Nakoda, the postposition functions much like the English preposition, specifying a relationship between two words in a sentence (e.g., Paul is ***in*** the house, Paul is ***at*** the theatre). However, Nakoda's postpositions come *after* the head word; this is why they are called "postpositions" (*post-* "after") instead of "prepositions" (*pre-* "before") like in English. For example, *mitákona **gicí*** "**with** my friend" or *šų́gatąga **agą́n*** "**on** the horse."

sám	*over, beyond*
mahén	*inside*
agą́n	*on*
gicí	*with*

ENCLITICS

In Nakoda, enclitics are not full words but unaccentuated elements that "lean" at the end of the verb. They indicate mood, aspect, negation, or small size.

-kta	*potential/future*
-ga	*durative aspect*
-šį	*negation*
-na	*small size*

In the following lessons we follow the orthographic convention of attaching the enclitics to the verb. This eases the reading of Nakoda texts.

Note on Spelling

You can see by looking at the chart of consonants on pages 6 and 7 that there are no *f, l, r, th,* or *v* sounds in Nakoda. Nevertheless, Nakoda does have several consonants that are lacking in English. These sounds are represented by letters with extra signs (called diacritics) over or under the basic letters, such as ǧ, ȟ, ž and '. In the following table, the sounds between slashes /p, pʰ/, /t, tʰ/, /k, kʰ/ and /c, cʰ/ are the sounds internalized by Nakoda speakers, but in certain contexts (e.g., between two vowels V__V, or at the beginning of a word #__) they are spelled differently as < b, p >, < d, t >, < g, k >, and < c, j >.

Internalized sounds	Spelling	Position
/ą́**p**a/ day	ą́**b**a	V__V
/**p**ahá/ hill	**b**ahá	#__
/a**pʰ**á/ she/he hits him/her/it	a**p**á	V__V
/**pʰ**ahá/ hair	**p**ahá	#__
/i**t**é/ face	i**d**é	V__V
/**t**ąyą́/ it is good, well	**d**ąyą́	#__
/i**tʰ**é/ forehead	i**t**é	V__V
/**tʰ**í/ she/he lives (in a house)	**t**í	#__
/a**k**ú/ she/he brings him/he/it	a**g**ú	V__V
/**k**aná/ those yonder	**g**aná	#__
/to**kʰ**én/ how	do**k**én	V__V
/**kʰ**úwa/ she/he chases him/her/it	**k**úwa	#__
/si**c**á/ it is bad	si**j**á	V__V
/**c**é/ always	**j**é	#__
/i**cʰ**ápʰe/ fork	i**c**ápe	V__V
/**cʰ**é/ penis	**c**é	#__

Chapter 1 Exercises

EXERCISE 1
Translate these Nakoda words into English and say them aloud.

1. waná _____
2. hą́ _____
3. ą́ba _____
4. mağážu _____
5. adé _____

6. maštá _____
7. pinámayaya _____
8. iná _____
9. micį́kši _____
10. micų́kši _____

EXERCISE 2
Translate these English words into Nakoda and say them aloud.

1. no _____
2. thank you _____
3. Mother! _____
4. my son _____
5. it rains _____

6. it snows _____
7. today _____
8. my daughter _____
9. outside _____
10. inside _____

EXERCISE 3
Pair with someone and introduce aloud some of your family members and friends (e.g., Micų́kši Mary egíyabi – *My daughter is called Mary*). Tell what the weather is like.

EXERCISE 4
Say the following words aloud. Be careful when pronouncing the nasal vowels in bold.

| micį́kši | micų́kši | hą́ | tągán |
| wáhįhą | tadéyąba | ą́ba | wącímnaga |

CHAPTER 2

Objectives

VOCABULARY

- Nouns for people
- Nouns for food, drinks, and animals
- Basic verbs
- Demonstratives

GRAMMAR

- Word order in Nakoda
- Structure of regular stem verbs (Class 1)

Dialogues

The following dialogues make use of the words seen in Chapter 1 plus some new ones. They also exemplify the sentence pattern, verb structure, and word order in Nakoda.

1. Wahą́bi yacį́ga he? *Do you want soup?*
   Hą́, wahą́bi wacį́ga. *Yes, I want soup.*

2. Wįcį́jana né waȟpé cįgá he? *Does this girl want tea?*
   Hą́, waȟpé cįgá. *Yes, she wants tea.*

3. Šų́gataga gá aktága he? *Is that horse over there running?*
   Hiyá, šų́gataga gá nážį. *No, that horse over there is standing.*

4. Mary eníjiyabi he?
   Hiyá, Charlotte emágiyabi.

   Are you called Mary?
   No, I'm called Charlotte.

5. Iná! Wíyą žé ağúyabi gáğa he?
   Hiyá, wíyą žé ḣuḣnáḣyabi gáğa.

   Mother! Is that woman making bannock?
   No, that woman is making coffee.

6. Adé, wįcá žé wóda he?
   Hą́, wįcá žé wóda.

   Father, is that man eating?
   Yes, this man is eating.

Vocabulary

NOUNS FOR PEOPLE

dáguškina	*baby, infant*	takónagu	*his/her friend*
hokšína	*boy*	wįcá	*man*
mitákona	*friend*	wįcíjana	*girl*
nitákona	*your friend*	wíyą	*woman*

FOOD AND DRINKS

asą́bi	*milk*	pąğí	*potato*
ağúyabi	*bread, bannock*	štušténa	*salt*
cąpásusuna	*pepper*	tanó	*meat*
ḣuḣnáḣyabi	*coffee*	waḣpé	*tea*

ANIMALS

búza	*cat*	šų́ga	*dog*
gugúša	*pig*	šų́gatąga	*horse*
hoğą́	*fish*	tatą́ga	*male buffalo*
pağų́da	*duck*	zitkána	*bird*

VERBS

aktága	*she/he/it runs*	nážį	*she/he/it stands*
cįgá	*she/he/it wants it*	ų́	*she/he/it is, stays*
gáğa	*she/he makes it*	wací	*she/he dances*
maní	*she/he/it walks*	wóda	*she/he/it eats*

Note that the simple and shortest form of a Nakoda verb corresponds to the English verb inflected for the third person singular (she/he eats; she/he sits; she/he walks) or the second person imperative in female speech (eat, sit, walk), but can sometimes be translated with the

-ing form of the verb (is eating, is sitting, is walking), as in dialogues 5 and 6 on page 14. For the sake of simplicity, the third person form will serve as the "citation form" in the rest of the chapters. However, in the Nakoda/English lexicon only the English infinitive meaning appears in an entry, as in **wóda** (VI) to eat. In reality, this verb means "she/he eats."

Word Order in Nakoda

The Nakoda word order differs greatly from that of English since demonstratives, prepositions, and adverbs are placed after the noun instead of before. The verb is almost always at the end of the sentence and this is why it is often said that Nakoda is a Subject—Object—Verb (SOV) language. The following table will help visualize the Nakoda word order. Note that the parentheses in the first and second positions indicate that the element is optional in a sentence.

First word	Second word	Third word
(Noun)	(Demonstrative) (Postposition) (Adverb)	Verb

Let us start with a simple sentence like *my son is eating*. In Nakoda, this would be expressed with two words *micį́kši* (noun) and *wóda* (verb). For this combination of words Nakoda has the same order as English.

Micį́kši	wóda.	*My son is eating; my son eats.*
my.son	he.eats	
NOUN	VERB	

Waná	nína	maštá.	*It is very hot now.*
now	very	to.be.hot	
ADVERB	ADVERB	VERB	

Wįcíjana	žé	tągán	maní.	*That girl is walking outside.*
girl	that	outside	he.walks	
NOUN	DEMONSTRATIVE	ADVERB	VERB	

We can see from the preceding examples that the word order is fairly rigid. The verb occurs in the last position (before enclitics), and adverbs occur before verbs. There are three more grammatical concepts (also known as "functions") that are important to understand, namely, "subject," "object," and "predicate." Examine the following sentences:

Wįcá	žé	tanó	yúda.
man	that.sg	meat	he.eats.it
NOUN	DEM	NOUN	VERB
SUBJECT		OBJECT	PREDICATE

One can see here that the words *wįcá žé* indicate the **subject** (the person doing the action), *tanó* is the **object** (the entity undergoing an action), while the verb *yúda* is a **predicate** which expresses the action or state. Thus, the word order is Subject—Object—Verb (or SOV); this order is rigid in Nakoda.

Demonstratives

Demonstratives are used to locate or point at a single thing or a plurality of things, according to the distance from the speaker. Included in the following table are three spatial adverbs derived from the simple demonstratives.

Demonstratives		Spatial Adverbs	
singular	plural	precise	general location
né – *this*	nená – *these*	nén – *here*	néci – *around here*
žé – *that*	žená – *those*	žén – *there*	žéci – *around there*
gá – *that over there*	ganá – *those over there*	gán – *over there*	gakí – *yonder, way over there*

As indicated in the following examples the demonstratives occur after the noun, for the most part. For instance, if you want to say *this fish* or *that fish* put the demonstratives *né* (close by) or *žé* (a little further) after the noun *hoǧą́* "fish":

hoǧą́	né	*this fish* (close by)
fish	this	

hoǧą́	žé	*that fish* (a little farther)
fish	that	

Now if you add a verb (action word), it will appear last in the sentence. Thus, a sentence like *that dog runs* would be expressed as *dog that runs* in Nakoda. Here are a few examples reflecting Nakoda word order.

Wįcá	žé	wóda.	*That man is eating.*
man	that	he.eats	
NOUN	DEM	VERB	
SUBJECT		PREDICATE	

Šúga	gá	aktága.	*That dog over there is running.*
dog	that.over.there	he.runs	
NOUN	DEM	VERB	
SUBJECT		PREDICATE	

Wíyą	né	nážį.	*This woman is standing.*
woman	this.here	she.stands	
NOUN	DEM	VERB	
SUBJECT		PREDICATE	

"Adjectival" verbs like *tall*, *big*, or *yellow*, come after the noun they qualify, and the demonstrative is placed after the combination of a noun and an adjectival verb. Here are some examples that include a demonstrative and one of the following adjectival verbs *šįtų́* "she/he/it is fat," *skána* "she/he/it is white," and *sába* "she/he/it is black."

Gugúša	šįtų́	žé	wóda.	*The fat pig is eating.*
pig	it.is.fat	that	he.eats	
NOUN	VERB	DEM	VERB	
SUBJECT			PREDICATE	

Búza	skána	žená	aktágabi.	*Those white cats are running.*
cat	it.is.white	those	they.run	
NOUN	VERB	DEM	VERB	
SUBJECT			PREDICATE	

Šų́gatąga	sába	gá	maní.	*That black horse over there is walking.*
horse	it.is.black	that.one.o.there	he.walks	
NOUN	VERB	DEM	VERB	
SUBJECT			PREDICATE	

Class 1: Regular Stem Verbs

The structure of the verb, or action word, is the most complex one in Nakoda. We already know that the simplest verbs, like *osní* "it is cold out" or *wóda* "she/he eats," are already inflected for the third person singular "she, he, it." To express first person singular (1SG) "I," second person singular (2S) "you," first person plural (1PL) "we," second person plural (2PL) "you all," or third person plural (3PL) "they," a prefix is placed in front of or inside the verb. The full set of markers and combinations is as follows:

Person Markers (Regular stem, Class 1)			
Singular		**Plural**	
1	-wa- *I*	-ų(g)-...-bi	*we*
2	-ya- *you*	-ya-...-bi	*you all*
3	-Ø- *she/he*	-Ø-...-bi	*they*

In the following examples you will find fully inflected verbs. The person and number markers are in bold. Note that the absence of a person marker (noted with the symbol Ø), as in the case of the third person, means "she/he/it" in Nakoda.

cįgá – *she/he wants it* (Regular stem, Class 1)

wacįga	*I want it*	**ų**cįga**bi**	*we want it*
yacįga	*you want it*	**ya**cįga**bi**	*you all want it*
cįgá	*she/he wants it*	cįgá**bi**	*they want it*

gáǧa – *she/he makes it* (regular stem, Class 1)

wagáǧa	*I make it*	**ų**gáǧa**bi**	*we make it*
yagáǧa	*you make it*	**ya**gáǧa**bi**	*you all make it*
gáǧa	*she/he makes it*	gáǧa**bi**	*they make it*

ų́ – *she/he is, stays* (regular stem, Class 1)

wa'ų́	*I am*	**ų**k'ų́**bi**	*we are*
ya'ų́	*you are*	**ya**'ų́**bi**	*you all are*
ų́	*she/he is*	ų́**bi**	*they are*

For some verbs the person prefix is placed inside the stem and not before it. The prefix, or in this case the *infix* (*in*-"inside"), is in bold in the following examples. Note that the "we" form *ų-...-bi* often does not follow this rule (e.g., **ų**gáktaga**bi** "we run" and not **a'***ų́**ktagabi*), and also that a *g* is used to connect with a verb stem that starts in a vowel (e.g., **ų**gáktaga**bi** "we run").

aktága – *she/he runs* (regular stem, Class 1)

a**wá**ktaga	*I run*	**ų**gáktaga**bi**	*we run*
a**yá**ktaga	*you run*	a**yá**ktaga**bi**	*you all run*
aktága	*she/he runs*	aktága**bi**	*they run*

maní – *she/he walks* (regular stem, Class 1)

ma**wá**ni	*I walk*	ma'**ú**ni**bi**	*we walk*
ma**yá**ni	*you walk*	ma**yá**ni**bi**	*you all walk*
maní	*she/he walks*	maní**bi**	*they walk*

nážį – *she/he stands* (regular stem, Class 1)

na**wá**žį	*I stand*	na'**ų́**žį**bi**	*we stand*
na**yá**žį	*you stand*	na**yá**žį**bi**	*you all stand*
nážį	*she/he stands*	nážį**bi**	*they stand*

wóda – *she/he eats* (regular stem, Class 1)

wó**wa**da	*I eat*	wó'**ų**da**bi**	*we eat*
wó**ya**da	*you eat*	wó**ya**da**bi**	*you all eat*
wóda	*she/he eats*	wóda**bi**	*they eat*

Šų́gatąga gá **wacíga**.	*I want that horse over there.*
Waȟpé **ųgáǧabi**.	*We are making tea.*
Dóken **ya'ų́** (he)?	*How are you?*
Wįcíjanabi nená **aktágabi**.	*These girls are running.*
Tągán **mawáni**.	*I'm walking outside.*
Mitákona gakí **nážį**.	*My friend is standing over there.*
Waná **wówada**.	*I'm eating now.*

The placement of person markers is a feature of the Nakoda verb that is a little complicated to master. Beginners will have to memorize which verbs require infixes or prefixes for first and second persons (*I* and *you*). We have numbered the different types of verbs as Class 1, 2, 3, and 4. To memorize which verbs belong to which class is an important aspect of Nakoda and is an essential part of any basic conversation. You can also ask a speaker of the language how to say "I do X," since the placement of the "I" form will tell you how to construct the verb forms for all other persons.

To facilitate this learning process, the person formation patterns and the four classes of verbs can be found in the appendix called *Classes of Verbs*. Verbs that require infixes are signaled with an underscore indicating the point of insertion (e.g., *wo_da* "eat" = *wówada* "I eat," *wóyada* "you eat").

Dual ų- "we two"

In this chapter we've learned that to express the "we" form of a verb one only needs to add ų(g)- and -bi on a stem, as in wóʼųdabi "we eat." However, Nakoda, like other Dakotan dialects, also has what is called the "dual," which means that only the speaker and one other person are doing something. This "we two" meaning is obtained by adding only ų(g)- on the stem, not -bi.

The dual (D) does not appear in the verb tables because it is not very frequent and many middle-age speakers do not use it anymore. You have to be careful, though, as it shows up in some chapters since the material gathered for this book was done with speakers of different ages, genders and levels of proficiency. The dual is especially frequent with the "let's X" constructions marked with the suffix -s.

Waná ųǧíštimas!	Let's sleep now!
Ųyás!	Let's go!
Waʼúci céyaga!	Let's dance!
Waná ųyíkta?	Shall we go?
Wanúȟ įšnáną įȟpéʼųya.	Maybe we should leave her alone.

Sounds: Uvulars ǧ and ȟ

In Chapter 1 we saw that some of the sounds found in Nakoda do not exist in English. Two of them may present some difficulty for beginners: ǧ and ȟ. These sounds are uvular consonants, and they are produced by a friction of the back of the tongue with the uvula, the small water-droplet-shaped piece of flesh located at the back of the mouth. The scratchy sound created by the friction of the tongue and the uvula can be either voiced ǧ (vibrations of the vocal cords) or unvoiced ȟ (no vibrations of the vocal cords). We have already encountered words that contain these two sounds:

maǧážu	it rains	paǧúda	duck
ȟuȟnáȟyabi	coffee	waȟpé	tea

Be aware that the sound ȟ is often spelled with an < x > by some speakers of Nakoda, not to mention that some speakers pronounce uvulars with the closest English equivalents [g] and [h].

Chapter 2 Exercises

EXERCISE 1
Find the subject (S), object (O), and predicate (P) in these English sentences.

1. I like chips.
2. The boys enjoyed their ride.
3. It is raining.
4. I am sick.
5. The clouds are now covering the sky.
6. They are late.
7. Love is what I want.
8. The horses are grazing on the hill.
9. My cats often kill mice.
10. The door broke.

EXERCISE 2
Translate the following sentences into Nakoda and read them aloud.

1. That man is over there. _____
2. This man is eating. _____
3. Those black cats are running. _____
4. These male buffaloes are standing. _____
5. Those women over there want coffee. _____
6. That girl is standing over there. _____
7. I want tea. _____
8. The dogs want meat. _____
9. Those boys over there are running. _____
10. The man is walking here. _____

EXERCISE 3

Translate the following sentences into English.

1. Hą́, Peter aké wącímnagįkta. _____
2. Ą́ba né mağážu. _____
3. Gugúša gá wóda. _____
4. Iná, ą́ba né maštá. _____
5. Hiyá, ȟuȟnáȟyabi ųcígabi. _____
6. Hiyá, ağúyabi cįgábi. _____
7. Tanó yacígabi he? _____
8. Šų́gatągabi ganá maníbi. _____
9. Nén na'ų́žįbi. _____

EXERCISE 4

Which three words do not belong in this set?

maštá	wáhįhą	osní	waȟpé	aktága
mağážu	búza	tadéyąba	nážį	šų́ga

Explain why using the correct terms seen in Chapter 1 (Parts of Speech):

EXERCISE 5
Conjugate the following verbs for all seven persons.

	wóda	maní	aktága
1SG	_____	_____	_____
2SG	_____	_____	_____
3SG	_____	_____	_____
1D	_____	_____	_____
1PL	_____	_____	_____
2PL	_____	_____	_____
3PL	_____	_____	_____

EXERCISE 6
Translate into English:

šų́ga žé _____   búza žé _____

wíyą né _____   hoǧą́ gá _____

tatága né _____   gugúša gá _____

EXERCISE 7
Translate this short story into Nakoda.

Hello, son! _____

Hello, mom! How is it going? _____

Well, I am very good. _____

Do you want coffee? _____

No, I want water (for) now. _____

Mother! I thank you! _____

CHAPTER 3

Objectives

VOCABULARY

- Common objects
- Interrogative pronouns, quantifiers, and conjunctions
- More basic verbs

GRAMMAR

- Asking questions with *what*, *how*, and *where*
- Orders and commands (imperatives)
- Structure of Y-stem verbs (Class 2)
- Future markers

Dialogues

1. Dóken ya'ų́ (he)? *How are you?*
   Dąyą́ wa'ų́. *I am fine.*

2. Dóken eníjiyabi (he)? *What is your name?*
   _____ emą́giyabi *My name is _____.*

3. Nitákona dágu yuhá? *What does your friend have?*
   Dágunišį! *Nothing!*

4. Ȟuȟnáȟyabi yacíga? — *Do you want coffee?*
   Hą́, edáhą wacíga. — *Yes, I want some.*

5. Micíkši, tín ú hį́kna nén iyódąga. — *My son, come inside and sit down here.*
   Iná waȟpé edáhą mak'ú. — *Mother, give me some tea.*

6. Gakí iyódągabi. — *They are sitting over there.*
   Dóken ų́bi (he)? — *How are they?*
   Dąyą́ šką́bi! — *They are feeling well!*

Vocabulary

COMMON OBJECTS

cąní	*tobacco*	icápe	*fork*
cąníska	*cigarette*	į'íjuna	*cup*
cąnúba	*pipe*	kiškána	*spoon*
gamúbi	*drum*	mína	*knife*
iyógapte	*plate*	wacą́ga	*sweetgrass*

INTERROGATIVE PRONOUNS, QUANTIFIERS, AND CONJUNCTIONS

dágu	*what*	edáhą	*some*
dágunišį	*none, nothing at all*	hiyá	*no*
dóken	*how*	nągų́	*and, more*
dóki	*where*	tín	*inside*

VERBS (CLASSES 1, 2)

egíya ~ ejíya	*she/he calls him/her* (Class 1)	yá	*she/he goes* (Class 2)
éyagu	*she/he takes it* (Class 2)	yatką́	*she/he drinks it* (Class 2)
iyódąga	*she/he sits down* (Class 2)	yúda	*she/he eats it* (Class 2)
šką́	*she/he moves, feels thus, tries* (Class 1)	yuhá	*she/he has it* (Class 2)
tí	*she/he lives there* (Class 1)	ú	*she/he comes (here)* (Class 1)

Interrogative Sentences

In Nakoda, interrogative sentences are formed by using a particle, differences in intonation, or interrogative pronouns.

HE – INTERROGATIVE PARTICLE (RISING INTONATION)

The use of the particle *he* differs from community to community. Traditionally, female speakers from White Bear and Pheasant Rump communities (in Saskatchewan) did not use *he*, while women from Carry The Kettle still use *he*. In this book, we use brackets where *he* is optional.

The interrogative particle *he* is placed after a verb. With the verb *cigá* "she/he wants it," the noun expressing the object is placed before the verb. If there is a quantifier like *edáhą* "some," it is placed after the noun. The verb always occurs last in simple sentences, but *he* is always after the verb.

Ȟuȟnáȟyabi yacíga **he**?	*Do you want coffee?*
Tanó edáhą yacíga **he**?	*Do you want some meat?*
Hą́, edáhą wacíga.	*Yes, I want some.*

The interrogative particle *he* can also be placed after an adverb like *waná* "now, already" to make a complete sentence as in *Waná he?* "Are you ready?" As a rule of thumb, in informal speech, *he* is not used after an interrogative pronoun (also known as D-word) like *dóken* "how" or *duktén* "where." However, *he* is used in formal speech after an interrogative pronoun, such as when asking how to say something in Nakoda.

For White Bear/Pheasant Rump female speakers, when no question words (such as the interrogative pronouns on the next page) are used it can be tricky to distinguish between declarative and interrogative sentences. In writing, the interrogative will be indicated by a question mark. In speech, intonation creates the distinction between the declarative (neutral intonation) and the interrogative (rising intonation), much like in the English example *This is a type of monkey?*

	Male speaker	**Female speaker (White Bear)**	**Meaning**
Declarative	Šų́ga né nitáwa.	Šų́ga né nitáwa.	*This is your dog.*
Interrogative	Šų́ga né nitáwa he?	Šų́ga né nitáwa?	*Is this your dog?*

NAKÓN-I'A WO! | BEGINNING NAKODA

INTERROGATIVE PRONOUNS

Another common way to form interrogative sentences is to use interrogative pronouns like *dágu* "what," *dóken* "how," or *dóki* "where." Again, not all speakers use the *he* particle with interrogative pronouns. (More interrogative pronouns will be studied in Chapter 8.)

Dágu – *what*

Dágu yacíga (he)?	*What do you want?*
Nitákona **dágu** yuhá?	*What does your friend have?*
Dágu nuhá (he)?	*What do you have?*

Dóken – *how*

Dóken ya'ų́ (he)?	*How are you?*
Dóken ya'ų́bi (he)?	*How are you all?*
Dóken ų́bi (he)?	*How are they?*
Dóken yašką́ (he)?	*How are you getting along/feeling?*

Dóki – *where*

Dóki ná (he)?	*Where are you going?* (after departure)
Micų́kši! **Dóki** inána (he)?	*My daughter! Where are you going?* (setting to go)
Dóki iyáyabi (he)?	*Where are they going?* (setting to go)

Imperative Particles *wo* and *bo*

Orders and commands are expressed using the third person singular form of the verb. There are no second person (*you*) markers for orders and commands. Even if, technically, the citation form is inflected for third person, the context and the intonation of the speaker make it clear that she/he is ordering someone to do something.

Two imperative particles are used only by male speakers: *wo* is used to give a command to one person (SG), and *bo* to more than one person (PL). These particles occupy the same place as the other particles (like *he*, *no*, and *c*) and all are mutually exclusive since one cannot ask and command at the same time. Female speakers use the third person singular form of the verb, as in *iyódąga* "Sit!" with a rising intonation.

	Female Speaker	**Male Speaker**	
Singular addressee	Yá!	Yá **wo**!	*Go!*
	Náži̧!	Náži̧ **wo**!	*Stand up!*
	Eyágu!	Eyágu **wo**!	*Take it!*
	Iyódąga!	Iyódąga **wo**!	*Sit down!*

With plural addressees (*all of you*), female speakers use the plural *-bi* while male speakers use *bo* which is a contraction of *-bi* (3PL) and *wo*.

	Female Speaker	Male Speaker	
Plural addressee	Yá**bi**!	Yá **bo**!	*You all go!*
	Nážį**bi**!	Nážį **bo**!	*All of you stand up!*
	Éyagu**bi**!	Éyagu **bo**!	*All of you take it!*
	Iyódąga**bi**!	Iyódąga **bo**!	*All of you sit down!*

Some female speakers from White Bear use another imperative enclitic *m* for plural addressees.

Néci'ú hį́kna iyódąga **m**!	*You all come in and sit down!*
Nážį **m**!	*You all stand up!*
Waná įštį́ma **m**!	*You all sleep now!*
Nén iyódąga **m**!	*You all sit down here!*

If some sort of precision is needed (e.g., where to sit, where to go, etc.), a spatial demonstrative (see Chapter 1) is placed before the verb.

| **Nén** iyódąga bo! | *You all sit down here!* |
| **Gakí** iyódąga! | *Sit down way over there!* |

Class 2: Y-Stem Verbs

In Chapter 2 we saw that Nakoda has a class of verbs called "regular stem" verbs, or Class 1 verbs (e.g., *wóda* "she/he eats"). The person markers for the regular stems are *-wa-* (1SG), *-ya-* (2SG) and *-Ø-* (3SG). There is another class of verbs called the "Y-stem" or Class 2 verbs. These verbs can be identified by looking at the 3SG or 1PL forms of the verb because both show a *y* sound in the stem. This is how one recognizes a Y-stem (Class 2) verb from the other classes of verbs. When you want to use the *I* or *you* forms, you have to delete the *y* of the Y-stem and add the appropriate set of person markers.

	Person Markers (Y-stem, Class 2)			
	Singular		**Plural**	
1	-mn-	*I*	-y(g)-...-bi	*we*
2	-n-	*you*	-n-...-bi	*you all*
3	-Ø-	*she/he*	-Ø-...-bi	*they*

Let us examine some Class 2 verbs. The marker for first person plural is *ų(g)-* plus the plural marker *–bi*. For the second person plural the marker is *n-…-bi*.

yúda – *she/he eats it* (Y-stem, Class 2)

mnúda	*I eat it*	**ų**yúda**bi**	*we eat it*
núda	*you eat it*	**n**úda**bi**	*you all eat it*
yúda	*eat it, she/he eats it*	yúda**bi**	*they eat it*

yuhá – *she/he has it* (Y-stem, Class 2)

mnuhá	*I have it*	**ų**yúha**bi**	*we have it*
nuhá	*you have it*	**n**uhá**bi**	*you all have it*
yuhá	*she/he has it*	yuhá**bi**	*they have it*

yá – *she/he goes* (Y-stem, Class 2)

mná	*I go*	**ų**yá**bi**	*we go*
ná	*you go*	**n**á**bi**	*you all go*
yá	*she/he goes*	yá**bi**	*they go*

yatką́ – *she/he drinks it* (Y-stem, Class 2)

mnatką́	*I drink it*	**ų**yátką**bi**	*we drink it*
natką́	*you drink it*	**n**atką́**bi**	*you all drink it*
yatką́	*she/he drinks it*	yatką́**bi**	*they drink it*

As with regular stem verbs, some Y-stem verbs require person infixes (i.e., elements inserted in the stem) instead of prefixes (i.e., elements placed before the stem). This is the case with the verbs *éyagu* and *iyódąga*. However, infixes are only used with the *I*, *you*, and sometimes *we* forms as shown below.

éyagu – *she/he takes it* (Y-stem, Class 2)

é**mn**agu	*I take it*	**ųg**éyagu**bi**	*we take it*
é**n**agu	*you take it*	é**n**agu**bi**	*you all take it*
éyagu	*she/he takes it*	éyagu**bi**	*they take it*

iyódąga – *she/he sits down* (Y-stem, Class 2)

i**mn**ódąga	*I sit down*	**ųg**íyodąga**bi**	*we sit down*
i**n**ódąga	*you sit down*	i**n**ódąga**bi**	*you all sit down*
iyódąga	*she/he sits down*	iyódąga**bi**	*they sit down*

Aǧúyabi nągų́ wahą́bi **ųyúdabi**.	We eat bannock/bread and soup.
Gamúbi nągų́ cąnúba **yuhábi**.	They have a drum and a pipe.
Búza né miní **yatką́**.	This cat is drinking water.
Búza sába gá asą́bi **yatką́**.	That black cat over there is drinking milk.
Éyagu wo!	Take it!
Tanó edáhą **ųgéyagubi**.	We took some meat.
Gakí **įmnódągįkta**.	I'll sit over there.
Mitúgaši! Nén **iyódąga**.	Grandfather! Sit here.

Note that, as a rule of thumb, when there is a *y* in the verb, normally it belongs to Class 2 verbs, and that *y* gets deleted by the first and second person markers. However, some Class 3 verbs also have a *y* in the stem, so it is hard to know for sure which class (2 or 3) a verb with a *y* belongs to.

Potential/Future Marker -*kta*

While in English the future tense is formed with *will* (as in *I will sleep, I will go to town*), in Nakoda the suffix -*kta* indicates either: (a) that an action will happen in the future; or (b) that a potential action might happen but has not at this point in time. The following sentences illustrate how -*kta* is used:

FUTURE

Ȟuȟnáȟyabi wacígį**kta**.	I will want coffee.
Cąní edáhą cigí**kta**.	She/he wants/needs some tobacco.
Aké wącímnagį**kta**.	I will see you again.

POTENTIAL

Dágu ecámų**kta**.	I have to do something.
Ȟtánihą wąyágį**kta**.	She/he would have seen him/her yesterday.

The potential/future -*kta* also provokes ablauting (i.e., sound change) of the last vowel of a verbal stem. More specifically, it changes *a* into *į*, as in the following examples. Remember that ablauting changes a vowel only if that vowel can be changed. If not, as in the case of *mağážu*, no ablauting happens when -*kta* is added.

ABLAUTING VERBS

wóda+kta	>	wódį_kta	she/he will eat
gáǧa+kta	>	gáǧį_kta	she/he will make it
iyódąga+kta	>	iyódągį_kta	she/he will sit down

NON-ABLAUTING VERBS

mağáž**u**+kta	>	mağáž**u_kta**	*it will rain*
man**í**+kta	>	man**í_kta**	*she/he/it will walk*
wak**ą́**+kta	>	wak**ą́_kta**	*she/he/it will be mysterious, holy*

Sounds: Glottal stop [']

The glottal stop IPA [?] (which is spelled here with an apostrophe [']) is produced by closing the glottis and suddenly releasing the airstream. In Nakoda, it is often used to link two vowels or two words together: one that ends in a vowel and another one that starts with a vowel. The glottal stop is a kind of natural linker just like *y* and this is why some words have two spellings in the lexicon: *tadéyąba* or *tadé'ąba* "it is a windy day," *miyáde* or *mi'áde* "my father." The inflection for the first person plural *-ų-…-bi* is linked with a glottal stop to the preceding element. Try to pronounce the following words aloud.

ya'ų̇   na'ų́žibi   wó'ųdabi   į'íjuna   tín ú

Chapter 3 Exercises

EXERCISE 1
Translate the following sentences from Nakoda into English.

1. Wįcíjana žé asą́bi yuhá. _____

2. Šúga sába wąží mnuhá. _____

3. Wįcábi žená wahpé yuhábi. _____

4. Búza skána wąží ųyúhabi. _____

5. Kiškána né éyagubįkta. _____

6. Dokí ná (he)? _____

EXERCISE 2

Pair with someone and transform these verbs into their potential/future version. One student does the first column and the other does the second one. You can also ask your partner to change the person (e.g., Q. *Will we sit down?* A. Hą ųgíyodągabįkta).

mağážu	_____	awáktaga	_____
wáhįhą	_____	maštá	_____
įštíma	_____	inódąga	_____
wówada	_____	ųgéyagubi	_____
nábi	_____	ųyátkąbi	_____
mná	_____	yacígabi	_____

EXERCISE 3

Translate the following sentences into Nakoda.

1. How are you? _____

2. How are they? _____

3. Do you want coffee? _____

4. Do you all want some meat? _____

5. Does she/he want some tea? _____

6. What is your name? _____

7. Where were they walking? _____

8. Where were you standing? _____

9. Do they want some? _____

Exercise 4

Match the correct English translations with the Nakoda commands.

a) Iyódąga bo!   _____ Drink tea!

b) Nén nážį!   _____ Walk over there!

c) Gakí maní!   _____ Stand here!

d) Ú wo!   _____ Move over there!

e) Iyódąga hįkna wóda!   _____ Sit down and eat!

f) Gakí šką́!   _____ Drink coffee!

h) Waȟpé yatką́ wo!   _____ You all sit down!

i) Ȟuȟnáȟyabi yatką́!   _____ Come (here)!

CHAPTER 4

Objectives

VOCABULARY

- Days of the week and the months
- Cardinal and ordinal numbers

GRAMMAR

- Telling time, dates, a person's age, distance, and height
- Mathematical operations
- Word order

Dialogues

1. Ába né ába įįíšakpe wįcógądu sųgágu hąwí he?
   Hiyá, micųkši, ába né įįíšagowį wįcógądu sųgágu hąwí no!

   Is today the sixth of November?
   No, my daughter, today is the seventh of November!

2. Huhúžubina mąkíyutabi wikcémna šákpe he?
   Hiyá, Huhúžubina mąkíyutabi wikcémna šaknóǧą no!

   Is Regina 60 kilometres distance?
   No, Regina is 80 kilometres away!

3. Dóken wįyą gá hąská (he)?
   Wįyą gá tacąkiyutabi šákpe hąská no!

   How tall is that woman over there?
   That woman over there is six feet tall!

4. Micųkši, dóna ehą'i (he)?
   Dóba ehą'i, iná!

   My daughter, what time is it?
   It is four o'clock, mother!

5. Iná! Waná ába ijínuba ehá'i he?
   Hiyá, ába né ába ijízaptą.

   Mother! Is it Thursday today?
   No, today is Friday.

6. Waníyedu dóna eháyakibi (he)?
   Waníyedu wikcémna ehą́'ukibi.

   How old are you all?
   We are ten years old.

Vocabulary

NOUNS AND ADVERBS

agé-	*added to* (prefix)	mąkíyutabi	*kilometre*
-cogą́n	*in the middle*	sám	*beyond, over*
dóna	*how many*	tacą́kiyutabi	*foot* (length)
hągé	*half*	waná	*now*
hąwí	*moon*	waníyedu	*winter, year*
Huhúžubina	*Regina*	wí	*sun, month*

VERBS

ehą́ki	*she/he reaches an age, is of a certain age* (Class 1)
ehą́'i	*she/he reaches or arrives at a point* (place or time) (Class 1)
éyagu	*she/he takes it* (Class 2)
hą́ska	*she/he is tall, of a certain height** (Class 4)

DAYS OF THE WEEK AND THE MONTHS

The days of the week are made with the word *ą́ba* "day" followed by a qualifying word, often an ordinal number like *ịnúba* "second" or an adjectival (stative) verb.

Day of the week	Nakoda	Translation
Monday	ą́bawaką gicúni	*when the holy day is finished*
Tuesday	ą́ba ịnúba	*second day*
Wednesday	ą́ba ịyámni	*third day*
Thursday	ą́ba ịdóba	*fourth day*
Friday	ą́ba ịzáptą	*fifth day*
	tanó yúdabišį	*they don't eat meat day*
	tacúba ą́ba	*animal marrow day*†

---

* For the person markers of the NV-conjugation (Class 4), see Chapter 5.

† There are two series of terms for "Friday" and "Saturday." Two of them refer to the fact that long ago the Indian agent would do some butchering on Friday (*tacúba ą́ba*) and distribute the meat rations on Saturday (*wowį́cak'u ą́ba*). The other terms for "Friday" (*tanó yúdabišį* lit., they don't eat meat, abstinence day) and "Saturday" (*ą́ba yužážabi* lit., washing day) were probably used by Christianized Nakoda people, or even made-up by priests who spoke Nakoda.

Saturday	ába yužáža	*laundry day*
	wowícak'u ába	*ration day*
Sunday	ábawaką	*holy day*

The structure for the names of the months usually requires the noun *hąwí* "sun, moon, month" with a qualifier in front.

Month	Nakoda	Translation
January	witéȟi hąwí	*hard time moon*
February	ąmháska hąwí	*long day moon*
March	wicísta yazą hąwí	*sore eyes moon*
April	tabéȟ'a tawí hąwí	*frog's wife moon*
May	įdú wiğá hąwí	*moon sits on its back*
June	waȟpé wóšma hąwí	*thick leaves moon*
July	wašáša hąwí	*berries ripening moon*
August	cąpásaba hąwí	*chokecherry moon*
September	waȟpé ǧí hąwí	*yellow leaves moon*
October	tašnáheja akída hąwí	*striped gopher looks back moon*
November	wicógądu sųgágu hąwí	*midwinter little brother's moon*
December	wicógądu hąwí	*midwinter moon*

Cardinal Numbers

Nakoda lower numbers (0 to 9) are displayed below. Teens (10 to 19) are obtained by adding the prefix *agé-* "on top" before the number. Here, it is important to remember that *wikcémna* "ten" (as in *two on top of ten = twelve*) is understood but not pronounced, thus *agénųba* "twelve" simply means "on top two" in Nakoda.

Lower numbers (0 to 9)		Teens (10 to 19)	
dágunišį	*zero*	wikcémna	*ten*
wążí	*one*	agéwąži	*eleven*
nųbá ~ núm	*two*	agénųba	*twelve*
yámni	*three*	agéyamni	*thirteen*
dóba ~ dóm	*four*	agédoba	*fourteen*
záptą	*five*	agézaptą	*fifteen*
šákpe	*six*	agéšakpe	*sixteen*
šagówį	*seven*	agéšagowį	*seventeen*
šaknóǧą	*eight*	agéšaknoǧą	*eighteen*
napcúwąga	*nine*	agénapcuwąga	*nineteen*

For numbers between 20 and 99, multiply ten by 2 (for 20), by 3 (for 30), by 4 (for 40), etc., and then add the postposition *sám* "over (more)" and the cardinal number, as in:

$$10 \times 2 \text{ over } 4 = 24 \qquad 10 \times 8 \text{ over } 8 = 88$$
$$10 \times 7 \text{ over } 9 = 79 \qquad 10 \times 3 \text{ over } 5 = 35$$

Twenties (20 to 29)

wikcémna núm	*twenty*
wikcémna núm sám wazí	*twenty-one*
wikcémna núm sám núba	*twenty-two*
wikcémna núm sám yámni	*twenty-three*
wikcémna núm sám dóba	*twenty-four*
wikcémna núm sám záptą	*twenty-five*
wikcémna núm sám šákpe	*twenty-six*
wikcémna núm sám šagówį	*twenty-seven*
wikcémna núm sám šaknóğą	*twenty-eight*
wikcémna núm sám napcúwąga	*twenty-nine*

For numbers between 30 and 100, follow the pattern of the Twenties above, using the appropriate decade as shown here:

Decades

wikcémna yámni	*thirty*
wikcémna dóba	*forty*
wikcémna záptą	*fifty*
wikcémna šákpe	*sixty*
wikcémna šagówį	*seventy*
wikcémna šaknóğą	*eighty*
wikcémna napcúwąga	*ninety*
obáwįğe	*hundred*

Numbers higher than 100 are formed according to the following pattern:

$$100 \; sám \; \text{number}_{hundred} \; \text{number}_{decimal}$$

obáwįğe sám sákpe wikcémna	610
obáwįğe sám yámni wikcémna dóba sám šagówį	347
obáwįğe sám wazí sám agénuba	112
obáwįğe sám napcúwąga wikcémna yámni sám šaknóğą	938

To count things, put the numeral after the noun. If a demonstrative like *né* is used, it is placed after the noun and the number word. Most of the time the plural number (e.g., four month<u>s</u>) is not indicated on the noun in Nakoda.

waníyedu **dóba**	*four winters*
šúga **wąží**	*one dog*
búza **yamní** žená	*those three cats*
Į'íjuna **dóba** émnagu.	*I took four cups.*

Ordinal numbers

The ordinal numbers are used to express the order of objects within a series. To form the Nakoda ordinal numbers, add the prefix *iji-* "ordinal" to the cardinal number. This prefix is often reduced to *i-* by some speakers.

ijidoba	*fourth*	**iji'**agezaptą	*fifteenth*
ijišaknoğą	*eighth*	**iji**wikcemna šákpe	*sixtieth*
ijišakpe	*sixth*	**iji**napcuwąga	*ninth*

When a cardinal number starts with a vowel, a glottal stop [ʔ] written ' is inserted after *i* as in *iji'agezaptą* "fifteenth." Note that "first" (as in an order) is *iwąži*, but when referring to time sequences one uses *togáhe*. Compare:

bispízana **iwąži**	versus	**Togáhe**, tanó ųyúdabi.
the first mouse		*First, we ate meat.*

Mathematical operations

One can express basic mathematical operations using the following words:

Nakoda Word	Literal Meaning	Mathematical Function
štén	*if, when* (also used to refer to a future event)	= (equals, results in)
aké	*again*	+ (plus)
énagu	*you take it*	– (take away)
cogą́n	*in the middle*	÷ (divided by)
-ȟ	(intensifier suffix)	× (indicates the process of multiplication)

The word order to express mathematical operations is shown here, followed by specific examples:

ADDITION (+)	SUBTRACTION (−)
number *aké* number *štén* number	number, number *énagu štén* number
+ =	− =

MULTIPLICATION (x)	DIVISION (÷)
number *ȟ* number *štén* number	number *cogą́n* number *štén* number
x =	÷ =

Dóba **aké** nų́ba štén šákpe.	*Four plus two equals six.*
Dóba, nų́ba **énagu** štén nų́ba.	*Four minus* (lit., you take) *two equals two.*
Dobáȟ nų́ba **štén** šaknóǧą.	*Four times two equals eight.*
Dóba **cogą́n** nų́ba štén nų́ba.	*Four divided by two equals two.*

Lastly, the idea of multiplication as in "twice" or "three times" is expressed by adding the intensifier *-ȟ* on a number: *Nų́baȟ yatką́.* "He drank it twice."

Age and Time

In English we count a person's age with the number of years she/he has lived so far, while in Nakoda it is done with the number of winters (*waníyedu*). The method of counting is the same, except that English and Nakoda use different words to indicate the unit of time measurement. Note that there is no plural marking on the word *waníyedu* "winter(s)." To ask a person's age, use the verb *ehą́ki* "she/he reaches an age, is of a certain age," as in the following examples:

Waníyedu dóna **eháyaki** (he)?	*How old are you?*
	(lit., How many winters have you reached?)
Waníyedu dóna **ehą́ki** (he)?	*How old is she/he?*
	(lit., How many winters has she/he reached?)

This verb is the possessive version of *ehą́'i* "she/he reaches or arrives at a point (place or time)" (see Chapter 17 under *-gi-* "dative"). It is a regular stem verb (Class 1) and requires infixes.

ehą́ki – *she/he reaches an age, is of a certain age* (regular stem, Class 1)

ehą́**wa**ki	*I reach a certain age*	ehą́'**ų**ki**bi**	*we reach a certain age*
ehą́**ya**ki	*you reach a certain age*	ehą́**ya**ki**bi**	*you all reach a certain age*
ehą́ki	*she/he reaches a certain age*	ehą́ki**bi**	*they reach a certain age*

Waníyedu wikcémna núba sám wąží **ehákįkta**.	*She/he will be twenty-one years old.* (lit., She/he will reach twenty-one winters.)
Waníyedu wikcémna dóba **eháwaki**.	*I am forty years old.* (lit., I reach(ed) forty winters.)

ehą́'i – *she/he reaches or arrives at a point* (place or time) (regular stem, Class 1)

ehą́**wa**'i	*I reach it*	ehą́'**ųgibi**	*we reach it*
ehą́**ya**'i	*you reach it*	ehą́**ya**'i**bi**	*you all reach it*
ehą́'i	*she/he reaches it*	ehą́'i**bi**	*they reach it*

This verb is also used to tell time and the days of the week. The unit of counting is not winters but the position of the hour and minute hands on a clock.

Dóna **ehą́'i** (he)?	*What time is it?*
Wąží **ehą́'i**.	*It is one o'clock.*

When it is 30 minutes past the hour, the noun *hągé* "half" is used, as in the following formula:

> [number of hours] + sám + hągé + ehą́'i
> over half it.reaches

Dóba sám hągé **ehą́'i**.	*It is four thirty* (4:30) (lit., four and a half).
Agéwąži sám hągé **ehą́'i**.	*It is eleven thirty* (11:30) (lit., eleven and a half).
Wąží **ehą́'i**.	*It is one o'clock* (1:00).

However, to tell a full date (day + month) Nakoda does not employ the verb *ehą́'i* but simply puts the day and the month side by side. To indicate a date in the past, add the enclitic -*'ehą* "then in the past" after the last word of the sentence.

Waná ąba įdóba **ehą́'i**.	*It is now Thursday.*
Ą́bawaką **ehą́'i**.	*It is Sunday.*
Ą́ba įįíšakpe wįcógądu sųgágu hąwí.	*It is the sixth of November.*
Ą́ba įįíšakpe wįcógądu sųgágu hąwí**'ehą**.	*It was on the sixth of November.*

Distance and Height

The noun *mąkíyutabi* "kilometre(s)" is used to tell distances and integrates into the following sentence pattern:

> destination + kilometre(s) + number of kilometres

Again, as with the expression of dates, there is no verb *to be* employed in telling distances in Nakoda. Instead, one puts side by side the words for destination, kilometre and number of kilometres, as shown above and in the following examples:

Huhúžubina **mąkíyutabi** wikcémna šaknóǧą.	*Regina is 80 kilometres distance.*
Lumsdén **mąkíyutabi** wikcémna núm sám wążí.	*Lumsden is 21 kilometres distance.*

To talk about the height of somebody, one uses the noun *tacąkiyutabi* "foot," which is placed before the numeral. The verb *hąska* "she/he is tall" (NV-conjugation, Class 4; *mahąska* "I am tall," *nihąska* "you are tall") ends the sentence. We will study person marking of Class 4 verbs in Chapter 6.

Hokšína né **tacąkiyutabi** záptą hąska.	*This boy is five feet tall.*
Tacąkiyutabi šákpe mahąska.	*I am six feet tall.*
Tacąkiyutabi šákpe nihąska.	*You are six feet tall.*

An alternative way of asking the height of somebody is by using the verb *ehą'i* "she/he reaches or arrives at a point (place or time)":

Dóna hąska **ehąya'i**?	*How tall are you?*
Tacąkiyutabi šákpe **ehąwa'i**.	*I am six feet tall.*

Both the nouns *mąkíyutabi* "kilometre" and *tacąkiyutabi* "foot" contain an element *-kiyutabi* "unit of measurement," which is added on *mą(ka)-* "earth" (earth + measurement = kilometre) and *tacą-* "body" (body + measurement = foot).

Chapter 4 Exercises

EXERCISE 1

Translate the following numbers into Nakoda:

65 _____

12 _____

34 _____

99 _____

56 _____

28 _____

81 _____

40 _____

9 _____

100 _____

69 _____

EXERCISE 2

Match the Nakoda number words with the numbers:

_____ agénapcuwąga   56

_____ wikcémna napcúwąga   88

_____ wikcémna záptą sám šákpe   100

_____ wikcémna šagówį sám yámni   42

_____ wikcémna šaknóğą sám šaknóğą   90

_____ obáwįğe   19

_____ wikcémna šaknóğą sám dóba   84

_____ wikcémna dóba sám núba   73

EXERCISE 3
Translate the following sentences into Nakoda:

1. It is the 3rd of October. _____
   _____

2. It is Tuesday. _____
   _____

3. It is the 30th of November. _____
   _____

4. It is the 3rd of August. _____
   _____

5. It was on the 1st of March. _____
   _____

6. It was on April 22nd. _____
   _____

7. It will be on the 24th of May. _____
   _____

8. It is Saturday the 23rd of July. _____
   _____

9. Saskatoon is 66 kilometres away. _____
   _____

10. Regina is 13 kilometres away. _____
    _____

11. This man is 6 feet tall. _____

_____

12. We (two) saw him four times. _____

_____

EXERCISE 4
Write the following operations in Nakoda and say them aloud.

1. 16 − 6 = 10 _____
2. 7 x 4 = 28 _____
3. 45 ÷ 5 = 9 _____
4. 3 + 8 = 11 _____
5. 9 x 0 = 0 _____
6. 15 ÷ 5 = 3 _____
7. 4 + 20 = 24 _____
8. 2 x 100 = 200 _____
9. 39 − 15 = 24 _____
10. 30 − 3 = 27 _____

EXERCISE 5
Say your age aloud, and then the age of your mother, father, and siblings (if you have any).

CHAPTER 5

Objectives

VOCABULARY

- More kinship nouns
- Adverbs expressing the time of the day
- More regular stem verbs (Class 1)

GRAMMAR

- Reference to time: past, present, future/potential
- Nasal conjugation verbs (Class 3)
- Plurality of demonstratives, nouns and verbs

Dialogues

1. Nikúši waná įštíma he? — *Is your grandmother sleeping now?*
   Hą́, nína įštíma. — *Yes, she is sleeping a lot.*

2. Mitímno, šų́gatągabi dóna nuhá (he)? — *My (female) older brother, how many horses do you have?*
   Mitą́kši, šų́gatągabi agédoba mnuhá. — *My (male) younger sister, I have fourteen horses.*

3. Mitą́gena, tatą́gabi ganá ną́žįbi he? — *My (male) elder sister, are those male buffaloes over there standing?*

   Hiyá, tatą́gabi ganá maníbi. — *No, those male buffaloes way over there are walking.*

4. Iyódąga hį́kna wóda!   *Sit down and eat!*
Hą́, nén imnódągikta.   *Yes, I will sit here.*
Ȟtayédu né dágu dókanųbi (he)?   *What are you all doing this evening?*
Wo'ų́dabi žehą́ štén, tągán ma'ų́nibįkta.   *After we have eaten, we will walk outside.*

5. Hąyákeji dágu yúdabįkta (he)?   *What will they eat tomorrow?*
Pasú agástaga né yúdabįkta.   *They will eat the turkey.*

6. Ą́bawaką žehą́ duwé wąnága (he)?   *Who did you see on Sunday?*
Nicį́na wąmnága.   *I saw your older brother.*

Vocabulary

NOUNS

ağúyabiskuya	*cake*	omáka	*year*
cijá	*child*	pąǧí	*potato*
dagúye	*relative*	pasú agástaga	*turkey*
koná	*friend*	taspą́	*apple*

ADVERBS AND OTHER FUNCTION WORDS

agą́n	*on top*	ȟtánihą	*yesterday*
ą́ba né	*today*	ȟtayédu	*evening*
dąyą́	*well*	į́š	*her/him/they/it too, also*
duwé	*who*	óda	*a lot; it is a lot*
hąyákeji	*tomorrow*	štén	*if, when*
hąhébi	*night*	žehą́, -c'ehą, -ehą	*then* (past)

VERBS (N-CONJUGATION, CLASS 3)

agą́n-yąga	*she/he rides a horse**	įyúǧa ~ įwúǧa	*she/he asks someone*
dóka'ų	*she/he does what?*	ų́	1) *she/he is, stays* (Class 1)
			2) *she/he wears it* (Class 3)
			3) *she/he uses it* (Class 3)
įštíma	*she/he sleeps*	yągá ~ yįgá (VI-N, AUX)	1) *she/he sits on it*
			2) *she/he does continuously*

---

* The full form of this verb is *šų́gatąga agą́n-yąga* "she/he sits on a horse," but the the noun *šų́gatąga* is omitted in front since a horse is one of the only animals one can sit on.

Here are four more regular stem verbs that will be used in the reading exercises at the end of this chapter. The future/potential *-kta* as well as the negative *-šį* enclitics are also included here but will be explained in Chapter 6. Note the infixed first and second person markers (*-wa-* and *-ya-*).

timáni – *she/he visits people* (regular stem, Class 1)

timá**wa**ni	*I visit*	timáni**kta**	*she/he will visit*
timá**ya**ni	*you visit*	timáni**bįkteší**	*they will not visit*
timá'**ų**ni**bi**	*we visit*		

awášpąya – *she/he cooks a feast* (regular stem, Class 1)

awášpą**wa**ya	*I cook a feast*	awášpąy**įkta**	*she/he will cook a feast*
awášpą**ya**ya	*you cook a feast*	awášpąya**bįkteší**	*they will not cook a feast*
awášpą'**ų**ya**bi**	*we cook a feast*		

gáğa – *she/he makes it* (regular stem, Class 1)

wagáğa	*I make it*	gağį́**kta**	*she/he will make it*
yagáğa	*you make it*	gáğa**bįkteší**	*they will not make it*
ųgáğa**bi**	*we make it*		

opétų – *she/he buys it* (regular stem, Class 1)

opé**wa**tų	*I buy it*	opétų**kta**	*she/he will buy it*
opé**ya**tų	*you buy it*	opétų**bįkteší**	*they will not buy it*
opé'**ų**tų**bi**	*we buy it*		

Kinship Nouns

Here is a list of all the main kinship terms for a family (mother, father, and children) including the grandparents. For *mother* and *father* there are distinct terms used in addressing someone (calling out that person) and referencing someone (talking about that person in her/his absence). Finally, some kinship terms for siblings differ according to the gender (male/female) of the possessor. Thus, these terms have to be read as: *my (I am a man) older sister; your (you are a woman) older brother*.

	Kinship Nouns		
Relation	**My**	**Your**	**His/Her**
grandfather	mitúgaši	nitúgaši	tugą́šicu ~ tugą́šitku
grandmother	mikúši	nikúši	kušícu ~ kugišiktu
father	adé (address) miyáde ~ mi'áde (reference)	niyáde ~ ni'áde	atkúgu ~ aktúgu
mother	iná (address) mihų́ (reference)	nihų́	hų́gu
Male possessor older brother	micína	nicína	cjcýna
older sister	mitągena	nitągena	tąkúna
younger brother	misų́ga	nisų́ga	sųgágu
younger sister	mitą́kši	nitą́kši	tąkšį́cu
Female possessor older brother	mitímno	nitímno	timnógo
older sister	micų́na	nicų́na	cųgų́na
younger brother	misų́ga	nisų́ga	sųgágu
younger sister	mitą́ga	nitą́ga	tągágu
son	micį́kši	nicį́kši	cjhį́tku ~ cjhį́ktu
daughter	micų́kši	nicų́kši	cųwį́tku ~ cuwį́ktu

To form the *my, your*, and *his or her* meanings, put a prefix *mi-* "my," *ni-* "your" or a suffix for the third person, either *-go, -gu*, or *tku* "his, her." We will survey the formation of other kinship terms, as well as other ways to indicate possession, in Chapter 9.

Reference to Time: Past, Present, and Future/Potential

In English, tenses are indicated in the verbal complex. Present tense has no special marker (*walk, eat*) except for the third person singular (*he walks*). Past tense is indicated by an inflection (*I walk > I walked*), or a change in the shape of the stem (*I bring > I brought*). Future tense is marked by the modal verb *will* (*I will eat*). In Nakoda, tenses are distinguished only in context and are not obligatory. Thus, if I say *ą́ba wašté* "it is a nice day," my addressee will induce that I am referring to today's weather and not yesterday or tomorrow's weather. A Nakoda verb with no elements added situates an event either in the past or present tense. Nevertheless, if you want to make it clear that something happened in the past, you can add the temporal adverb *žehą́*, or enclitics *-c'ehą, -'ehą́* "just then, at a certain point in the past," but again it is not obligatory.

PRESENT

    awášpąya   *she/he eats, cooks a feast*
    gáǧa   *she/he makes it*
    wówada   *I eat*

PAST

    Awášpąya **žehą́**.   *Then she/he cooked a feast.*
    Gáǧa **žehą́**.   *Then she/he made it.*
    Žéci wa'í **žehą́**.   *I arrived there.*
    Ą́bawaką **žehą́** owácegiya žéci wa'í.   *I went to church on Sunday.*

Žehą́ has a similar variant, *-ehą* or *-c'ehą*, the latter being an enclitic that attaches to some adverbs, such as *dóhącʼehą* "when in the past."

    Dóhąc**'ehą** wąnága?   *When did you see him?*
    Dóhąc**'ehą** tanó núda?   *When did you eat meat?*
    Dóhąc**'ehą** wahpé yagáǧa?   *When did you make tea?*
    Hąhébic**'ehą** wagáǧa.   *I made it last night.*
    Asą́bi eháš**'ehą**.   *There was too much milk.*
    Wanágašʼ**ehą** omáka agénapcuwąga   *Long ago, in the year 1968.*
       wikcémna šákpe sám šaknóǧaʼ**ehą**.

Class 3: Nasal Conjugation Verbs (or N-Conjugation)

We already know about the regular stem verbs (Class 1) as well as the Y-stem verbs (Class 2). Class 3 verbs have few members, although they are very frequent. This set of verbs is called the "Nasal conjugation" (or N-conjugation) because the person markers are stand-alone nasal consonants[*]: *-m-* (1SG) and *-n-* (2SG) and *-Ø-* (3SG). These person markers delete any following *w* or *y* of the stem and replace it by the first and second person markers. Here are the prefixed person markings for N-conjugation verbs:

	Person Markers (Class 3)			
	Singular		**Plural**	
1	-m-	I	-ų(g)-...-bi	we
2	-n-	you	-n-...-bi	you all
3	-Ø-	she/he	-Ø-...-bi	they

---

[*] Nasal consonants like *m* and *n* are produced when the airstream goes through the nasal cavity, as in the word *nnnnose*.

Below are some very common N-conjugation verbs inflected for the six persons (singular and plural). We start with the verbs that require the prefixed person markers.

yagá ~ yigá – 1) *she/he sits on it*; 2) *she/he does continuously* (Class 3)

magá	I am sitting on it	ųyágabi	we are sitting on it
nagá	you are sitting on it	nagábi	you all are sitting on it
yagá ~ yigá	she/he is sitting on it	yagábi	they are sitting on it

įštíma – *she/he sleeps* (Class 3)

mįštíma	I am sleeping	ųgįštímabi	we are sleeping
nįštíma	you are sleeping	nįštímabi	you all are sleeping
įštíma	she/he is sleeping	įštímabi	they are sleeping

ų́ – 1) *she/he wears it*; 2) *she/he uses it* (Class 3)

mų́	I wear it	ųgų́bi	we wear it
nų́	you wear it	nų́bi	you all wear it
ų́	she/he wears it	ų́bi	they wear it

As with other verb classes the person markings can be infixed in the stem. Note that in the case of *įwų́ǧa* "she/he asks someone" the semi-vowel *w* is deleted like in the Y-stem (Class 2) verbs.

įyų́ǧa ~ įwų́ǧa – *she/he asks him/her about it* (Class 3)

įmų́ǧa	I ask him/her	ųgíyuǧabi	we ask him/her
įnų́ǧa	you ask him/her	įnų́ǧabi	you all ask him/her
įyų́ǧa ~ įwų́ǧa	she/he asks him/her	įyų́ǧabi	they ask him/her

dóka'ų – *she/he does what* (Class 3)

dókamų	I do what?	dóka'ųgųbi	we do what?
dókanų	you do what?	dókanųbi	you all do what?
dóka'ų ~ dókų	she/he does what?	dókųbi	they do what?

Šų́gatąga agą́n-**yąga** no!	*Ride the horse!*
Žén **yįgá**.	*He is sitting there.*
Žéci **yįgábi**.	*They are sitting around there.*
Gakí **mągį́kta**.	*I'll sit way over there.*
Búza gá **įštíma**.	*That cat over there is sleeping.*
Aké **nįštíma**.	*You are sleeping again.*
Wapáha né **nų́kta** he?	*Are you going to wear this hat?*
Šiná žé **ų́šį**.	*She did not wear that blanket.*
Micína **įmų́ǧįkta**.	*I will ask my (male) older brother.*
Nitága **įnų́ǧįkta**.	*You will ask your (female) younger sister.*
Šų́ga gá dágu **dókų** (he)?	*What is that dog over there doing?*
Dágu **dókanų**? Dágunišį!	*What are you doing? Nothing at all!*

Note that for the verb *dóka'ų* "she/he does what?" there is a shortened version, *dókų*, used in fast speech, and the last vowel is often inaudible.

Plural of Subjects

As can be seen from the preceding examples, whenever the subject of a verb (i.e., the person doing the action) is plural, the verb takes the suffix -*bi*. In Nakoda, the subject of a verb can be pluralized on the verb and on the subject noun with the suffix -*bi* and also on the demonstrative with -*na* (PL). One should keep in mind that the nominal -*bi* (as shown below) is not commonly used; speakers prefer the plural demonstrative -*na* or the verbal -*bi* alone.

ANIMATE SUBJECT

Cijá**bi** žená įštíma**bi**.	*Those children are sleeping.* (not common)
Cijá žená įštíma**bi**.	*Those children are sleeping.* (common)
Wíyą**bi** žená nážįbįkta.	*Those women will be standing.* (not common)
Wíyą žená nážįbįkta.	*Those women will be standing.* (common)
Wíyą né wóda**bi**.	*The women were eating.* (very common)

The suffix -*bi* appears on some nouns but not on others. The distribution is conditioned by whether the noun refers to an **animate** entity (those that possess life and free will, like humans and animals) or to an **inanimate** entity (those that do not possess life, like objects and concepts).

ANIMATE NOUNS

cijá	child	>	cijá**bi**	children
búza	cat	>	búza**bi**	cats
šúga	dog	>	šúga**bi**	dogs

Cijá**bi** dóna nuhá (he)?	How many children do you have?
Cijá**bi** yámni**bi**.	There are three children.
Búza**bi** asą́bi yatką́**bi**.	The cats are drinking milk.

As mentioned above, speakers often drop the -*bi* on nouns but never on verbs. Thus, it is more common to hear *búza asą́bi yatką́bi* "the cats are drinking milk" than the version shown above. Note also that when nouns are built with the diminutive -*na* "small" or the nominalizer -*na* (these suffixes are homophones*), the pluralizer -*bi* is inserted before -*na*:

hokšína	boy	>	hokší**bi**na	boys
mitúgašina	my grandfather	>	mitúgaši**bi**na	my grandfathers

For inanimate nouns indicating the subject of a verb, plural demonstratives such as *žená* and *nená* can be used, or a cardinal number *dóba* "four," but -*bi* is never employed. Instead, the process of reduplication—which means to copy a syllable of the word as in the fictive words *trala*$_{SG}$ > *tralala*$_{PL}$, *gitosa*$_{SG}$ > *gitotosa*$_{PL}$—indicates plurality, among other things, in Nakoda. However, in some instances no indication of plurality is used, although the speaker is referring to a plurality of inanimate objects.

INANIMATE NOUNS

pąǧí **šá**	a red potato
Pąǧí **šašá** žená éyagu!	Take those red potatoes!
Pąǧí yuhá.	She/he has potatoes.
Tašpą́ né tága.	This apple is big.
Tašpą́ ne**ná tąktága**.	These apples are big.
Tašpą́ wąží wacíga.	I want an apple.
Pąǧí **nų́ba** wacíga.	I want two potatoes.

---

* Homophones are two words or elements that have the same pronounciation but different meanings, like *sent* and *cent* in English.

Lastly, the plural suffix -*bi* (3PL) should not be confused with the homophone -*bi* "nominalizer." The suffix -*bi* "nom." appears on nouns that are made from a verb (see Chapter 10). More specifically, this -*bi* changes a verb into a noun that expresses the end product or result of an activity, much like the English -*er*: to run > runner; to flip > flipper.

Verb			**Noun**	
ağúya	*to brown it*	>	ağúya**bi**	*bread* (lit., that which is browned)
ȟuȟnáȟya	*to roast it*	>	ȟuȟnáȟya**bi**	*coffee* (lit., that which is roasted)
tí	*to dwell*	>	tí**bi**	*house* (lit., that in which one lives)
wací	*to dance*	>	wací**bi**	*dance* (lit., that which is danced)
wóda	*to eat*	>	wóda**bi**	*meal* (lit., the eating)

That the resulting words are nouns and not verbs—even though they sound exactly the same—is clearly indicated by the fact that one can add a singular demonstrative after a derived noun, as in *ağúyabi né* "this coffee" or *tíbi né* "this house," but not after a verb *tíbi né "the they live."

Chapter 5 Exercises

EXERCISE 1

Translate these sentences into Nakoda using the correct time markers.

1. When did you eat? _____

2. Who wanted coffee? _____

3. When did you walk over there? _____

4. My grandfathers sat there. _____

5. It rained yesterday. _____

6. How are the boys doing? _____

7. I slept a lot yesterday._____

8. Tomorrow the women will cook for a feast. _____
_____

9. Yesterday we walked outside. _____

EXERCISE 2
Conjugate these verbs:

	gáǧa	**įštíma**	**ų́** –*wear it*
1SG	_____	_____	_____
2SG	_____	_____	_____
3SG FUT/NEG	_____	_____	_____
1PL	_____	_____	_____
2PL FUT/NEG	_____	_____	_____
3PL NEG	_____	_____	_____

EXERCISE 3
Match the correct phrases with their English translations:

cijá žé	pąǧí nená	šų́gabi ganá	cąníska žená
those dogs over there	those cigarettes	these potatoes	that child

EXERCISE 4
Translate the following kinship terms into Nakoda (M = male; F = female):

my son	_____	his grandmother	_____
his older brother	_____	your grandfather	_____
her older sister	_____	my (M) younger sister	_____
your (M) older sister	_____	my daughter	_____
Mother!	_____	his (M) younger brother	_____
her son	_____	my mother	_____
her (F) older brother	_____	her (F) younger sister	_____

EXERCISE 5

Read the following sentences aloud and translate them into English. (žéca cén – *because she/he is of a certain kind*)

Hąhébi štén mikúši nągų́ mitúgaši timánibįkta.

___

Nená gáǧįkta: tanó, paǧí, waȟpé į́š.

___

Mihų́ aǧúyabiskuya į́š opétų.

___

Dąyą́ wó'ųdabįkta.

___

CHAPTER 6

Objectives

VOCABULARY

- Clothing
- More objects, animals, and persons
- Verbs for states and colours

GRAMMAR

- Negative marker -šį
- Active and stative verbs
- How to say "to be" in Nakoda

Dialogues

1. Dóken yašką (he)?
   Nína mayázą no! Ȟtánihą osní žehą́.

   How is it going?
   I am very sick! It was cold yesterday.

2. Wašíju tíbi tó né duwé opétų (he)?
   Wįcá gá wašíju tíbi žé opétų.

   Who bought the blue house?
   That man over there bought that house.

3. Duwé cąní yuhá (he)?
   Miyáde cąní yuhá. Cąní waką́ no!

   Who has tobacco?
   My father has tobacco. Tobacco is sacred!

4. Šiná né sága (he)?
   Hiyá, šiná né sagéšį.

   Is this blanket dry?
   No, this blanket is not dry.

5. Šúgatąga né waníyedu dóna ehą́ki (he)? — *How old is this horse?*
Šúgatąga né nínaȟ gána. — *This horse is very old.*

6. Wįcíjana gá nitą́kši (he)? — *Is that girl over there your (male) younger sister?*
Hą́, wįcíjana gá mitą́kši. — *Yes, that girl over there is my younger sister.*
Hukwááǃ Nitą́kši nína tágašį. — *Wow! She is not very big.*

Vocabulary

NOUNS

asą́bi súda	cheese	midáguyabi	my relatives
agícida	soldier, police	owį́ža	quilt, bedding
cáhąba	shoe	sąksája	dress
cuwį́knąga	coat, shirt	šiná	blanket
hába	moccasin	šųkcúkʼana	coyote
hųská	pants	šųgašána	red fox
įkcé wįcášta	Indigenous person	wapáha	hat, cap
maštį́ja	rabbit	wašíju	white person
mató	bear	zitkána	bird

VERBS (NV-CONJUGATION, CLASS 4)

dąyą́	she/he/it is well, good	miní įtʼá áya	she/he is thirsty
é	she/he/it is	téjana	she/he/it is young, new
gána ~ gą́na	she/he/it is old	šįtų́	she/he/it is fat
hą́ska	she/he/it is tall, long, of a certain height	tą́ga	she/he/it is big
įdúka	she/he is hungry	waką́	she/he/it is sacred, holy, mysterious
ípi	she/he/it is full	yazą́	she/he/it is sick
júsina	she/he/it is small	žéca	she/he is of that kind, tribe, trade

MISCELLANEOUS

hį́į́ǃ	Wow! (female speaker)	jé	always, habitually
hukwááǃ	Wow! (male speaker)	okná	through, in
iyé	she/he/it is the one	no	declaration (male speaker)
iyúhana	everything	wanágaš	long ago

Negation

Negative statements are expressed by putting the suffix *-šį* after the verb. As with *-kta* 'future/potential' the negation marker *-šį* is an ablauting element which provokes a change in the final vowel of the stem. In other words, *a* changes to *e*, *a* to *į*, and *i* to *į* when *-šį* is added. Ablauting (or vowel change) can be illustrated as such:

núd**a** + šį	=	núd**e**šį	*you did not eat it*
wącímnag**a** + kta	=	wącímnag**į**kta	*I will see you*

Positive form		**Negative form**	
wóda	*she/he is eating*	wód**e**šį	*she/he is not eating*
yacíga	*you want it*	yacíg**e**šį	*you do not want it*
yaškáda	*you play with it*	yaškád**e**šį	*you do not play with it*
iyódąga	*she/he sits down*	iyódąg**e**šį	*she/he does not sit down*
yá	*she/he goes*	y**é**šį	*she/he does not go*

For some verbs that end in a nasal vowel there is no change, as with *šką́* "she/he moves" > *šką́šį* "she/he does not move" or *yatką́* "she/he drinks" > *yatką́šį* "she/he does not drink."

There is a strict order for the placement of the plural *-bi*, future/potential *-kta* and negation *-šį* markers. Note the change from *i* to *į* of the *-bi* suffix.

VERB STEM + -bį- + -kte- + -šį

Positive forms		**Future + Negative forms**	
yá	*she/he goes*	yį́**-kte-šį**	*she/he will not go*
ná-**bi**	*you all go*	ná-**bį-kte-šį**	*you all will not go*
wóda-**bi**	*they are eating*	wóda-**bį-kte-šį**	*they will not eat*

Active and Stative Verbs

Verbs are words that are used to talk about an activity (*she **walks**, she **kicked** it*), a state (*she **is** tall*), or a natural phenomenon (*it **is** raining, it **is** muddy*). If you did not have any knowledge of English there would be no way to know if the verbs *she **walks*** or *she **kicked** it* or *she **is** tall* are actions or states, since they all have *she* as the subject. Nakoda works differently than English since the person markers tell you—to some extent—if the verb describes an **action** (e.g., *to think, live, take it*) or a **state** (e.g., *to be nice, black, sad*). Nakoda marks the distinction between active and stative verbs with different person markers for the first and second persons.

In Chapters 2, 3, and 5 we studied the formation of three types of active verbs: i) regular stem (Class 1); ii) Y-stem (Class 2); and iii) N-conjugation (Class 3). In this chapter we will study the last set of person markers, that of stative verbs, or Class 4 verbs (NV-conjugation). Like the N-conjugation verbs, the subject of stative verbs is exclusively expressed with a **N**asal consonant (either *m* or *n*) and a **V**owel (either *a* or *i*), hence the label NV-conjugation. Again, the third person (*he, she, it*) is expressed with a zero marker Ø independently of the verbal class.

	Active (regular stem)	**Active (Y-stem)**	**Active (N-conjugation)**	**Stative (NV-conjugation)**
	Class 1 (Chapter 2)	**Class 2 (Chapter 3)**	**Class 3 (Chapter 5)**	**Class 4 (Chapter 6)**
1SG	-wa-	-mn-	-m-	-ma-
2SG	-ya-	-n-	-n-	-ni-
3SG	-Ø-	-Ø-	-Ø-	-Ø-
	wacíga – *I want it*	**mn**á – *I go*	**m**ų́ – *I wear it*	**ma**šį́tų – *I am fat*

Like any other active verbs, the *I* and *you* person markers in stative verbs can be prefixed or infixed. The placement of these person markers is hard to predict just by looking at the verb form of the third person singular. However, it is possible to know if a verb belongs to the NV-conjugation if you ask yourself the following question: Does the verb express an action like *eat, sleep, run* (Class 1, 2, or 3) or a state like *to be blue, big, holy* (Class 4)? If the verb expresses a state, then add the following person markers:

		Person Markers (NV-conjugation, Class 4)		
1	-ma-	*I*	-ų(g)-...-bi	*we*
2	-ni-	*you*	-ni-...-bi	*you all*
3	-Ø-	*she/he*	-Ø-...-bi	*they*

Below you will find some common stative verbs of the NV-conjugation (Class 4), inflected for person, negation, and future/potential. This will give you a precise idea of how to form and use them.

šį́tų́ – *she/he/it is fat* (Class 4)

mašį́tų	*I am fat*	šį́tų́**kta**	*she/he will be fat*
nišį́tų	*you are fat*	šį́tų́**bįkteší**	*they will not be fat*
ųšį́tų**bi**	*we are fat*		

dąyá – *she/he is well* (Class 4)

madáyą	*I am well*	dąyá**kta**	*she/he will be well*
nidáyą	*you are well*	dąyá**biktešį**	*they will not be well*
ųdáyą**bi**	*we are well*		

tága – *she/he/it is big, large* (Class 4)

matága	*I am big, large*	tági**kta**	*she/he will be big, large*
nitága	*you are big, large*	tága**biktešį**	*they will not be big*
ųtága**bi**	*we are big, large*		

júsina – *she/he/it is small* (Class 4)

majúsina	*I am small*	júsina**kta**	*she/he will be small*
nijúsina	*you are small*	júsina**ktešį**	*she/he will not be small*
ųjúsina**bi**	*we are small*		

yazą́ – *she/he is sick* (Class 4)

mayázą	*I am sick*	yazą́**kta**	*she/he will be sick*
niyázą	*you are sick*	yazą́**ktešį**	*she/he will not be sick*
ųyázą**bi**	*we are sick*		

hą́ska – *she/he/it is tall, long* (Class 4)

mahą́ska	*I am tall*	hą́ski**kta**	*she/he will be tall*
nihą́ska	*you are tall*	hą́ski**ktešį**	*they will not be tall*
ųhą́ska**bi**	*we are tall*		

gána ~ gą́na – *she/he is old* (Class 4)

magána	*I am old*	gána**kta**	*she/he will be old*
nigána	*you are old*	gána**ktešį**	*she/he will not be old*
ųgána**bi**	*we are old*		

téjana – *she/he/it is young, new* (Class 4)

matéjana	*I am young*	téjana**kta**	*she/he will be young*
nitéjana	*you are young*	téjana**ktešį**	*they will not be young*
ųtéjana**bi**	*we are young*		

Nína **nišį́tų**.	*You are very fat.*
Gugúša **šį̇tų́** žé įštíma.	*The fat pig is sleeping.*
Nína **mayázą** jé.	*I am always very sick.*
Ą́ba šagówį **yazą́bi** žehą́.	*They were sick for seven days.*
Nína **payážą**.	*She/he has a big headache.*
Dóna **hą́ska** ehą́yaki?	*How tall are you?*
Mahą́skešį.	*I'm not tall.*
Waną́gaš, miyáde wįcášta **hą́ska**, **yazą́**-c'ehą.	*Long ago, my father (who was called Tall Man), was very sick.*
Cįhį́tku žé **hą́ska**.	*His/her son is tall.*
Nahą́ȟ **magánešį**.	*I'm not old yet.* (nahą́ȟ – still, yet)

The verb *dąyą́* can also be used as an adverb meaning "nice, fine, well," and in this role it modifies the verb. It occurs frequently in this adverbial function, and like any other adverb, it precedes the verb. The same applies to the verbs *wašté* "nice, good" (> "nicely") and *waką́* "holy, mysterious" (> "sacredly, in a holy manner").

Dąyą́ wacímnagįkte no!	*It's good to see you!*
Dąyą́ wa'ų́.	*I am fine.*
Dąyą́ wací no!	*She/he dances well!*
Waką́ iyódągabi.	*They are fasting.* (lit., they sit sacredly)
Waką́ imnódągešį.	*I don't fast.*
Wašté įštímabįkte no!	*They will sleep well!*

waką́ – *she/he is holy, mysterious* (Class 4)

wa**má**ką	*I am holy*	waką́**kta**	*she/he will be holy*
wa**ní**ką	*you are holy*	waką́**bįktešį**	*they will not be holy*
wa'**ų́ką**bi	*we are holy*		

į́pi – *she/he is full* (Class 4)

į́**ma**pi	*I am full*	į́pi**bikta**	*she/he will be full*
į́**ni**pi	*you are full*	į́pi**bįktešį**	*they will not be full*
ųgį́pi**bi**	*we are full*		

įdúka – *she/he/it is hungry* (Class 4)

į**má**duka	*I am hungry*	įdúka**kta**	*she/he will be hungry*
į**ní**duka	*you are hungry*	įdúka**bįktešį**	*they will not be hungry*
ųgį́duka**bi**	*we are hungry*		

miní įt'á áya – *she/he/it is thirsty* (Class 4)

miní **mat**'á áya	*I am thirsty*	miní **įt'į́kta** áya	*she/he will be thirsty*
miní **ni**t'á áya	*you are thirsty*	miní **įt'ábišį** áya	*they are not thirsty*
miní **ųt'ábi** áya	*we are thirsty*		

Dágu iyuhána **waką́** no!	*Everything is holy!*
Midáguyabi **į́pibi**.	*My relatives are full.*
Waná nína **į́mapi** no!	*Now I'm really full!*
Búza nená **miní įt'ábišį áya**.	*Those cats are not thirsty.*
Dáguškina **miní įt'į́kta áya** no!	*The baby will be thirsty!*
Miní mak'ú wo, nína **miní mat'á áya**.	*Give me some water, I'm very thirsty.*

The complex verb *miní įt'á áya* translates as "she/he is starting to die for water" and will be explained in Chapter 16.

Stative Verbs: Colours

Unlike English, there are no adjectives in Nakoda. To indicate the colour, shape, or size of something a stative verb like *tó* "it is blue" or *waką́* "it is sacred, holy, or mysterious" is placed after the word you want to qualify, as in: *búza sába* "it is a black cat." There are also a lot of compounds built by combining a noun with a stative verb of colour, such as *hųskáto* "jeans, denims" (leggings + blue). All colour verbs are stative and thus belong to Class 4: **mas**ába "I am black," **ni**tó "you are blue."

Colours (NV-conjugation, Class 4)

ǧí	*it is light yellow*	šá	*it is red*
ȟóda	*it is grey*	ša'į́mna	*it is pink*
pežíto	*it is grass green*	tó	*it is blue, green*
sába	*it is black*	tósaba	*it is dark blue*
ská	*it is white*	zí	*it is brown, dark yellow*

Pąǧí **šašá** žená éyagu.	*Take those red potatoes.*
Búza **sába** gá asą́bi yatką́.	*That black cat over there is drinking milk.*
Cuwį́knąga **sába** né duwé táwa?	*Whose black coat is this?*
Maštį́ja **skána** né nitáwa he?	*Is this white rabbit yours?*
Mihų́ wašíju tíbi **tó** wążí okná tí.	*My mother lives in a blue house.*
Ma**tó** hį́kna nis**kána**.	*I am blue and you are black.*

Stative verbs can serve as nominal subject or object when a demonstrative is placed after, such as "the [stative verb] one". The verb cannot be inflected with person prefixes and mood markers. Stative verbs are in bold in the following examples.

Skána žé waná iyáya.	*The white one is leaving now.*
Zí žé nitáwa.	*Yours is yellow.*
Mitáwa žé júsina.	*Mine is small.*
Tága žé nitáwa.	*The big (one) is yours.*
Wąží **júsina** né įštímes'a.	*That small one is a sleeper.*

As indicated in the preceding examples the word order is:

STATIVE VERB + DEMONSTRATIVE + VERB

Noun compounds are made up of two parts: ENTITY (animal, thing) + COLOUR. They are pronounced as a single word and have only one stress point, as with *greenhouse* (where one grows vegetables) compared to *green house* (a green-coloured house). In order to have a better grasp at this technique of word formation we have put the literal meaning in brackets. Note that *šųk-* roughly means "canine, dog-like" but also "horse" (see Chapter 16).

cąníska	*cigarette* (tobacco + white)
šųksába	*black horse* (horse + black)
šųgašána	*red fox* (canine + red + small)
wapáska	*white hat* (hat + white)
zitkánato	*bluebird* (bird + blue)
zitkásaba	*blackbird* (bird+black)

How to Say "To Be" in Nakoda

There are a few ways to translate the English verb "to be" in Nakoda. We will review here three ways to do so.

1. Impersonal weather verbs are always translated with *to be* in English:

Mağážu he?	*Is it raining?* (lit., raining + INTERROGATION)
Nína osní no!	*It is very cold outside!* (lit., very + cold.outside + DECLARATIVE)

2. Stative verbs are always translated with *to be* in English:

Makóce né nína **waką́** no!	*The land is very sacred!*
Gugúša né **šį̱tų́**.	*This pig is fat.*
Zitkána žé **tó**.	*That bird is blue.* (compare *zitkána tó žé* "that blue bird")

3. Active verbs *nážį* "she/he stands" (Class 1), *žéca* "she/he is one a kind (ethnic group, trade)," and *yągá* "she/he sits on it" (Class 3) can also be translated with *to be* in English:

Mitákona gakí **nážį**.	*My friend is (standing) over there.*
Bahágąn **mągį́kta**.	*I will be (sitting) on a hill.*
Agícida **žéca**.	*He is a soldier.*

4. To ask for the identity of an object, one can also use a demonstrative (*né, ganá*) with a question particle *he* (for male speakers):

Dágu **né** he?	*What is this (close)?*
Duwé **né** he?	*Who is this (close)?*
Dágu **nená** he?	*What are these?*
Dágu **ganá** he?	*What are those over there?*

5. Nouns and some pronouns can be used as stative verbs (Class 4):

Įkcé wį**mácašta**.	*I am Indigenous.*
Wamášiju no!	*I'm a white person,* of European descent.*
Mamáto.	*I'm a bear.*
Maduwé he?	*Who am I?*

6. Finally, there are two *to be* verbs in Nakoda: *é* "she/he is" (Class 4) and *ų́* "she/he is, stays" (Class 1). The first one is not frequent and mostly used to specify the identity of a participant.

Né'**e** no!	*Here it is!* (something previously mentioned)
Žé'**e** he?	*Is that the one?* (something previously mentioned)
Wįcá gakí'**e**.	*It is that man over there.*
Waná wíyą gicí **wa'ų́**.	*I'm with a woman now.*
Dóken **ya'ų́** (he)?	*How are you?*

---

* *Wamášiju* is translated as "I am a Whiteman," but in this text that term is considered archaic and we have changed all instances of *Whiteman* to *white person* to be consistent with Gregory Younging's important writing guide, *Elements of Indigenous Style: A Guide for Writing By and About Indigenous Peoples* (Edmonton: Brush Education, 2018).

Sounds: Nasal Spread

In the previous chapters you probably noticed that some vowels like *a* became nasalized as *ą* in some words but stayed as *a* in others. This is the case with the person marker *-ma-* (1SG); it becomes nasalized in **emą́giya** "she/he told me" but not in **ma**stústa "I'm tired." Nasalization or "nasal spread" is very frequent in Nakoda and occurs whenever *a*, *i*, or *u* follows or precedes a nasal consonant like *m* or *n*. However, there are variations between speakers on this matter.

maká	>	mąká ~ maká	*earth*
gána	>	gą́na ~ gána	*she/he/it is old*
yábi	>	yą́bi ~ yábi	*they go*
iníbi	>	inį́bi	*sweat lodge*

Chapter 6 Exercises

EXERCISE 1

Translate the following sentences into Nakoda and read them aloud.

1. The blue house is big. _____

2. My (male) younger brother is very fat. _____

3. The black coat is very big. _____

4. The white dog is old. _____

5. That black rabbit over there is running. _____

6. Tobacco is sacred. _____

7. They don't dance well. _____

8. I was sick for three days. _____

9. Those rabbits over there are really small. _____

10. My (female) older brother is not tall. _____

EXERCISE 2
Fill in the following table with the correct verb forms.

	yazą́	dąyą́	ípi
1SG FUT	_____	_____	_____
2SG FUT	_____	_____	_____
3SG FUT/NEG	_____	_____	_____
1PL FUT/NEG	_____	_____	_____
2PL FUT/NEG	_____	_____	_____
3PL FUT/NEG	_____	_____	_____

EXERCISE 3
Translate the following verbs into English.

yá	_____	wódabįkteší	_____
háskįkta	_____	yį́kteší	_____
wódabi	_____	nábi	_____
ųdą́yąbi	_____	dąyą́kta	_____
šįtų́kta	_____	šįtų́bįkteší	_____

EXERCISE 4
Which words (3) do not belong in this set? Explain why, using the correct terms seen in Chapter 1 (parts of speech).

cą́hąba	asą́bi súda	wįcášta	šiná	súda
háska	hųská	tadéyąba	zitkána	šų́ga

EXERCISE 5
Read the following sentences aloud and translate them into English.

Šúgatągabi dóna nuhá (he)?
_____

Waná šúgatągabi dóba mnuhá.
_____

Sába žé nína gána no!
_____

Waníyedu agéšagowį ehą́ki.
_____

Ská žé dąyą́šį, nína yazą́.
_____

Ą̨bá šagówį yazą́.
_____

Šką́šį no!
_____

CHAPTER 7

Objectives

VOCABULARY

- More words for objects
- Words indicating the position of something

GRAMMAR

- Declarative and imperative enclitics
- "Let's" construction
- Conjunction markers: *įš* "and, also, him/her/it too"; and *eštá* "or"
- Spatial adverbs and postpositions

Dialogues

1. Taspą ǧí duktén yągá (he)?
   Taspą ǧí awódabi agą́n yągá.

   Where are the oranges sitting?
   The oranges are sitting on the table.

2. Nisų́ga, nikúši įš dókųbi (he)?

   Nisų́ga timáhen šųktí gakná škáda hį́kna mikúši owókšubi én ų́!

   What are your (female) younger brother and your grandmother up to?
   My younger brother is playing beside the barn and my grandmother is in the garden!

3. Waȟpé eštá miní yacíga (he)?
   Waȟpé edáhą wacíga hį́kna mihų́ įš waȟpé cįgá.

   Do you want tea or water?
   I want some tea and my mother, too, wants tea.

4. Cąníska éyagu bo! — *All of you take some cigarettes!*
Duktén iyódągabįkte (he)? — *Where will they be sitting?*
Iyécįgayena timáhen iyódągabįkte no. — *They will be sitting in the car.*

5. Háu koná! Dágu dókanų? — *Hello, friend! What are you doing?*
Dágunišį! — *Nothing!*
Ųyįkte owóde tíbi no! — *Let's go to the restaurant!*

6. Dágu né (he)? — *What is this?*
Né wahábi gicí tanó. — *This is soup with meat.*
Wašté! Nągáhą wó'ųdas! — *Neat! Let's eat now!*

Vocabulary

NOUNS

awódabi	*table*	owókšubi	*garden*
bahá	*hill*	owópetų tíbi	*store*
cą́ágąn	*chair*	peží	*hay, grass*
iyécįgayena	*car*	šųktí	*barn*
íyą	*stone*	tá	*moose*
makóce	*land, ground*	taspą́ ǧí	*orange*
miní	*water*	taspą́ ǧí tóta	*lemon*
océti	*fireplace, stove*	tíbi	*house, dwelling*
ocągu	*road*	wahábi	*soup*
owóde tíbi	*restaurant*	wašíju tíbi	*framed house*

VERBS

dókų	*she/he does what?* (Class 3)
įštíma	*she/he sleeps* (Class 3)
kní	*she/he goes back home* (Class 1)
ú	*she/he comes (here)* (Class 1)
yá	*she/he goes (there)* (Class 2)

FUNCTION WORDS AND INTERJECTIONS

eštá	*or*	iyuhána	*all of them, everybody*
dukté	*what, which*	į́š	*and, also, him/her/it too*
Háu koná!	*Hello, friend!*	nągáhą	*now*
hók	*yes (male speaker)*		

Declarative Male Enclitic *no*

In Nakoda, some verbal enclitics indicate that a sentence is a declaration. Most of them are used only by male speakers while others are used by both male and female speakers. As mentioned in Chapter 3 the enclitic *he* indicates a question and is gender neutral while the imperative enclitics *wo* and *bo* are used by male speakers only. These enclitics do not carry stress and are separated from the host word to ease the reading.

Pinámayaya!	*I thank you!*
Pinámayaye **no**!	*I thank you!* (male declaration)
Wa'úkte **no**!	*I'm going to come!*
Iná, imnámnįkteši̧ **no**!	*Mother, I won't go!*

As you can see from the following examples, the declarative male enclitic *no* is an ablauting element (indicated by an underscore) which changes the final vowel of a preceding verb.

wa'ú + kta + no	>	wa'úkte_**no**!	*I'm going to come!*
mağážu + kta + no	>	mağážukte_**no**!	*It's going to rain!*
wącímnaga + kta + no	>	wącímnagįkte_**no**!	*It will see you!*

Lastly, some female speakers produce a glottal stop ['] after a verb to indicate a declaration: *Tatą́ga'!* "It was big!"

"Let's" Constructions

The "let's" construction is related to the imperative since it is used to suggest to a group of people to do something. As opposed to the pure imperatives seen above, "let's" constructions include the speaker and are translated into English by the verb phrase *let's*, as in *Let's go to town!* In Nakoda, this type of construction is obtained by suffixing *-s* on a verb already inflected for the first person dual (1D). The template is the following: 1D VERB + *-s*.

	Stem	**1D**	**"Let's X"**
eat	wóda	wó'ų̨da	wó'ų̨da**s**
sleep	įštíma	ų̨gį́štima	ų̨gį́štima**s**
go	yá	ų̨yá	ų̨yá**s**
go walk	ománi yá	ománi ų̨yá	ománi ų̨yá**s**

Waná wó'ųdas!	Let's eat now!
Waná ųgíštimas!	Let's sleep now!
Ųyás owóde tíbi!	Let's go to the restaurant!
Ųnáȟ'ųs!	Let's listen to it!

As can be seen in the preceding examples, the dual form "we two" (without the plural -bi) is wó'ųda "we two eat." For some speakers who don't use the dual at all, it nevertheless appears in this type of verb form. Some speakers don't use the -s suffix but only a verb with -kta "potential/future," as in ųgíštimabįkta "we will sleep, let's go to bed."

Conjunction Markers: *íš* "and, also, him/her/it/they too"; *híkna* "and"; *eštá* "or"

In English, there are small function words like *and* and *or* that are used to connect nouns, verbs, and other parts of speech, as in:

*I want meat **and** soup.*	noun **and** noun
*Do you want tea **or** coffee?*	noun **or** noun
*She likes riding horses **and** swimming.*	verb **and** verb
*Do want to eat **or** continue driving?*	verb **or** verb
*Is it here **or** there?*	demonstrative **or** demonstrative

In Nakoda, the words that fulfill these two functions are *íš* "and, also," *híkna* "and," and *eštá* "or." The conjunction *híkna* "and" usually connects verbs together, but there are some variations between speakers from different communities. Some use *íš* "and" to connect two nouns together while others use *íš* to connect verbs too, but speakers who use *híkna* "and" do it to connect verbs only.

íš – *and, also, him/her/it/they too*

Tanó **íš** wahábi yacíga (he)?	Do you want meat and soup?
Paul **íš** Mary wódabi.	Paul and Mary are eating.
Iyódąga **íš** nągáhą wóda wo!	Sit down now and eat!
Iyódąga **íš** wóda wo!	Sit down and eat!
Wįcá gá **íš** aǧúyabi yúda.	That man over there, too, is eating bread.
Íš ú!	She is coming, too!
Íš įdúkabi.	They are hungry, too.

HÍKNA ~ HÍK – *and*

Iyódąga **híkna** wóda wo!	Sit down and eat!
Tín ú **híkna** wóda!	Come in and eat!
Ȟuȟnáȟyabi yatką́ wo, **híkna** taspą́ ǧí yúda!	Drink your coffee and eat your orange!

CHAPTER 7

EŠTÁ – *or*

This conjunction has a rather free position and can host some suffixes like *-š* "contrast, on the other hand".

Tanó **eštá** wahábi yacíga (he)?	*Do you want meat or soup?*
Ȟuȟnáȟyabi yacíga **eštá** waȟpé?	*Do you want coffee or tea?*
Dukté yacíga, júsina žé **eštáš** tága žé?	*Which one do you want, a small one or a big one?*

Spatial Adverbs and Postpositions

In English, adverbs of positions and prepositions indicate a general location or the location of something in relation to a point of reference. We call them "prepositions" because the locative expressions (e.g., *inside*, *beside*, etc.) come *before* the point of reference (*the house*) as indicated by the following examples:

English adverbs	English prepositions
come **inside**	**beside** the barn
play **outside**	**around** the corner
come **over here**	**in** the house
here she sat	**on, under** the couch

In Nakoda, adverbs and postpositions can indicate the position of something in relation to a point of reference. However, unlike English prepositions, the Nakoda postpositions (e.g., *to*, *beside*, etc.) come *after* the point of reference (*the house*). This is why we use the term "postposition."

Adverbs		Postpositions	
héktam	*behind*	agą́n	*on*
hokún	*below, down*	ektá	*in, to, at*
į́hokun	*beneath*	én	*in, here*
kún	*down*	gakná	*beside*
ókšą	*around*	mahén	*in, inside something*
tągán	*outside*		
timáhen ~tín	*inside; in a house*		

1. **Adverbs** do not necessarily have a point of reference, which may be expressed or not.

Šųktí **héktam** nážį.	He is standing behind the barn.
Héktam nážį nén.	He stands here behind it.
Hokún yá!	Go downstairs!
íyą **įhokun**	beneath the stone
iyécįgayena **įhokun**	beneath the car
Kún ú!	Come down (here)! (e.g., downstairs)
Kún a'ú!	Bring it down (here)!
Duwé iyuhána nén **ókšą** iyódąga bo!	Everybody sit around here!
tí **ókšą**	around the house
Tągán škáda bo!	You all play outside!
Tągán nína maštá no!	It is very hot outside!
Tągán iyáya.	She/he sets to go outside.
wacégiya tíbi **timáhen**	inside the church
Tín ú wo!	Come in!

2. **Postpositions** have a preceding point of reference, which may be expressed or not.

(Šúgatąga) **agą́n**-yąga.	She/he rides a horse.
íyą **agą́n**	on the stone
cą'ágąn **agą́n**	on the chair
Tá bahágąn nážį.*	The moose is standing on top of a hill.
Húgu Céǧa K'ína **ektá** tí.	His/her mother lives in Carry The Kettle.
Wiyóhpaya **ektá** timáni mnįkta.	I am going to visit people in the West.
Wanágaš Šiyóša **ektá** wa'í.	Long ago I went to Red Pheasant.
Žé **én** ųhíbi.	We arrived here.
Én yįgá!	Sit here!
Mikúši **én** ų́.	My grandmother is here.
Peží žé wašíju tibí **gakná**.	The hay is beside the house.
iyógapte **gakná**	beside the plate
ocą́gu **gakná**	beside the road
Océti **gakná** nawážį.	I'm standing beside the stove.
Šúgatąga **gakná** nawážį.	I'm standing beside the horse.
océti **mahén**	in the stove
iyécįgayena **máhen**	in the car
mahén ų́bi	underwear (ų́ "she/he wears it" + -bi "nom.")
Owį́ža **mahén** yįgá!	Stay under the blanket!

---

* Note that the postposition *agą́n* can fuse with a noun that ends in *a*: bahá + **agą́n** = *bahágąn* "on a hilltop."

Chapter 7 Exercises

EXERCISE 1

Translate the following sentences into Nakoda.

1. Let's walk beside the road. _____

2. Let's sleep in the car. _____

3. The cat is sleeping under the table. _____

4. The horse is standing beside the house. _____

5. That cat over there is sleeping under the chair. _____

6. That man over there is standing on the hill. _____

7. Take it! It's sitting beside the house. _____

8. Do you want tea or coffee? _____

9. I want coffee. _____

10. I want meat and bread. _____

11. What is your mother doing? _____

EXERCISE 2

Translate the following words into English.

1. peží _____
2. wó'ųdas _____
3. gakná _____
4. iyécįgayena _____
5. owóde tíbi _____
6. makóce _____
7. cąníska _____
8. ųgį́štimas _____

9. taspą́ ǧí _____
10. tá _____
11. wa'úkte no _____
12. íyą _____
13. yá bo _____
14. į́š _____
15. šųktí _____
16. cą́ágąn _____

EXERCISE 3

Translate the following phrases into Nakoda:

	beside	**inside**
barn	_____	_____
house	_____	_____
car	_____	_____
school	_____	_____

	on top	**under**
table	_____	_____
chair	_____	_____
stone	_____	_____
car	_____	_____

EXERCISE 4
Translate this short story into English.

Háu koná, dóken ya'ų́ (he)?
Dąyą́ nína wa'ų́.
Waȟpé eštá ȟuȟnáȟyabi yacíga he?
Ȟuȟnáȟyabi wacíga no!
Nén océti gakná ųgíyodągas!
Dágu né (he)?
Né íyą waką́ no!

_____

_____

_____

_____

_____

_____

CHAPTER 8

Objectives

VOCABULARY

- Names of towns/places
- Adverbs expressing times of the day
- Verbs of departing, going, and arriving

GRAMMAR

- Two types of active verbs: transitive and intransitive
- Inflections of transitive verbs (with third person singular object)
- Interrogative pronouns *where*, *when*, and *who*

Dialogues

1. Nitímno duktén tí? — *Where does your (female) older brother live?*
   Hókuwa O'ínaží ektá tí. — *He lives in Fort Qu'Appelle.*

2. Dóhąc'ehą yahí? — *When did you arrive (here)?*
   Ába né yámni ehą́'i wahí. — *I arrived (here) today at three o'clock.*
   Duwé gicí yahí? — *Who did you arrive with?*
   Micúna gicí wahí. — *I arrived (here) with my (female) older sister.*

3. Hąhébic'ehą šųktógeja wąmnága no! — *Last night I saw a wolf!*
   Duktén wąnága (he)? — *Where did you see it?*
   Gakí Wazíhe no! — *Over there in the Cypress Hills!*

4.Hą adé, dóken ya'ų́? — *Hello father, how are you?*
Dąyą́ wa'ų́ no! Dágu nihų́ yak'ú (he)? — *I am fine! What did you give your mother?*
Tanó wak'ú. — *I gave her meat.*
Wašté, pinámayaye no! — *That is good, thank you very much!*

5. Dóhąni wacíbi žé hokšínabi híbi? — *When did the boys arrive (here) from the dance?*
Kníbįkteší no! — *They did not come home!*

Vocabulary

TOWNS/PLACES

Huhúžubina	*Regina*	Šiyónide	*Pheasant Rump*
Céǧa K'į́na	*Carry The Kettle*	Hokúwa O'įnaži	*Fort Qu'Appelle*
Taȟé	*Moose Mountain*	Waziȟe	*Cypress Hills*

NOUNS

mázaska tíbi	*bank*	šųktógeja	*wolf*
wayáwa tíbi	*school*	niyá-wašte	*good health* (lit., good breath)
hokšína	*boy*	onówą	*song*
wacíbi	*dance*		

VERBS OF COMING AND GOING

hí	*she/he arrives (here)* (Class 1)	timáni	*she/he visits* (Class 1)
hiyú	*she/he is coming over (here)* (Class 1)	ú	*she/he is coming (here)* (Class 1)
í	*she/he arrives (there)* (Class 1)	yá	*she/he is going (there)* (Class 2)
iyáya	*she/he sets to go (there)* (Class 2)		

ADVERBS

aškán	*recently*	hąhébic'ehą	*last night*
ába yámni	*in three days*	hąyákena	*early this morning*
-dahą	*from*	štén	*if, when*
gicí	*with another person*	wanúȟ	*maybe*
hącógądu	*midnight*	wiyódahą	*noon, midday*

DIRECTIONALS

ektá	*at, to*	žéciya	*over that way*
néci	*around here, over here*	žéci	*around there, over there*
néciya	*over this way, over here*	gakí	*around there, in a distant area*

Asking Questions with *Where, When,* and *Who*

In Chapter 3 we studied interrogative pronouns and interrogative adverbs or "D-words": *dágu* "what," *dóken* "how," and *dóki* "where." Oftentimes the interrogative particle *he* is not used with these pronouns.

DÓKI – *where, to where* (i.e., when asking about a destination—dynamic)

Dóki ná (he)?	*Where are you going?* (in progress)
Micúkši **dóki** inána (he)?	*My son, where are you going?* (slightly after departure)
Nitákona **dóki** iyáya?	*Where is your friend setting to go?* (slightly after departure)

The suffix *-ya* can be added on *dóki* meaning "where to" (i.e., when putting focus on the exact location): *Dókiya ná he?* "**Where** are you going **to**?"

DÓKIYADAHĄ – *where from* (movement toward the speaker + source location)

Dókiyadahą yahí?	*Where are you arriving from?*
Dókiyadahą híbi (he)?	*Where are they arriving from?*

DUKTÉN – *where* (i.e., when asking about a location, like a place of birth, place of residence—static)

Duktén yatí?	*Where do you live?*
Duktén šųktógeja žé wąnága (he)?	*Where did you see the wolf?*
Nikúši **duktén** tí?	*Where does your grandmother live?*
Hokšína žé **duktén** wací iyáya?	*Where is the boy going to dance?*

DOHÁDA ~ DÓHĄ – *when in the future* (hypothetical, potential, unrealised). This pronoun requires the suffix *-kta* "potential/future" on the verb.

Doháda yawácibįkta?	*When will you all dance?*
Doháda tugášina timáyanįkta (he)?	*When will you visit grandpa?*
Doháda wayáwa tíbi inánįkta (he)?	*When will you go to school?*
Dóhą wa'úcibįkta (he)?	*When are we going to dance?*
Dóhą úbįkta (he)?	*When are they coming?*

Since they sound alike, beware not to confuse *doháda* and *dóhą* with **dóhąni** "never": *Dóhąni ecámųkteši!* "I will never do it again!"

DÓHĄC'EHĄ – *when in the past* (realised)

Midáguyebi! **Dóhąc'ehą** yahíbi?	*My relative! When did you all arrive here?*
Dóhąc'ehą wahpé yagáǧa?	*When did you make tea?*
Dóhąc'ehą yúda?	*When did she/he eat it?*

DUWÉ – *who* (can also function as a stative verb: *duwé* "she/he is someone")

Duwé wąnága?	*Who did you see?*
Ába įyámni žehą́ **duwé** wąnága?	*Who did you see last Tuesday?*
Duwé né (he)?	*Who is this?*
Duwé hí (he)?	*Who is arriving?*
Duwé waȟpé cįgá (he)?	*Who wants tea?*
Ma**dúwe** he?	*Who am I?*

Verbs of Departing, Going, and Arriving

Nakoda verbs of departing, going, and arriving are more numerous and more complex than in English and constitute a very important part of the Nakoda language. There are six basic verbs which can be classified according to two parameters: a) departure, movement in progress, and arrival; b) away from or towards the speaker/here.

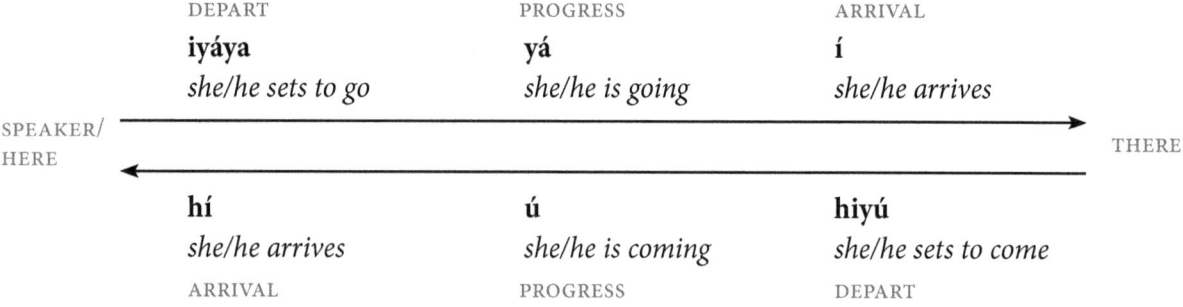

Following are conjugations for the six basic verbs for departing, going, and arriving, along with a few examples for each to help you understand the formation of these verbs. The verbs *yá* and *iyáya* are Y-stems which require -mn- and -n- person markers, while the others are all regular active verbs which take -wa- and -ya-. Note that for *iyáya* the inflection occurs twice, as shown in bold for the first and second persons.

iyáya – *she/he is setting to go (there)* (Y-stem, Class 2)

imnám**n**a	*I am setting to go*	iyáyį**kta**	*she/he will be setting to go*
inána	*you are setting to go*	iyáya**bį**kte**šį**	*they will not be setting to go*
ųgíyaya**bi**	*we are setting to go*		

Imnámnįktešį no!	*I will not be setting to go!*
Mitágena dóki **iná**na (he)?	*My (male speaker) older sister, where are you setting to go?*
Owópetų tíbi **imná**mna.	*I'm setting to go to the store.*
Dóki **ųg**íyayabi (he)?	*Where are we setting to go?*
Nikúši dóki **iyáyį**kta (he)?	*Where will your grandmother be setting to go?*
Wayáwa tíbi dóhą **inánį**kta (he)?	*When will you be setting to go to school?*

yá – *she/he is going (after departure)* (Y-stem, Class 2)

mná	*I am going*	**y**į́**kta**	*she/he will be going*
ná	*you are going*	**yá**bį**kteš**į̌	*they will not be going*
ųgí**yabi**	*we are going*		

Yá wo!	*Go!*
Yábi!	*You all go!*
Wayáwa tíbi dóki **ná** (he)?	*Where do you go to school?*
Ųgíyįkte no owóde tíbi ektá.	*Let's go to the restaurant.*

í – *she/he arrives (there)* (regular stem, Class 1)

wa'í	*I arrive*	**í**kta	*she/he will arrive*
ya'í	*you arrive*	**í**bįkteš̨į	*they will not arrive*
ųgí**bi**	*we arrive*		

Dóhąc'ehą **ya'í**?	*When did you arrive (there)?*
Šiyónide aškán nén **í**.	*She/he arrived (there) in Pheasant Rump recently.*
Ą́bawaką žehą́ owácegiye tíbi žecí **wa'í**.	*I went to church over there last Sunday.*
Hąyákeji wanúȟ **wa'íkte** no.	*Maybe I will arrive (go) there tomorrow.*

hiyú – *she/he is coming over, departing (from there)* (regular stem, Class 1)

wahíyu	*I am coming over*	**hiyú**kta	*she/he will come over*
yahíyu	*you are coming over*	**hiyú**bįkteš̨į	*they will not come over*
ųhíyu**bi**	*we are coming over*		

Hiyú wo!	*Come!*
Hiyú bo!	*Come, you all!*
Midáguyabi néci **hiyú** bo!	*My relatives, come over here!*

ú – *she/he is coming (from there)* (regular stem, Class 1)

wa'ú	*I am coming*	**ú**kta	*she/he will come*
ya'ú	*you are coming*	**ú**bįkteš̨į	*they will not come*
ų'ú**bi**	*we are coming*		

Wa'úkte no!	*I am coming!*
Ya'úkte he?	*Are you coming?*
Nén **úbįkta** (he)?	*Are they coming here?*
Néci **ú**.	*Come here.*
Ą́bawaką štén **wa'úkta**.	*I will come next Sunday.*
Tín **ú** bo!	*Come in, all!*
Úkta he?	*Will he come?*

CHAPTER 8

hí – *she/he arrives (from there)* (Y-stem, Class 1)

wahí	*I arrive*	hí**kta**	*she/he will arrive*
yahí	*you arrive*	hí**bįkteší**	*they will not arrive*
ųhí**bi**	*we arrive*		

Dóhągeja **yahíkta**?	*At what time will you arrive?*
Ába né wąží ehą́'i **wahí**.	*I arrived at one o'clock today.*
Duwé gicí **yahí**?	*Who did you arrive with?*
Duwé **hí** (he)?	*Who is arriving?*
Hokšína žé hąhébic'ehą **hí**.	*That boy arrived last night.*
Nén **wahí**.	*I arrived here.*

Lastly, there are two other very frequent verbs of departing, going, and arriving in Nakoda. One very common verb is *timáni* "to visit people." The verb *kní* "to come home" was introduced in Chapter 7, but we give its conjugations here. Note that some speakers put the noun *tída* "home" (which is often pronounced *cída* TSHEEDA) in front of *kní* to reinforce the idea of "coming home."

kní – *she/he is coming, returning home* (regular stem, Class 1)

wakní	*I am coming home*	kní**kta**	*she/he will come home*
yakní	*you are coming home*	kní**bįkteší**	*they will not come home*
ųkní**bi**	*we are coming home*		

Hącógądu žehą́ wacíbi žé dahą́ **wakní**.	*I came home from the dance at midnight.*
Waná tída **waknikta**.	*I am going home now.*
Yakní c!	*You came back home!* (strong assertion)
Ába iyámni **ųkníbįkta**.	*We will go home on Wednesday.*
Aké **cída** kníbįkta.	*They will come home again.*

Active Verbs: Intransitive and Transitive

In Chapter 6 we saw that some verbs belong to Class 4 **stative** (like *to be tall, fat, sacred*) and were inflected with the markers *-ma-* (1SG), *-ni-* (2SG), and *-Ø-* (3SG). Other verbs belong to the **active classes** (like *to eat, walk, take it*) and necessitate either *-wa-*, *-mn-*, or *-m-* "1SG," *-ya-*, *-n-*, or *n-* (2SG), and *-Ø-* (3SG). There is another distinction that exists between verbs that require an object—a thing or person acted upon—and those that do not. Those that require an object will be called "transitive" and those that do not, "intransitive."

Transitivity is a notion that relates to a transfer of power. For instance, in the sentence *I hit a ball*, we can identify a subject (*I*) and an object (*the ball*), and we see that there is a transfer of power. Similarly, we can identify subjects and objects in these sentences: *you* (subject) push *her* (object), or *I* (subject) talk to *my mom* (object). We say that *hit*, *push*, and *talk* are **transitive** verbs requiring both a subject and an object, as shown in the following English (SVO) and Nakoda (SOV) sentence structures:

English	The man	saw	a wolf.
	SUBJECT	VERB	OBJECT
Nakoda	Wįcá žé	šųktógeja	wayága.
	SUBJECT	OBJECT	VERB

On the contrary, intransitive verbs may imply a transfer of power (like *walk*) but it is not always the case (like *wait*). Intransitive verbs necessitate only a subject, as in *I sleep, you yawn, he is tall*. Thus, we say that *sleep*, *yawn* and *be tall* are **intransitive** verbs. The following table will serve to expand on transitive inflections. Note that all four types of inflections can occur on intransitive verbs to express the subject, but the active (regular stem, Class 1), Y-stem (Class 2) and the stative (NV-conjugation, Class 4) are the most common ones occurring on transitive verbs to express the subject and object.

	Intransitive subject			
	Transitive subject			**Transitive object**
	Active (regular stem) Class 1	**Active (Y-stem) Class 2**	**Active (N-conjugation) Class 3**	**Stative (NV-conjugation) Class 4**
1SG	-wa-	-mn-	-m-	**-ma-**
2SG	-ya-	-n-	-n-	**-ni-**
3SG	-Ø-	-Ø-	-Ø-	-Ø-
	wak'ú – *I give it to him/her*	wą**mn**ága – *I see him/her/it*	**m**ų́ – *I wear it*	**ma**šį́tų – *I am fat*

Inflections of Transitive Verbs (Third Person Object)

Transitive verbs (e.g., *Peter loves Mary*) are the most complex verbs to inflect since both the subject and the object are marked on the verb in Nakoda. In this chapter we will learn how to inflect a verb when the object is a third person *him/her/it*. Since person marking of transitive verbs is intricate, the steps have been broken down as such:

1. to indicate the subject of a transitive verb, use the **active regular stem** (Class 1), the **active Y-stem** (Class 2), or the **active N-conjugation** (Class 3) markers (shown in the table above);

2. to indicate the object of a transitive verb use only the **stative NV-conjugation** markers;

3. put the markers in the following order: OBJECT + SUBJECT. With some verbs, like *see* and *ask*, the order is reversed.

Here are a few examples of transitive verbs from each class, inflected for the first three persons, along with the internal analysis:

CLASS 1 (PREFIX)

Ø-	**wa-**	k'ú	>	wak'ú	*I give it to him/her*
3SG.OBJECT	1SG.SUBJECT	GIVE			
Ø-	**ya-**	k'ú	>	yak'ú	*you give it to him/her*
3SG.OBJECT	2SG.SUBJECT	GIVE			
Ø-	**Ø-**	k'ú	>	k'ú	*she/he gives it to him/her*
3SG.OBJECT	3SG.SUBJECT	GIVE			
Ø-	**ų-**	k'ú-bi	>	ųk'úbi	*we give it to him/her*
3SG.OBJECT	1PL.SUBJECT	GIVE-PL			

CLASS 2 (PREFIX) – *y* is deleted

Ø-	**mn-**	(y)uha	>	mnuhá	*I have him/her/it*
3SG.OBJECT	1SG.SUBJECT	HAVE			
Ø-	**n-**	(y)uha	>	nuhá	*you have him/her/it*
3SG.OBJECT	2SG.SUBJECT	HAVE			
Ø-	**Ø-**	yuha	>	yuhá	*she/he has him/her/it*
3SG.OBJECT	3SG.SUBJECT	HAVE			
Ø-	**ų-**	yuha-bi	>	ųyúhabi	*we have him/her/it*
3SG.OBJECT	1PL.SUBJECT	HAVE-PL			

CLASS 3 (INFIX) – *w* is deleted; *ųg–* is placed before the stem

į-	Ø-	m-	(y)ųǧa	>	įmúǧa	*I ask him/her*
ROOT	3SG.OBJECT	1SG.SUBJECT	ASK			

į-	Ø-	n-	(y)ųǧa	>	įnúǧa	*you ask him/her*
ROOT	3SG.OBJECT	2SG.SUBJECT	ASK			

į-	Ø-	Ø-	yųǧa	>	įyúǧa	*she/he asks him/her*
ROOT	3SG.OBJECT	3SG.SUBJECT	ASK			

ųg-	Ø-		įyųǧa-bi	>	ųgį́yųǧabi	*we ask him/her*
1PL.SUBJECT	3SG.OBJECT		ASK-PL			

The following tables comprise the inflections (in bold) for four frequent verbs.

	-k'u- – *to give it to him/her/it* (regular stem, Class 1)		**wayaga- – *to see him/her/it* (Y-stem, Class 2)**	
1SG	**wa**k'ú	*I give it to him/her/it*	wą**mn**ága	*I see him/her/it*
2SG	**ya**k'ú	*you give it to him/her/it*	wą**n**ága	*you see him/her/it*
3SG	k'ú	*she/he gives it to him/her/it*	wąyága	*she/he sees him/her/it*
1PL	**ų**k'ú**bi**	*we give it to him/her/it or she/he gives it to us*	wą'**ų́**yaga**bi**	*we see him/her/it or she/he sees us*
2PL	**ya**k'ú**bi**	*you all give it to him/her/it*	wą**n**ága**bi**	*you all see him/her/it*
3PL	k'ú**bi**	*they give it to him/her/it*	wąyága**bi**	*they see him/her/it*

	snohya- – *to know him/her/it* (regular stem, Class 1)		**ųspekiya- – *to teach him/her/it* (regular stem, Class 1)**	
1SG	snoh**wá**ya	*I know him/her/it*	ųspé**wa**kiya	*I teach him/her/it*
2SG	snoh**yá**ya	*you know him/her/it*	ųspé**ya**kiya	*you teach him/her/it*
3SG	snohyá	*she/he knows him/her/it*	ųspékiya	*she/he teaches him/her/it*
1PL	snoh**ų́**ya**bi**	*we know him/her/it or she/he knows us*	ųspé'**ų**kiya**bi**	*we teach him/her/it or she/he teaches us*
2PL	snoh**yá**ya**bi**	*you all know him/her/it*	ųspé**ya**kiya**bi**	*you all teach him/her/it*
3PL	snohyá**bi**	*they know him/her/it*	ųspékiya**bi**	*they teach him/her/it*

Yak'úbi he?	*What did you all give him?*
Niyá-wašte **yak'ú** no!	*You give him/her a good life!*
Wįcíjana gá búza wążí **k'úbi.**	*They gave that girl a cat.*
Asą́bi edáhą **k'úbi.**	*They gave him/her/it some milk.*
Nitúgaši miní edáhą **k'ú.**	*Give your grandfather some water.*
Wįcá gá į́š ağúyabi edáhą **k'ú.**	*Give that man some bread/bannock also.*
Duwé **wąnága?**	*Who did you see?*
Duktén šúga žé **wąnága** (he)?	*Where did you see the dog?*
Ą́ba iyámni žehą́ duwé **wąnága?**	*Who did you see last Wednesday?*
Dáguni **snohyábįšį** no!	*They don't know anything!*
Wįcá žé opétų **snohwáyešį.**	*I don't know the man who bought it.*
Waná duwé ecų́ žé **snohwáya.**	*Now I know who did it.*
Nicį́kši nakón-i'a **ųspéwakiya**'ecą.	*I taught the Nakoda language to your son.*
Dąyą́ **ųspé'ųkiyabi** no!	*We taught him well!*
Há, mázaska **mnuhá.**	*Yes, I have money.*
Mína **nuhá** he?	*Do you have a knife?*
Wasé Wakpá ekta wótijağa **yuhábįkta.**	*They will have a Sun Dance at Lodge Pole.*
Ą́ba né, tadéyąba **ųyúhabi.**	*We have a windy day today.*
Hokšína gá šųkcíjana zí wążí **yuhá.**	*That boy over there has a brown puppy.*
Sába žé **ųgéyagubi** no!	*We took the black one!*
Dąyą́ **nawáȟ'ų** štén, wašté no!	*When I hear well, it is good!*

Sounds: Ejective Consonants

Ejective consonants are voiceless consonants which are produced by closing the lips or the tongue against the palate and the glottis and by suddenly releasing the airstream. A common way to produce them is by holding your breath and trying to pronounce a *p*, *s*, or *t*. Try pronouncing these words aloud: ma**k'**ú, dohą́**c'**ehą. For the ejective *k'*, you should hear a soft click. Practise pronouncing the following syllables aloud:

k'u　 t'u　 s'a　 t'a　 t'ų　 p'i　 p'u

Chapter 8 Exercises

EXERCISE 1
Translate the following sentences into Nakoda and pronounce them aloud.

1. They came back home yesterday. _____
2. Give these boys some water. _____
3. Did you see the buffalo? _____
4. He did not come home last night. _____
5. We will be leaving in two days. _____
6. Where do they go to school? _____
7. I will arrive there at noon. _____
8. Will you visit your grandmother out west? _____
9. I gave her oranges and coffee. _____
10. They did not see him yesterday. _____
11. I arrived there at midnight. _____
12. Where does his older brother live? _____

EXERCISE 2
Find the correct English translation for the following time adverbs.

1. hącógądu   ____ noon, midday
2. hąhébic'ehą   ____ early this morning
3. hąyákena   ____ tomorrow
4. wiyódahą   ____ midnight
5. ȟtánihą   ____ night
6. ą́ba né   ____ yesterday
7. ȟtayédu   ____ evening
8. hąhébi   ____ today
9. hąyákeji   ____ last night

EXERCISE 3

Fill in the blank boxes in the following inflection tables.

	-k'u- – give	-wąyaga- – see	-snohya- – know
1SG		wą**mn**ága – I see him/her/it	snoh**wá**ya – I know him/her/it
2SG	**ya**k'ú – you give it to him/her/it		
3SG	k'ú – she/he gives it to him/her/it		
1PL	**ų**k'ú**bi** – we give it to him/her/it	wą'**ų́**yaga**bi** – we see it	
2PL			snoh**yá**ya**bi** – you all know him/her/it
3PL			

EXERCISE 4

Translate the following short story into English. (žécų - *having done that*)

Hąyákena štén ağúyabi nągų́ asą́bi wacíga.
Žécų hį́kna owáyawa tíbi mnį́kta.
Wayáwa tíbi gakná mitákona wąmnága.
Wįcį́jana gicí škáda.
Dóba ehą́'i, waná wakní no!

_____

_____

_____

_____

CHAPTER 9

Objectives

VOCABULARY

- Body parts
- Animals
- More common objects

GRAMMAR

- More verbs expressing states and bodily functions
- Ownership and possession: inflecting nouns
- Using and inflecting the verbs *táwa* "she/he owns, possesses it"; *yuhá* "she/he has it"
- Part/whole relations
- Noun modifiers *edáhą* "some" and *dóna* "some, many"

Dialogues

1. Duwé iyécįgayena tó žé táwa? — *Who owns that blue car?*
   Mitą́ga né iyécįgayena tó žé táwa. — *This blue car belongs to my (female) younger sister.*

2. Háu adé! Šų́gatąga gá duwé táwa he? — *Hi Father! Who owns that horse over there?*
   Mitákona šų́gatąga gá táwa no! — *My friend owns that horse over there.*

3. Obáwįge mázaska nuhá he? — *Do you have a hundred dollars?*
   Hą́ iná, mázaska wacíga no! — *Yes, Mother, I have money! I'll give some to my father!*
   Miyáde edáhą wak'ú no!

4. Cijábi dóna nuhá (he)?   *How many children do you have?*
Cijábi wikcémna ųyúhabi no!   *We have ten children!*

5. Háu koná, dóken ya'ų́ (he)?   *Hello, friend! How are you?*
Madáyąšį, nína mapáyažą no!   *I'm not doing well. I have a big headache!*

Vocabulary

BODY PARTS

cądé	*heart*	nigé	*stomach*
ceží	*tongue*	núğe	*ear*
hí	*tooth*	pá	*head*
hú	*leg*	pahá	*hair*
í	*mouth*	póğe	*nose*
įdé	*face*	sihá	*foot*
įštá	*eye*	sipá	*toes*
įstó	*arm*	šubé	*guts, intestines*
nąbé	*hand*	tacą́	*body*
nąpsíhu	*finger*	wé	*blood*

OBJECTS

iyécįgayena	*car*	océti	*fireplace, stove*
hú (mįmámina)	*wheel*	otókšu ~ tokšú ~ įwátokšu	*truck*
mázaska	*money*	wáda	*canoe*
minískuya	*soda pop*		

ANIMALS

bizéna	*gopher*	ptecíjana	*calf*
įkmų́	*lynx*	ptewánu	*domestic cow*
maštíja	*rabbit*	šųkcíjana	*puppy*
mató	*bear*		

More Verbs Expressing States and Bodily Functions

In Chapter 6 we studied some stative verbs expressing states (*dąyą́* "she/he is well," *tága* "she/he is big," *payázą* "she/he has a headache," *háska* "she/he is tall," *gána* "she/he is old," *yazą́* "to be sick"). In this section the conjugations are given for verbs expressing states as well as bodily functions. Some of them belong to Class 1 (*-wa-* "I," *-ya-* "you") while others belong to Class 4 (*-ma-* "I," *-ni-* "you") as seen in Chapter 6.

cesní – *she/he defecates* (Class 4)

macésni	*I am defecating*	cesní**kta**	*she/he will defecate*
nicésni	*you are defecating*	cesní**bįkteš į**	*they will not defecate*
ųcésni**bi**	*we are defecating*		

néža – *she/he urinates* (Class 1)

wanéža	*I urinate*	nežį́**kta**	*she/he will urinate*
yanéža	*you urinate*	nežį́**kteš į**	*they will not urinate*
ųnéža**bi**	*we urinate*		

stustá – *she/he is tired* (Class 4)

mastústa	*I'm tired*	stustį́**kta**	*she/he will be tired*
nistústa	*you are tired*	stustá**bįkteš į**	*they will not be tired*
ųstústa**bi**	*we are tired*		

káda – *she/he is feverish, hot* (Class 4)

makáda	*I am feverish*	kádį**kta**	*she/he will feverish*
nikáda	*you are feverish*	kádį**kteš į**	*they will not be feverish*
ųkáda**bi**	*we are feverish*		

Dóki **yanéžįkta** (he)?	*Where are you going to urinate?*
Nína **mastústa** no!	*I'm very tired!*
Stustá (he)?	*Is she tired?*
Micų́kši nína **káda** no!	*My daughter is really feverish!*
Nína **káda** no!	*It's really hot!*

Some verbs expressing a state pertaining to a body part have the noun for the body part in question compounded with a verb. This is the case of *payázą* "to have a headache," which is made of *pa* "head" and *yazą́* "to be sick." To indicate numbness in a body part the verb *t'á* "to die" is reduplicated (or doubled), as in *t'at'á* "to be paralyzed," and the noun for the body part is put in front; sometimes it is truncated, as in *sihá* "foot" > *si*.

payázą – *she/he has a headache* (Class 4)

mapáyazą	*I have a headache*	payázą**kta**	*she/he will have a headache*
nipáyazą	*you have a headache*	payázą**bįkteší**	*they will not have a headache*
ųpáyazą**bi**	*we have a headache*		

sit'át'a – *she/he has a numb foot* (Class 4)

si**má**t'a	*I have a numb foot*	sit'át'a**kta**	*she/he will have a numb foot*
si**ní**t'a	*you have a numb foot*	sit'át'a**bįkteší**	*they will not have a numb foot*
si'**ų́**t'a	*we have a numb foot*		

Finally, two of the most basic verbs expressing human feelings show the compounding of the noun *cądé* "heart" with the verbs *wašté* "to be good" or *síja* "to be bad," such as *Nidáguyabi cądéwašte wo!* "Be kind to your relatives!"

cądéwašte – *she/he is kind, good-hearted* (Class 4)

cądé**ma**wašte	*I am kind*	cądéwašte**kta**	*she/he will be kind*
cądé**ni**wašte	*you are kind*	cądéwašte**bįkteší**	*they will not be kind*
cądé'**ųgi**wašte**bi**	*we are kind*		

cądésija – *she/he is sad, broken-hearted* (Class 4)

cądé**ma**sija	*I am sad*	cądésij**kta**	*she/he will be sad*
cądé**ni**sija	*you are sad*	cądésija**bįkteší**	*they will not be sad*
cądé'**ų**sija**bi**	*we are sad*		

Ownership and Possession

Possession refers to the notion of ownership, a situation where a person or entity owns something, or is in relation to someone. In English, possession can be expressed with possessive adjectives (*my, your, his/her*, etc.), possessive pronouns (*mine, yours, his*, etc.) or verbs of possession (*I own, you have*, etc.).

My car is red.
Their house is on the left.
This is *yours*.
This money is *his*.
I have a debt.
They own three horses.

In Nakoda, there are also several ways to express the notions of ownership and possession: 1) use of a noun with possessive person markers (e.g., *my dog*); 2) use of the intransitive verb *táwa* "to own, possess it"; 3) use of the verb *yuhá* "to have it."

1A. POSSESSIVE MARKERS FOR BODY PARTS AND OBJECTS

There are two sets of possessive affixes. There are those which indicate a relation of possession between a person and a body part (e.g., *my head*) or an object (e.g., *my truck*), and those which indicate kinship relations (e.g., *my father*). Note that *ma-* or *mi-* and *ni-* are similar to Class 4 person markers.

Body-part possessive markers

hí	*tooth*	**pá**	*head*
mihí	*my tooth*	**ma**pá	*my head*
nihí	*your tooth*	**ni**pá	*your head*
hí	*his/her/its tooth*	pá	*his/her/its head*
ųgíhi**bi**	*our tooth*	**ųgí**pa**bi**	*our head*
nihí**bi**	*your (pl.) tooth*	**ni**pá**bi**	*your (pl.) head*
hí**bi**	*their tooth*	pá**bi**	*their head*
hú	*leg, stem*	**páha**	*hair*
mahú	*my leg(s)*	**ma**páha ~ **mi**páha	*my hair*
nihú	*your leg(s)*	**ni**páha	*your hair*
hú	*his/her/its leg(s)*	pahá	*his/her/its hair*
ųhú**bi**	*our leg(s)*	**ųgí**paha**bi**	*our hair*
nihú**bi**	*your (pl.) leg(s)*	**ni**páha**bi**	*your (pl.) hair*
hú**bi**	*their leg(s)*	pahá**bi**	*their hair*

Note that for nouns starting with a vowel, a glottal stop ['] is inserted before the stem in order to make a connection with the possessor prefix: *í* "his/her mouth," *mi'í* "my mouth," *ni'í* "your mouth"; *įdé* "his/her face," *mi'įdé* "my face," *ni'įdé* "your face." For object possession the prefix *-ta-* is inserted before the noun but after the person prefixes, while for body parts this prefix is not used. This prefix means that the entity in question is not permanently attached as with most objects.

Object and animal possessive markers

tokšú	*truck**	**šúgataga ~šúga**	*horse*
mit**a**tokšu	*my truck*	**mi**t**á**šuga	*my horse*
nit**á**tokšu	*your truck*	**ni**t**á**šuga	*your horse*
(t**a**)tókšu	*his/her truck*	tašúga	*his/her horse*
ugítatokšu**bi**	*our truck*	**ugí**tašuga**bi**	*our horse*
nit**á**tokšu**bi**	*your (pl.) truck*	**ni**t**á**šuga**bi**	*your (pl.) horse*
(t**a**)tokšu**bi**	*their truck*	t**á**šuga**bi**	*their horse*

Šúga óda **ugí**tawa.   *We have many dogs.*
Ugídaguškina wikcémna wicóyuhabi† no!   *We have ten children together.*

1B. POSSESSIVE MARKERS FOR KINSHIP NOUNS

The possessive markers for kinship terms resemble that of Class 4 forms. They are *mi-* "my," *ni-* "your," but for the third person "her/his" they are irregular. Some nouns require a prefix Ø- 'her/his' (although they are few), but the vast majority take a suffix (or infix), which has different forms: *-tku*, *-ktu*, *-gu*, *-co*, *-ju*, or *-cu*. The first person plural "our" is *ug-* or *ugi-...-bi* (with a linking vowel *i*).

-tawíju-	*wife*	-hikna-	*husband*
mitáwiju	*my wife*	**mi**hikna	*my husband*
nitáwiju	*your wife*	**ni**hikna	*your husband*
tawíju	*his wife*	hikná**gu**	*her husband*
ugítawiju**bi**	*our wives*	**ugí**hikna**bi**	*our husbands*
nitáwiju**bi**	*your (PL) wives*	**ni**hikna**bi**	*your (PL) husbands*
tawíju**bi**	*their wives*	hikná**gu**bi	*their husbands*

As shown with the kinship root *-cina-* "male's older brother," the suffix *-cu* is infixed inside the root.

-timno-	*female's older brother*	-cina-	*male's older brother*
mitímno	*my older brother*	**mi**cína	*my older brother*
nitímno	*your older brother*	**ni**cína	*your older brother*
timnó**gu**	*her older brother*	ci**cú**na	*his older brother*
ugítimno**bi**	*our older brother*	**ugí**cina**bi**	*our older brother*
nitímno**bi**	*your (PL) older brother*	**ni**cína**bi**	*your (PL) older brother*
tímno**gu**bi	*their older brother*	ci**cú**na**bi**	*their older brother*

Other kinship terms like "grandmother" and "grandfather" show the element *-gi-*, which has no meaning. This is often dropped by some speakers, resulting in *kúšicu* "his/her grandmother" and *tugášicu* "his/her grandfather."

---

* Oftentimes the alienable prefix *-ta-* is left out, as in *tokšú* "his/her truck" or *tokšúbi* "their truck." Moreover, this word is often truncated to be *tokšú* from the long form *iwátokšu*.

† This is a contraction of *wica-u-yuha-bi* > *wicóyuhabi* "we have them."

tugáši	*grandfather*	-kuši-	*grandmother*
mitúgaši	*my grandfather*	**mi**kúši	*my grandmother*
nitúgaši	*your grandfather*	**ni**kúši	*your grandmother*
tugágiši**ktu** ~ tugáši**cu**		kúgiši**ktu** ~ kúši**cu**	
	his/her grandfather		*his/her grandmother*
ųgítugaši**bi** ~ **mi**túgaši**bi**		**ųgí**kugiši**bi** ~ **mi**kúši**bi**	
	our grandfather		*our grandmother*
nitugaši**bi**	*your (PL) grandfather*	**ni**kúgaši**bi**	*your (PL) grandmother*
tugágiši**ktubi**	*their grandfather*	kúgiši**ktubi**	*their grandmother*

Nihį́kna dóki iyáya?	*Where did your husband go?*
Jim **tawíju** wací iyáya.	*Jim's wife went dancing.*
Mikúši waȟpé gáǧa.	*My grandmother is making tea.*
Nitúgašibi dágu yuhá?	*What does your (PL) grandfather have?*
Ųgítugašibi šų́gatąga zí wążí yuhá.	*Our grandfather has one brown horse.*

In order to master the formation of the third person possessor one has to refer to the Kinship Table in Appendix 1. Remember that many, if not all, of the kinship terms have specificities that cannot be guessed out and have to be memorized. Note also that some semi-fluent speakers will tend to regularize the kinship terms. That is, they will avoid the irregular forms and replace them with the third person Ø- "his/her" prefix.

2. INTRANSITIVE VERB *TÁWA* "TO BE ONE'S OWN"

To express possession or ownership, use the intransitive verb *táwa* (sometimes written as *itáwa*), which means "to be one's own" or "his/her." Unlike other intransitive verbs, it has *mi-* as first person prefix (instead of *ma-*) and *ni-* as second person prefix.

táwa – *she/he owns it, it is his/hers* (irregular verb, similar to Class 4)

mitáwa	*it's mine*	**ųgí**tawa**bi**	*it's ours*
nitáwa	*it's yours*	**ni**táwa**bi**	*it's yours all*
táwa	*it's his/hers/its*	táwa**bi**	*it's theirs*

Duwé né **táwa**?	*Who owns this?*
Žé **táwa**.	*She/he owns that.*
Žé **táwabi**.	*They own that.*
Šųkcíjana skána né **nitáwa** he?	*Is this white puppy yours?*
Šúga zí gá **nitáwabi** he?	*Does that brown dog over there belong to you all?*
Šúga zí né **ųgítawabi**.	*This brown dog is ours.*
Šúga sába **mitáwabi**.	*My dogs are black.*
Wáda **ųgítawabi**.	*our canoes / We own canoes.*
Wįcá žé gugúša šįtų́ gá **táwa**.	*The man owns that fat pig over there.*
Wįcíjana né minískuya žé **táwa**.	*This pop belongs to that little girl. / The little girl owns the pop.*

3. TRANSITIVE VERB *YUHÁ* "TO HAVE, TO CARRY"

To express the state of possession or ownership one can also use the transitive verb *yuhá* "to have it."

yuhá – *she/he has it, carries it* (Y-stem, Class 2)*

mnuhá	*I have it*	yuhá**kta**	*she/he will have it*
nuhá	*you have it*	yuhá**bįkteši**	*they will not have it*
ųyúha**bi**	*we have it*		

Niyáde dágu **yuhá**?	*What does your father have?*
Miyáde šų́gatąga zí wažį́ **yuhá**.	*My father has a brown horse.*
Mázaska **nuhá** (he)?	*Do you have money?*
Hiyá, mázaska **mnuhéšį**.	*No, I don't have money.*
Hą́, mázaska **mnuhá**.	*Yes, I have money.*

Part/Whole Relations

Part/whole relations refer to things that are part of a whole, such as the *leg of a chair*, the *guts of a bear*, etc. There are two ways to express this idea in English and Nakoda. In English, there is a difference between *the skull of a bear* (specified; e.g., the one that is in front of the speaker) and *bear skull* (unspecified; i.e., bear skulls in general). Nakoda, too, makes this distinction between specified and unspecified things.

1. Specified (*the X of a Y*) as seen in the previous section: the verb *táwa* "to own, possess" is used. The words are placed in the following order: POSSESSOR + THING POSSESSED + TÁWA.

mató pá táwa	*the bear's head*
Mary hí táwa	*Mary's tooth/teeth*
Mary pá táwa	*Mary's head*
Mary įštá táwa	*Mary's eye(s)*

2. Unspecified (*a Y$_{possessor}$ X$_{thing\ possessed}$*): the words for the possessor and the thing possessed are simply put together:

mató šubé	*bear guts*
mató pá	*bear head*
įkmų́ šagé	*lynx claw*
iyécįgayena hú mįmámina	*car wheel*
iyécįgayena įštá	*car headlights*

---

* This verb can also be compounded with the noun *hokšína* "boy," which is contracted to *hokši-*: *hokšíyuha* "she is delivering" (Class 2).

Noun Quantifiers *edáhą* "some" and *dóna* "some, many"

There are two very frequent noun quantifiers in Nakoda: a) *edáhą* is used with mass nouns (entities that are not countable like *water, sand, snow,* etc.) and b) *dóna* is used with count nouns (entities that are countable like *winters, children, apples,* etc.). While in English the modifiers come before the noun (e.g., *some water, some apples*), in Nakoda they occur after it, as shown in the following examples (the nouns are underlined):

Miní **edáhą** mak'ú.	*Give me some water.*
Nitúgaši miniskuya **edáhą** k'ú.	*Give your grandfather some pop.*
Ȟuȟnáȟyabi **edáhą** wak'úkta no!	*I'll give him some coffee!*
Cijábi **dóna** nuhá (he)?	*How many children do you have?*
Dóna yacíga?	*How many do you want?*
Waníyedu **dóna** eháyaki (he)?	*How old are you?*

Chapter 9 Exercises

EXERCISE 1

Translate the following possessive nouns into English.

1. his grandfather _____
2. my toes _____
3. your nose _____
4. our bodies _____
5. her eyes _____
6. their hair _____
7. their legs _____
8. your (PL) arms _____
9. my grandchildren _____
10. your (female) (PL) younger brother _____

EXERCISE 2

Translate the following sentences into English.

1. Šúgatąga gá táwa he! _____
2. Búzabi dóna nuhá (he)? _____
3. Miyáde nína káda. _____
4. Wíyąbi␣ganá stustábi he? _____
5. Mázaska yuhábi? _____
6. Žé táwabi. _____
7. Hokšína né minískuya žé táwa. _____
8. Miyáde edáhą wak'ú no! _____
9. Mitúgašina šúgatąga zí wąží yuhá. _____
10. Waníyedu dóna eháki (he)? _____
11. Šúgatąga dóna nuhá (he)? _____
12. Waná šúkcíjanabi dóba mitáwa. _____
13. Cijábi dóba ųyúhabi no! _____
14. Dąyášį, nína payážą! _____
15. Hąhébic'ehą tá wąmnága. _____

EXERCISE 3
Complete the following verbal paradigms.

	-tawa- – to own it	-yuha- – to have it	-stusta- – to be tired
1SG		**mn**uhá – I have it	
2SG			
3SG			
1PL	**ųgí**tawa**bi** – we own it		
2PL			**ni**stústa**bi** – you all are tired
3PL			

EXERCISE 4
Read the following Nakoda story aloud and translate it into English.

Cįjábi dóna nuhá (he)? Cįjábi núba wįcá'ųyuhabi. Céǧa K'ína ektá tíbi. Iyécįgayena yuhábi hį́kna ą́bawaką žehą́ timánibi. Micį́kši nína stústa hį́kna payážą cén úšį. Maštį́ja tanó įš hą́bi wašpą́wįcawakiya hį́kna óda wódabi no! Ųgítagožabi įš timaní úbi. Nína dąyą́ ųgį́pibi.

_____

_____

_____

_____

_____

_____

CHAPTER 10

Objectives

VOCABULARY

- People and occupations
- Animals and birds
- Food and drinks

GRAMMAR

- Complex noun formation
- Noun incorporation
- Independent pronouns for focus and contrast
- Intensifiers -ȟ and -ȟtįyą

Dialogues

1. Nihų́ dágu dókų (he)?
   Tągán pahá gisų́ no.
   Ni'áde he?
   Hokúwa iyáya.

   What is your mother doing?
   She is braiding her hair outside.
   And your father?
   He is gone fishing.

2. Dóken owágiyįkta (he)?
   Wacís'a gá ógiya wo!

   How can I help?
   Help that dancer over there!

3. Duwé tíbi né ógiya gáǧįkta (he)?
   Duwénišį, tíbi né iyé gáǧįkta no.
      Mitúgaši tigáǧes'a žéca no!

   Who will help him build this house?
   Nobody; he will build this house himself.
      My grandfather is a carpenter!

4. Nį́š wóyadįkta yacíga he?
   Ağúyabi, tanó edáhą, wį́bazuką į́š wacíga.

   As for you, what do you want to eat?
   I want bannock, some meat, and saskatoon berries too.

5. Šų́gatągabi dóna ni'ádena yuhá (he)?
   Mi'ádena tašų́ga yámni táwa. Šųksába wažį́ į́š šųkskána núba táwa.

   How many horses does your uncle have?
   My uncle owns many horses. He has a black one and two white ones.

Vocabulary

PERSONS

adéna	my uncle (father's brother)	nową́s'a	singer
ağóbas'a	snorer	ógiyes'a	servant
eyés'a	blabbermouth	wacís'a	dancer
gisų́na	Asian person	wadópena ~ wadópana	band of Nakoda called the "Paddlers"
inána	my aunt (mother's sister)		
įštímes'a	sleeper	yatkés'a	drunkard

ANIMALS AND BIRDS

hįhą́	owl	šųksába	black horse
hįhą́hana	pigmy owl	šųkskána	white horse
hįhą́ ohnóga otís'a	burrowing owl	ųkcékiğa	magpie
įkmų́na	bobcat	wamní	eagle
kąǧí	raven	zitkána	bird
pağų́da	duck	zitkánato	bluebird
sihásaba	Canada goose	zitkásaba	blackbird
snohéna	snake		

OBJECTS

awódabi	table	škoškóbena	banana
hąbí	juice	wį́bazuką	saskatoon berries
hųská	pants	wakmúhaza	corn
hųskána	leggings, stockings	wítka	egg
o'į́	beads	wožábi	gravy

VERBS

ağóba	*she/he snores* (Class 1)
i'á	*she/he talks, speaks (to him/her)* (Class 1)
wadópa	*she/he paddles* (Class 1)
gisų́	*she/he braids his/her own hair* (irregular)
nową́	*she/he sings* (Class 1)
snohá	*she/he crawls* (Class 1)
tóȟtįyą	*it is purple* (Class 4)
ípį	*she/he is full, satiated* (Class 4)
ȟuȟnáȟya	*she/he burns, roasts it* (Class 1)
wa'áyaza	*she/he is beading* (Class 2)
žéca	*she/he is of a tribe, kind, trade* (Class 4)

Complex Noun Formation

We will study here three suffixes, *-s'a* or *-bi* and *-na*, that are used to derive nouns from verbs or nouns from nouns.

1. **-S'A ~ -S'Ą** "agent, one who does X" is used to form an agentive noun from an active or stative verb. It is similar to the English suffix *-er*, which may indicate a profession (*to bake > a baker*; *to surf > a surfer*) or a habit (*to snore > a snorer*; *to drink > a drinker*). This suffix provokes ablauting and sometimes the resulting noun has a pejorative meaning, depending on the meaning of the stem.

ağóba	*she/he snores*	>	ağóba**s'a**	*snorer*
awáyaga	*she/he watches it*	>	awáyages**'a**	*guard, bodyguard*
i'á	*she/he talks*	>	i'és**'a**	*chatterbox, blabbermouth*
ištíma	*she/he sleeps*	>	ištímes**'a**	*sleeper*
nową́	*she/he sings*	>	nową́s**'a**	*singer*
ógiya	*she/he helps him/her*	>	ógiyes**'a**	*servant*
wací	*she/he dances*	>	wacís**'a**	*dancer*
wašpáya	*she/he cooks a feast*	>	wašpáyes**'a**	*cook, chef*
yatką́	*she/he drinks it*	>	yatkés**'a**	*drunkard*

    The suffix *-s'a* also occurs with complex nouns such as *hįhą́ oȟnóga otís'a* "burrowing owl" (lit., *hįhą́* "owl" + *oȟnóga* "hole" + *otí* "dwelling" > *otís'a* "dweller"). Finally, *-s'a* can also be used with verbs to indicate that the action is a habitual or continuous one (see Chapter 12).

wacíbi	*they dance*	>	wacíbis**'a**	*they dance all the time*
nową́bi	*they sing*	>	nową́bis**'a**	*they sing all the time*

2. **BI** "nominalizer" is used to form nouns from verbs. The agent is left unspecified and those nouns can be translated as "someone did it to make it thus" or "the thing used to." Beware not to confuse -*bi* "nominalizer" with -*bi* "third person animate plural."

tí	she/he lives there	>	tí**bi**	a dwelling
ḣuḣnáḣya	she/he burns it	>	ḣuḣnáḣya**bi**	coffee
wóda	she/he eats	>	awóda**bi**	table
wací	he/he dances	>	wací**bi**	dance

3. **NA** "agent which has a given quality." The suffix -*na* is used to form nouns from verbs that indicate that the agent referred to has the quality indicated by the verb. Note that -*na* is an ablauting element. It often appears on personal names.

snohá	she/he crawls	>	snohé**na**	snake
wadópa	she/he paddles	>	wadópe**na**, wadópa**na**	Band of Nakoda
gisų́	she/he braids his/her own hair	>	gisų́**na**	Asian person
céǧa k'í	she/he carries a kettle	>	Céǧa K'į́**na**	Carry The Kettle (Nakoda chief)

4. **NA** "diminutive, small size, endearment, sympathy" occurs on the names of some birds and animals to indicate their small size. On kinship terms -*na* carries the idea that a person is somehow parallel (in status and duties) to another one (e.g., the maternal aunt *inána* is like a mother *iná*)* or that the speaker has sympathy for that person (usually old people or very young ones). Beware not to confuse the diminutive -*na* and the nominal -*na* "agent" seen above. A way to distinguish between the two is that -*na* "nominalizer" provokes ablauting while the diminutive -*na* does not.

PARALLEL STATUS, ENDEARMENT, SYMPATHY

iná	mother	>	iná**na**	my aunt (mother's sister)
adé	father	>	adé**na**	my uncle (father's brother)
mihų́	my mother	>	mihų́**na**	my dear mother
mitúgaši	my grandfather	>	mitúgaši**na**	my dear grandfather

SMALL SIZE

įkmų́	lynx	>	įkmų́**na**	bobcat
huská	leggings	>	huská**na**	stockings
hįhą́	owl	>	hįhą́ha**na**	pigmy owl
ų́	she/he wears it	>	ų́**na**	it (baby) wears it

---

* Some words like *zitkána* "bird" exist only with the diminutive -*na*.

The diminutive -*na* has been lexicalized (i.e., frozen) for some words, since the counterpart without the diminutive does not exist (anymore): *wįcą́ȟtiyąną* "old man"; *hokšína* "boy"; *dáguškina* "baby"; *júsina* "she/he/it is small."

Noun Incorporation

In Nakoda, some nouns, functioning as the object of a verb, can be integrated into simple verbs to form complex verbs. This process is known as "noun incorporation." The following English verbs display noun incorporation: *I like **fox** hunting*, *I'm **baby**sitting*, *I **name**-called him*, etc. As can be seen here, the so-called direct object of the verb has become generic or unspecified and the noun acts more like an adverb: *What kind of hunting do you like? I like **fox** hunting. I like **spring** hunting*. Nakoda has noun incorporation as well. As is the case with English, the incorporated-object noun also displays a lesser degree of specificity:

No incorporation	Noun incorporation
Šų́ga né manų́.	Šųkmánų.
He stole this horse.	*He is horse-stealing.*
SPECIFIC HORSE	UNSPECIFIC HORSE

As can be seen in the preceding examples, there are two major features of noun incorporation: i) shift in stress; ii) truncation of nouns; and iii) change from transitive (subject + object) to intransitive (subject only).

When incorporated into a verb the noun loses its stress and the stress shifts to the second syllable. The final vowel of the noun is truncated, and the consonant of the last syllable will become devoiced: *b > p*; *g > k* or *j*; *ǧ > ȟ*; *d > t*; *z > s*, etc.

Tí né iyé **g**áǧa.	*He is building this house himself.* (VT)
Ti**j**áǧa.	*He builds houses.* (VI)
Tá**b**a né nąpsíja.	*He kicked that ball.* (VT)
Ta**p**nápsija.	*He ball-kicks./He plays football.* (VI)
Má**z**aska žé watų́.	*I bear/carry that money.* (VT)
Ma**s**wátųga.	*I'm rich.* (VI)
Má**z**a žé **g**adódo.	*He is pounding on that piece of metal.* (VT)
Ma**sk**ádo.	*He pounds metal. He is a blacksmith.* (VI)

Wįcá šų́ga né įkóyakya.	*The man harnessed this horse.* (VT)
Šųkį́koyakya.	*He is horse-harnessing.* (VI)
Cą́ né oné.	*She/he is looking for this tree.* (VT)
Cąné.	*She/he is looking for wood.* (VI)

In some cases it is the final syllable of the full noun (consonant + vowel) that is truncated:

Hokší**na** yuhá.	*She has a boy.* (VT-Y)
Hokšíyuha.	*She delivers a baby.* (VI-Y)
Hoǧą́ né kuwá.	*He chased/pursued this fish.* (VT)
Hokúwa.	*He is fishing.* (VI)
Hokúwa O'į́nažį	*Fort Qu'Appelle* (lit., the place where one stops to fish)
Wíyą né wakúwa.	*I'm chasing this woman.* (VT)
Wįkúwešį wo!	*Don't be a womanizer!* (VI)

Independent Pronouns for Focus and Contrast

In the previous chapters we saw that person markers occurred on verbs (e.g., *mawáni* "I walk") and not as separate pronouns as in English (e.g., *I love you*). However, Nakoda has independent focus pronouns that are used to put emphasis on a participant. They can be translated using the suffix -*self*. In fact, *iyé* "she/he is the one" is a stative verb (Class 4) that can be used as a pronoun.

miyé	*I, myself*	**ųg**íye	*we, ourselves*
niyé	*you, yourself*	**n**iyé**bi**	*you all, yourselves*
iyé	*he, himself, her, herself*	iyé**bi**	*they, themselves*

As seen in the preceding table, the independent pronouns are formed by adding the Class 3 (N-conjugation) person markers *m-* (1SG), *n-* (2SG), *ųg-*... (1D) on the root *-iyé-* "self." These pronouns appear before the verb, as can be seen in the following examples, and can be used like an existential "be" verb:

Awódabi né wagáǧa.	*I'm building this table.*
Wáda né **miyé** wagáǧa.	*I'm building this canoe myself.*
Škoškóbena wążí yúda.	*She/he is eating a banana.*
Wįbazuką **iyé** yúda.	*She/he, herself, is eating saskatoon berries.*
Stustá?	*Are you tired?* (female speaker)
Hą́ **miyé**!	*Yes, I am.*

CHAPTER 10

In Chapter 5 we saw that the pronoun *íš* means "she, he, they, it too, also," but that it is also used to join two nouns (e.g., *ȟuȟnáȟyabi* **íš** *waȟpé* "coffee and tea too"). The root *-įš-* indicates a contrast or a comparison and may be inflected for some of the persons, as shown in the following examples.

mį́š	me too	į́š	him, her, they, it too
nį́š	you too	ųgį́š	us too

Micíkši nína dąyą́ ų́no! **Mį́š** dąyą́ wa'ų́.	My son is doing very well! Me, too, I'm doing well.
Nį́š wóyadįkte no!	You will eat as well! You, too, will eat!
Wožábi **íš** gáǧa.	She made gravy as well.

Intensifiers -ȟ and -ȟtįyą

In Nakoda, there are two suffixes, *-ȟ* and *-ȟtįyą*, known as "intensifiers." They attach at the end of a pronoun (like *iyé*), verb, or adverb and are used in different contexts.

INTENSIFICATION (*-ȟ* "really, very, specifically")

Tíbi né wagáǧa miyé**ȟ**.	I'm building this house specifically myself.
Sąksája né waámnaza miyé**ȟ**.	I beaded this dress specifically myself.
Nį́š wóyadįkta**ȟ** yacíga he?	As for you, what do you want to eat?
Nína**ȟ** įmápį no!	I'm really full! (lit., I'm well filled.)

MULTIPLICITY (*-ȟ* can be translated as a multiplier [times])

Žéci yámni**ȟ** wa'í.	I went there three times.
Nųbá**ȟ** žé i'á.	He spoke twice.

DESIRE TO TO DO SOMETHING

Verbs marked with *-kta* indicate "potential/future" but also "intentionality to do something." The verbal intensifier *-ȟtįyą* enhances the intentional meaning of *-kta*. Thus, speakers often translate the sequence *-kta* + *-ȟtįyą* as "want, desire, very." Note that this suffix ablauts a preceding vowel *a > e* while *-ȟ* does not.

Mį́š wówadįkte**ȟtįyą**.	I want to eat too.
Huhúzubina ųyábįkte**ȟtįyą**.	We want to go to Regina.
Wašté ųskádabįkte**ȟtįyą**.	They want to have fun.
Šiyónide mnį́kte**ȟtįyą**.	I want to go to Pheasant Rump.

Some words have the suffix lexicalized: *tóȟtįyą* "it is purple" (blue + INTENSIFIER), *sábaȟtįyą* "it is pitch black" (black + INTENSIFIER), *wįcáȟtįyąna* "old man" (man + INTENSIFIER + NOMINALIZER).

Chapter 10 Exercises

EXERCISE 1
Translate the following sentences into Nakoda.

1. I want some saskatoon berries. _____
2. That woman wants to go to Carry The Kettle. _____
3. My uncle is a drinker. _____
4. I intend to build a house myself. _____
5. As for them, what do they want to eat? _____
6. Ask your aunt too! _____
7. I, too, saw a bobcat yesterday. _____
8. We want to eat too! _____
9. My uncle, too, is a singer. _____
10. She has many things. _____
11. My friend is Chinese. _____
12. I'm really tired. _____
13. I really want to do that. _____
14. I did it three times. _____

EXERCISE 2
Circle the four words that do not belong in the following list and explain why.

aǧóbas'a	hihá	tóhtiya	gisú
wamní	awódabi	kaǧí	wacís'a
zitkásaba	i'á	snohéna	wítka
ípi	adéna	huská	haská
gisúna	zitkána	habí	Tahé

EXERCISE 3

Complete the following table.

	-wa'ayaza- – bead	X-self	X too
1SG	wa'ámnaza		
2SG			niyé – you too
3SG			
1PL		ųgíš – ourselves	
2PL			
3PL			

EXERCISE 4

Match the English sentences with their Nakoda counterpart.

1. Micų́kši nína káda no!   _____ She is eating a banana.

2. Stustá he?   _____ I'm building this table.

3. Mikúši wahpé gáǧa.   _____ Jim's wife went dancing.

4. Awódabi né wagáǧa.   _____ My daughter is really feverish!

5. Wáda né miyé wagáǧa.   _____ Where did your husband go?

6. Škoškóbena wąží yúda.   _____ Is she tired?

7. Wį́bazuką wąží iyé yúda.   _____ She, herself, is eating saskatoon berries.

8. Nihį́kna dóki iyáya?   _____ I'm building this canoe myself.

9. Jim tawíju wací iyáya.   _____ My grandmother is making tea.

EXERCISE 5

Give the noun incorporated version of the following verbs. Make changes in the stress pattern and the sounds of the incorporated noun, if required.

1. Tába žé nąpsíjabi. *They kicked the ball.* _____

2. Tába žé nąwápsijabi. *I kicked the ball.* _____

3. Hokšína mnuhá. *I have a boy.* _____

4. Hokšína yuhábi. *They have a boy.* _____

5. Mázaska edáhą mnuhá. *I have some money.* _____

6. Šúgatąga gá ųmánų. *We (two) stole that horse yonder.* _____

CHAPTER 11

Objectives

VOCABULARY

- Ceremonies and dances
- Adverbs of time/space and manner
- Verbs of speaking

GRAMMAR

- Formation of irregular verbs
- Inflections of transitive verbs (third person subject)

Dialogues

1. Mitímno! Dóki ináninkta (he)?　　　　　　*My (female) older brother! Where are you going?*
   Huhúžubina nagáhą imnámnikte no.　　　　*I am going to Regina now. Do you want to go?*
   　Yábi yacíga he? Acáštubi ecúbikta no.　　　*They will do a naming ceremony.*
   Snohwáyešį, iná įmúǧikta.　　　　　　　　*I don't know, I will ask my mother.*
   Nihų́ įš gicó wo!　　　　　　　　　　　　*Invite your mother too!*

2. Iná omágiya wo! *Black horse* nakón-i'a　　*Mother, help me! How do they say/does one say*
   　dóken eyábi (he)?　　　　　　　　　　*"black horse" in Nakoda?*
   "Šųksába" eyábi. Nį́š nakón-i'a!　　　　　*They/one say(s) šųksába. You, too, say it in Nakoda.*

3. Mitúgaši nawáȟ'ų. Duktén náži̧ (he)?　　　*I hear my grandfather. Where is he standing?*
   Įnį́bi nén iyódąga. Waná nową́ no!　　　　*He is sitting here in the sweat lodge. He is singing.*
   Wašté! Nitúgaši dąyą́ nína nową́s'a.　　　*Good! Your grandfather is a really good singer.*

4. Nitímno dókʼų (he)? — *What is your older brother up to?*
Naháḣ įštíma no! — *He is still sleeping!*
Dágucen? — *Why?*
Hąyákena nų́ba ehą́ʼi kní. — *He came home at two o'clock this morning.*
Hįį! Ába né nína stustį́kte no! — *Oh! He will be very tired today.*

Vocabulary

NOUNS AND ADVERBS

cądéskuya	sweetheart	owáyawa tíbi	school*
dágucen	why	oyáde	nation
doháda ~ dóhą	when	šųkšóšo ~ šóšona	mule, donkey
hokšítogapa	firstborn son	šųkcíjana	puppy
hú	voice	táȟca	deer
iyúhana	all	wagíyą	thunderbird
niyá-wašte	health	wahíkiyabi	radio
owácegiye tíbi	church	wanáǧi	spirit

VERBS

ahídųwą	she/he looks on him/her/it (Class 1)
ahópa	she/he respects him/her/it (Class 1)
apá	she/he hits him/her/it Class 1)
basí	she/he drives it (Class 1)
ecų́	she/he does, uses it (Class 3, irregular)
eyá	she/he says it (irregular)
gicó	she/he invites him/her (Class 1, irregular)
kté	she/he kills him/her/it (Class 1)
naȟʼų́	she/he listens to him/her/it (Class 1)
snokyá ~ snohyá	she/he knows him/her/it (Class 1)
teȟína	she/he loves him/her/it (Class 1)
wacégiya	she/he prays (Class 1)

---

* Some speakers pronounce the word for "school" *wayáwa* instead of *owáyawa*.

NAKODA CEREMONIES

The Nakoda language is called *nakón-iyabi* or *nakón-wįco'i'e*, while Nakoda customs and traditions are referred to as *nakón-wįcoȟ'ąge*. Ceremonies and dances are numerous, each being held for specific occasions in the communities.

acáštųbi ecúbi	*naming ceremony*	įwážikte ecúbi	*first kill ceremony*
cąnúba oȟpáǧa ecúbi	*pipe ceremony*	wótijaǧa	*medicine lodge, sun dance*
įnįbi ecúbi	*sweat lodge ceremony*	zuyés'a tíbi	*warrior lodge society*

The words *ecúbi* and *ecúbina* are derived nouns indicating that a contest, ceremony, or event is taking place. Note that *-bi* in *ecúbi* is the "nominalizer" rather than *-bi* "plural." Thus, in the examples above *ecúbi* occurs after the word describing a given ceremony, as in *įwážikte ecúbi* "first kill ceremony."

Įnįbi nén iyódąga.	*They are sitting here in the sweat lodge.*
Įnįbi wagaǧa štén, miní óda wacíga no!	*When I make a sweat lodge, I want a lot of water!*
Nakón-wįcoȟ'ąge tewáȟina cá no!	*I really cherish my Nakoda traditions!*
Nakón-i'a ecúgųbįkte no!	*We will use the Nakoda language!*

TYPES OF DANCES

The terms for the different types of dances show a modifier (Omaha, round, scalp, etc.) followed by the noun *wacíbi* "a dance." Like *ecúbi*, the noun *wacíbi* is made of *wací* "she/he dances" and *-bi*, which changes a verb into a noun.

gahómni wacíbi	*round dance, courting dance*	omáha wacíbi	*Omaha dance*
hąwácibi	*women dance, moon dance*	wamní wacíbi	*eagle dance*
mįméya wacíbi	*round dance*		

Mįméya wacíbi ecúbįkte no!	*They will do a round dance!*
Dąyą **wawáci**.	*I dance well.*
Wanágaš **wacíbi** né ecén.	*Long ago they danced like this.*
Hącógądu žehą **wacíbi** žé daȟą wakní.	*It was midnight when I came home from the dance.*

Finally, here are more conjugated transitive and intransitive verbs dealing with ceremonial activities, along with examples of their use in sentences.

ahópa – *she/he respects it, honours it* (Class 1)

ahó**wa**pa	*I respect it*	ahópį**kta**	*she/he will respect it*
ahó**ya**pa	*you respect it*	ahópį**ktešį**	*she/he will not respect it*
ahó'**ų**pa**bi**	*we respect it*	ahópa**bi**	*they respect it*

nową – *she/he sings* (Class 1)

wanówą	*I sing*	now**į́kta**	*she/he will sing*
yanówą	*you sing*	now**į́ktešį**	*she/he will not sing*
ųnówą**bi**	*we sing*	nową́**bi**	*they sing*

wacégiya – *she/he prays* (Class 1)

wacé**wa**giya	*I pray*	wacégiy**įkta**	*she/he will pray*
wacé**ya**giya	*you pray*	wacégiy**įktešį**	*she/he will not pray*
wacé'**ų**giya**bi**	*we pray*	wacégiya**bi**	*they pray*

wací – *she/he dances* (Class 1)

wa**wá**ci	*I dance*	wací**kta**	*she/he will dance*
wa**yá**ci	*you dance*	wací**ktešį**	*she/he will not dance*
wa'**ų́**cibi	*we dance*	wacíbi	*they dance*

Makóce né **ahópa** bo!	*All of you respect the land!*
Nakón-i'abi **ahówapa** no!	*I respect the Nakoda language!*
Ą́bawaką štén, wįcášta **nową́bįkta**.	*On Sunday, people are going to sing.*
Nową́ wo!	*Sing!*
Dóhąda **yanówąbįkta**?	*When will you sing?*
Dóhągeja **yanówąbįkta** (he)?	*At what time are you all singing?*
Dąyą́ **wayáci** no!	*You dance well!*
Nągáhą **wacé'ųgiyabi**.	*Now we pray together.*

Adverbs of Time/Space and Manner

Adverbs are words that specify a verb. They are not obligatory, although they provide a finer gradation of meaning and often clarify when, where, and how an activity is done. The adverbs fall into two categories: time/space and manner. Place adverbs and postpositions were studied in Chapter 7. Adverbs are usually placed before the verb they modify.

TIME/SPACE ADVERBS

Time/space adverbs express when an action is or will take place:

aškán	*recently*	téhąduwa ~ téhąn	*a long distance, far*
éstena	*early*	téhądahą	*from a distance, far from over there*
nągáhą	*now*	wanágaš	*long ago*
téhą	*long ago*		

Huhúžubina **aškán** nén wahí.	I arrived here in Regina recently.
Éstena gíkta no!	She/he wakes up early!
Nągáhą wacé'ųgiyabi hą́da.	Now we pray together.
Huhúžubina **nągáhą** imnámnįkte no!	I am going to Regina now!
Nągáhą owáyawa tíbi imnámnįkte no!	I am going to school now!
Téhąduwa wa'íšį.	I didn't go far.
Makóce **téhądahą** híbi.	They come from a faraway land.
Huhúžubina gakí **téhąda**.	Regina is far over there.

MANNER ADVERBS

Manner adverbs give more precision as to how an activity is done:

awánųka	accidentally	inína ~ a'ínina	quietly, softly
ektášį	wrongly	įknúhana	suddenly
įdú	only, just, simply	nahą́ȟ	still, yet

Tȟáȟca **awánųka** wakté.	I accidentally killed a deer.
Ektášį ecámų.	I did it wrongly.
Ektášį ecánų.	You use it wrongly.
Mitímno **ektášį** ecų́.	My older brother is using it wrongly.
Įdú wacís'a	the only dancer
Įdú ecų́ wo!	Simply do it!
Įknúhana awápa.	I hit him suddenly.
Inína mawáni	I walk quietly, softly.
Inína mawánįkta.	I will walk quietly.
Mihų́ **inína** i'á.	My mother speaks softly.
Nahą́ȟ waná he?	Are you ready yet?
Nahą́ȟ wagáǧįkte no!	I am still going to make it!

As you can see from the preceding examples, manner adverbs are close to the verb—closer than the time adverb when both occur in a sentence. The word order for sentences containing two types of adverbs is as follows:

TIME ADVERB + SUBJECT + OBJECT + MANNER ADVERB + VERB

Awánųka kté.
M.ADV VERB
He killed it accidentally.

Tȟáȟca **awánųka** kté.
OBJECT M.ADV VERB
He accidentally killed a deer.

Adé	táȟca	**awánuka**	kté.
SUBJECT	OBJECT	M.ADV	VERB

Dad accidentally killed a deer.

Ȟtánihą	adé	táȟca	**awánuka**	kté.
T.ADV	SUBJECT	OBJECT	M.ADV	VERB

Yesterday, Dad accidentally killed a deer.

Formation of Irregular Verbs

In Chapters 2 and 5 we studied the structure and inflections of four types of verbs (i.e., regular stem, Y-stem, N-conjugation and NV-conjugation). There is a type of verb that shows irregularity in its formation. The verb *ecú* "she/he uses it, does it" is an N-conjugation verb (see Chapter 6) and slightly irregular, especially for the first and second person markers.

ecú – *she/he uses it, does it* (irregular, similar to a Class 3)

ecámu	*I do it*	ecúkta	*she/he will do it*
ecánu	*you do it*	ecúkteši	*she/he will not do it*
ecúgubi	*we do it*	ecúbi	*they do it*

You can see here that *ecú* requires the insertion of a linking vowel *a* before the first and second person markers. The role of this sound is to avoid the sequence of consonants *cm* (**ecmú*).

Iníbi háda **ecánukte** (he)?	*When will you do a sweat lodge?*
Dágucen žé **ecánu**?	*Why did you do that?*
Ecúši!	*Don't do it!*
Ecámukteši no!	*I will not do it!*
Ecúkteši no!	*She/he will not use it!*
Waná duwé **ecú** žé snohwáya.	*Now I know who did it.*
Dąyą́ **ecánu**!	*You did well!*
Dąyą́ **ecánuši**!	*You did not do well!*

Another highly frequent but completely irregular verb is *eyá* "she/he says it." As with *ecú* only the first *-p-* and second *-h-* person markers are irregular. The third person form of this verb is used to quote somebody's words.

eyá – *she/he says it* (irregular verb)

epá	*I say it*	eyį́kta	*she/he will say it*
ehá	*you say it*	eyį́kteši̦	*she/he will not say it*
u̦géyabi	*we say it*	eyábi	*they say it*

"Dágu yatkábi yacígabi (he)?" **eyá**.	*"What do you all want to drink?" he said.*
Nakón-i'a dóken **eyábi** (he)?	*How is it said in Nakoda?*
	(lit., *How do they say it in Nakoda?*)
Dóken **eyábi** žé?	*How do they say that?*
Aké **eyá** wo!	*Say it again!* (also Aké i'á wo! – *Speak again!*)
Dóken **epį́kta** né_____.	*What I'm saying is_____.*

Another similar verb is *žeyá* "she/he says that." *Žeyá* is used in stories to quote what a person has said and is made up of *žé* "that" and *eyá* "she/he says it." As seen in the following examples, it can be placed at the beginning or at the end of a sentence.

Mihú̦ **žeyá**, "Nén iyódą̱ga!"	*My mother said, "Sit down here!"*
"Mázaska iyúhana mak'ú!" **žeyá**.	*"Give (me) all your money!" he said.*

Yet another associated verb of speaking is *gáya* "she/he/they said that" (*gá* + *eyá*). While *žeyá* can be inflected for persons, *gáya* is used only for third person. It is intensively used in storytelling to indicate second-hand sources:

"Néci ų́bi," **gáya**.	*"They are here," he said.*

Lastly, the verb *gicó* "she/he invites him/her" also presents some irregularities in the first and second persons. As with almost all verbs starting with the sequence *gi*, the *gi* merges with *wa* and *ya* to yield *wéco* and *yéco*, although some speakers have regularized it to *wáco* and *yáco*. Note that the accent is on the person marker for first and second persons.

gicó – *she/he invites him/her* (irregular verb, similar to Class 1)

wéco ~ **wá**co	*I invite him/her*	gicókta	*she/he will invite him/her*
yéco ~ **yá**co	*you invite him/her*	gicókteši̦	*she/he will not invite him/her*
u̦gícobi	*we invite him/her*	gicóbi	*they invite him/her*

Wi̦cá žé **wáco**.	*I invited that man.*
Wi̦cábi žená **u̦gícobi**.	*We invited these men.*
Nená iyúhana **u̦gícobi**.	*We invited all of these people.*
Á̦ba né **wéco**.	*I invited him/her today.*
Gicó wo!	*Invite him/her!*

Inflections of Transitive Verbs (Third Person Subject)

As seen in Chapter 8, in Nakoda the most complex verbs to inflect are the transitive ones (e.g., *Peter loves Mary*) since both the subject and the object are marked on the verb. We have already seen the inflections of transitive verbs with a third person singular object. In this chapter we will study the formation of transitive verbs with a third person singular subject doing an action on a first person *me* and second person *you*, and third person *him/her* object. Again, the steps to build up a transtitive verb are as follow:

1. to indicate the <u>subject</u> of a transitive verb, use the **active regular stem** (Class 1), the **active Y-stem** (Class 2), or the **active N-conjugation** (Class 3) markers (shown in the table above);

2. to indicate the <u>object</u> of a transitive verb, use the **stative NV-conjugation** inflections. This means that whenever you want to express the object of a verb you will use the stative NV-conjugation forms -*ma*- "me" (*mastústa* "I am tired") and -*ni*- "you" (*nistústa* "you are tired") as seen in Chapter 8;

3. put the markers in the following order: OBJECT + SUBJECT

Here are a few examples from each class of verb with the transitive verb *k'ú* inflected for the first three persons, along with the internal analysis:

CLASS 1 (PREFIX)

ma-	Ø-	k'ú	>	mak'ú	*she/he gives it to me*
1SG.OBJECT	3SG.SUBJECT	GIVE			
ni-	Ø-	k'ú	>	nik'ú	*she/he gives it to you*
2SG.OBJECT	3SG.SUBJECT	GIVE			
Ø-	Ø-	k'ú	>	k'ú	*she/he gives it to him/her*
3SG.OBJECT	3SG.SUBJECT	GIVE			
ų-	Ø-	k'ú-bi	>	ųk'úbi	*she/he gives it to us*
1PL.OBJECT	3SG.SUBJECT	GIVE-PL			

CLASS 2 (PREFIX)

ma-	Ø-	yuha	>	mayúha	*she/he has me*
1SG.OBJECT	3SG.SUBJECT	HAVE			
ni-	Ø-	yuha	>	niyúha	*she/he has you*
2SG.OBJECT	3SG.SUBJECT	HAVE			
Ø-	Ø-	yuha	>	yuhá	*she/he has him/her/it*
3SG.OBJECT	3SG.SUBJECT	HAVE			
ų-	Ø-	yuhá-bi	>	ųyúhabi	*she/he has us*
1PL.OBJECT	3.SG.SUBJECT	HAVE-PL			

CLASS 3 (INFIX) (*ųg-* is placed before the stem)

į-	**ma-**	Ø-	yųǧa	>	įmáyųǧa	*she/he asks me*
ROOT	1SG.OBJECT	3SG.SUBJECT	ASK			
į-	**ni-**	Ø-	yųǧa	>	įníyųǧa	*she/he asks you*
ROOT	1SG.OBJECT	3SG.SUBJECT	ASK			
į-	Ø-	Ø-	yųǧa	>	įyúǧa	*she/he asks him/her*
ROOT	3SG.OBJECT	3SG.SUBJECT	ASK			
ųg-	Ø-	**į'-**	yųǧa-bi	>	ųgíyųǧabi	*she/he asks us*
1.PL.OBJECT	3SG.OBJECT	ROOT	ASK-PL			

The following table exemplifies the verb formation of two common verbs of Class 1 and 2, respectively. Note that the third person plural object marker *-wįca-* will be studied in Chapter 13.

	-snohya- – *to know him/her/it* (regular stem, Class 1)		**-wąyaga- – *to see him/her/it*** (Y-stem, Class 2)	
1SG	snoh**má**ya	*she/he knows me*	wą**má**yaga	*she/he sees me*
2SG	snoh**ní**ya	*she/he knows you*	wą**ní**yaga	*she/he sees you*
3SG	snohyá	*she/he knows him/her/it*	wąyága	*she/he sees him/her/it*
1PL	snoh**ų́**ya**bi**	*she/he knows us* or *we know him/her/it*	wą'**ų́**yaga**bi**	*she/he sees us* or *we see him/her/it*
2PL	snoh**ní**ya**bi**	*she/he knows you all*	wą**ní**yaga**bi**	*she/he sees you all*
3PL	snoh**wįca**ya	*she/he knows them*	wą**wįca**yaga	*she/he sees them*

Mázaska óda **mak'úbi**.	*They gave me a lot of money.*
Miní edáhą **mak'ú**!	*Give me some water!*
Niyáwašte **wįcáyak'u** no!	*You gave them a good life!*
Dágu **nik'úbi** (he)?	*What did they give you?*
Dágu **nik'ú** (he)?	*What did he/she give you?*
Dágucen šúga žé **nik'úbi** (he)?	*Why did they give you the dog?*
Duwé škoškóbena né **nik'ú** (he)?	*Who gave you this banana?*
Nitúgaši dágu **nik'ú** (he)?	*What did your grandfather give you?*
Nitúgaši miní edáhą **k'ú**.	*Give your grandfather some water.*
Wįcá gá íš ağúyabi edáhą **k'ú**.	*Give that man there some bread/bannock also.*
Wįcíjana gá búza wążí **k'úbi**.	*They gave that girl a cat.*
Asábi edáhą **k'úbi**.	*They gave him/her/it some milk.*
Iyúhana gakí šóšobina **wąwįcayaga**.	*He saw a whole bunch of mules yonder.*
Šúgatągabi nená **wąníyagabi**.	*Those horses see you.*
Macóbi cén imnámna.	*They invited me, so I went.*
Nągáhą né duwéni šúgatąga **ųwįcábasibišį**.	*Nowadays, none of us drives horse teams.*
Dóken **eníjiyabi** (he)?	*What is your name? (lit., how do they call you?)*
Jimmy **emágiyabi**.	*My name is Jimmy. (lit., they call me Jimmy)*

In order to gain a full grasp of transitive verb formation, here are some conjugation tables with the forms for both the third person object (as those of Chapter 8) and the third person subject.

naȟ'ų́ – *she/he hears, listens to him/her/it* (transitive, regular stem, Class 1)

Third Object

nawáȟ'ų	*I hear him/her/it*
nayáȟ'ų	*you hear him/her/it*
naȟ'ų́	*she/he hears him/her/it*
na'ų́ȟ'ųbi	*we hear him/her/it or she/he hears us*
nayáȟ'ųbi	*you all hear him/her/it*
naȟ'ų́bi	*they hear him/her/it*

Third Subject

namáȟ'ų	*she/he hears me*
naníȟ'ų	*she/he hears you*
naȟ'ų́	*she/he hears him/her/it*
na'ų́ȟ'ųbi	*we hear him/her/it or she/he hears us*
naníȟ'ųbi	*she/he hears you all*
nawįcaȟ'ų	*she/he hears them*

Hó **namáȟ'ų** wo!	*Hear my voice!*
Dáguškina ųgítawabi **na'ų́ȟ'ųbi**, ecén edáhąȟ **na'ų́ȟ'ųbišį**.	*Our children listen to us, but others don't listen to us.*
Micį́kši **namáȟ'ų**.	*My son heard me.*

teȟína – *she/he loves him/her/it* (transitive, regular stem, Class 1)

Third Object
tewáȟina	*I love him/her/it*
teyáȟina	*you love him/her/it*
teȟína	*she/he loves him/her/it*
te'ų́ȟina**bi**	*we love him/her/it or she/he loves us*
teyáȟina**bi**	*you all love him/her/it*
teȟína**bi**	*they love him/her/it*

Third Subject
te**má**ȟina	*she/he loves me*
te**ní**ȟina	*she/he loves you*
teȟína	*she/he loves him/her/it*
te'ų́ȟina**bi**	*we love him/her/it or she/he loves us*
te**ní**ȟina**bi**	*she/he loves you all*
te**wį́ca**ȟina	*she/he loves them*

Wį́yą žé **teníȟina**.	*That woman loves you.*
Wįyą́ žé **teyáȟina** he?	*Do you love that woman?*
Macą́de-skuya **tewáȟina** no!	*I love my sweetheart!*
Nakón-wįcoh'aǧe **teȟína** cá no!	*She/he really cherishes Nakoda traditions!*

snohyá – *she/he knows him/her/it* (transitive, regular stem, Class 1)

Third Object
snohw**á**ya	*I know him/her/it*
snohy**á**ya	*you know him/her/it*
snohyá	*she/he knows him/her/it*
snohų́ya**bi**	*we know him/her/it or she/he knows us*
snohy**á**ya**bi**	*you all know him/her/it*
snohyá**bi**	*they know him/her/it*

Third Subject
snoh**má**ya	*she/he knows me*
snoh**ní**ya	*she/he knows you*
snohyá	*she/he knows him/her/it*
snohų́ya**bi**	*we know him/her/it or she/he knows us*
snoh**ní**ya**bi**	*she/he knows you all*
snoh**wį́ca**ya	*she/he knows them*

Žé **snohwáya**.	*I know that.*
Snohwáyešį no!	*I don't know!*
Wįcá žé **snohwáyešį** wašíju tíbi žé opétų žé.	*I don't know the man who bought the house.*
Ȟtánihą wį́yą nową́ žé wahíkiyabi **snohwáya**.	*I know the woman who sang on the radio yesterday.*
Wįcá zé **snohníyešį**.	*That man doesn't know you.*
Dáguni **snohyábįšį** no!	*They don't know anything!*

Chapter 11 Exercises

EXERCISE 1

Translate the following sentences into Nakoda.

1. I arrived here recently. _____
2. The man arrived here yesterday. _____
3. Long ago my grandfather had many horses. _____
4. Now he has some mules too. _____
5. This evening they are doing a round dance. _____
6. Tomorrow we will do an Omaha dance. _____
7. The girl hit the boy accidentally. _____
8. At night time, my son walks quietly. _____
9. My grandmother still dances. _____
10. Everything on earth is sacred. _____
11. I respect the land! _____
12. They always dance on Friday. _____
13. They will dance at seven o'clock. _____

EXERCISE 2

Circle the words (3) that do not belong in the following set and explain why.

ą́ba né	škoškóbena	epá	edáhą	éstena
jé	ecúbi	ȟtayédu	ȟtánihą	aškán
hąhébi	wanágaš	tągán	žéci	búza

EXERCISE 3

Match the Nakoda words with the proper English translation.

hí	ceží	iyécįgayena	wé	mázaska	minískuya
bizéna	nąpsíhu	otókšu	océti	ptecíjana	hųská
įštá	núǧe	wáda	wíbazuką	wožábi	škoškóbena
wagíyą	cądé	hó	póǧe	įstó	įkmų́
maštíja	ptewánu	awódabi	hųskána	wakmúhaza	wítka
hąbí	mató	iyúhana	dágucen	šųkcíjana	šųkšóšo
í	niyá-wašte				

all _____

why _____

health _____

mule _____

puppy _____

gopher _____

voice _____

tooth _____

tongue _____

ear _____

thunderbird _____

mouth _____

heart _____

nose _____

eye _____

arm _____

finger _____

blood _____

car _____

lynx _____

money _____

bear _____

soda pop _____

stove _____

rabbit _____

truck _____

calf _____

canoe _____

domestic cow _____

table _____

juice _____

leggings _____

stockings _____

corn _____

banana _____

egg _____

saskatoon berries _____

gravy _____

EXERCISE 4
Translate the following text into English.

Wowícak'u ába štén, ṇnówąbįkte no! Micína íš hį́kta. Dąyą́ wašté nową́s'a. Nakón-i'abi ṇnówąbįkta hį́kna wacé'ųgiyabįkta. Tíbi gakná įníbi wagáǧįkta. Cą́ óda héktam tíbi nážį. Micį́kši į́š omágiya. Nitą́ga, nihų́ į́š wįcágico wo!

_____

_____

_____

_____

_____

_____

CHAPTER 12

Objectives

VOCABULARY

- More weather verbs
- Land and hydrographic features
- Tribes and tribal affiliation

GRAMMAR

- Transitive verb inflections: -*ci*- "I on you"; -*maya*- "you on me"
- Aspectual markers

Dialogues

1. Nisúga dóki yá (he)?
   Snohwáyešį. Makóce mnaská gakí manís'a, né ptéǧa ókšą.
   Oné wo! Ošíjeja hí ot'į apá į́š nawáȟ'ų no!

   Where did your (male) younger brother go?
   I don't know. He usually walks over there on the prairies, around the slough.
   Go look for him because there is a storm coming and I heard a thunderclap!

2. Ába ú háda wamákaškąšką wąnága he?
   Há, minítąga žéci šųkcúk'ana wąmnágas'a.

   Do you see animals at dawn?
   Yes, I often see coyotes by the lake.

3. Háu iná! Dóken ya'ú (he)?
   Há micíkši! Duwé né? Wįkóške snohwáya?
   Hiyá! Jane egíyabi macáde-skuye no!
   Dágu žéca (he)?
   Téhąn Nakóda žéca, duká húgu Iháktųwąna žéca. Waná Huhúžubina tí.
   Hą́!

   Hello mother! How is it going?
   Good my son, who is this? Do I know this girl?
   No! My sweetheart is called Jane.
   Of what tribe is she?
   She is a Stoney Nakoda, but her mother is a Yanktonai Dakota. She lives in Regina now.
   Okay!

4. Iná, šiná né cic'ú no!
   Hį́į́! Micíkši! Nína pinámayaya.
   Tecíȟina no!
   Mį́š tecíȟina! Iyógipimayayabi jé hą́dahą nén yahíbi.

   Mother! I give you this blanket.
   Oh! Son! Thank you very much!
   I cherish you a lot!
   Me too, I cherish you a lot! You guys always make me happy whenever you all come here.

Vocabulary

WEATHER VERBS

aʼóžążą	*it shines from sunlight*	mąkóškąšką	*it is an earthquake*
ą́ba ú	*it is dawn*	ošíjeja	*it is a storm*
aházi	*it is dusk*	otį́ apá	*it is a thunderclap*
amáȟpiya	*it is cloudy*	owáhįkna	*it is lightning*
maȟpíyato	*it is a blue sky*	wasú hįhą́	*it is hailing*

LAND AND HYDROGRAPHIC FEATURES

cąwóhą ~ cążóhą	*in a wooded area* (ADV)	oná	*prairie fire*
įyáȟe ~ įyáȟe	*mountain, hill*	owóšma	*thick vegetation*
maká ~ mąká	*earth, soil*	ptéǧa	*slough, lake*
mąkázi	*sand*	šošéna	*waterfall*
makóce mnaská	*prairies, flat land*	wakpá	*river*
minítąga	*lake*	wída	*island*
ocáguhe	*gravel road*	wiwí	*swamp, marsh*

OTHER WORDS

a'í	*she/he takes him/her/it there* (Class 1)
basí	*she/he drives* (Class 1)
ecágen	*always, in such a manner* (ADV)
gicí	*with* (POST)
gú	*she/he comes back* (Class 1)
oné	*she/he looks for it* (Class 1)
oyáde	*tribe, nation*
ptéjena	*she/he/it is short* (Class 4)
tiwáhe	*family*
ti'óšpaye	*extended family*
yušíkna	*she/he angers him/her by teasing, poking* (Class 2)
žéca	*she/he is of a certain kind* (Class 4)

Tribes and Tribal Affiliation

The following tables contain the names for other Indigenous as well as non-Indigenous groups. We have included some of the etymologies for these terms since they are relelvant culturally and historically.

Indigenous groups		Translation
Téhąn Nakóda	*Stoney Nakoda*	far away Nakoda
I'ášija	*Dakota*	bad talkers
Įhą́ktųwąna	*Yanktonai Dakota*	
Ką́ǧí Tóga	*Crow*	crow enemy
Šahíya	*Cree*	
Šahíyena	*Cheyenne*	little Cree (those who speak like the Cree)
Sihásaba	*Blackfoot*	black foot
I'ášijana	*Chippewa, German, French*	bad talkers
Mahpíyato	*Arapaho*	blue sky

Non-Indigenous groups		Translation
Wašíju	*white person*	minor spirit, fat gatherer
Gisýna	*Asian*	the braided
Špe'óna	*Mexican, Spaniard*	from French *Espagñol*
Wašíjusaba ~ Hásaba	*Black person, African*	black white person ~ black skin

Along with greetings, questions about tribal affiliation and origins are very important aspects of a person's social life. In Nakoda, the stative verb *žéca* "to be of a certain kind" is used when asking a person's origin, or work.

žéca – *she/he is of a certain kind* (NV-conjugation, Class 4)

že**má**ca	*I am of that kind*	že'**ú̜**cabi	*we are of that kind*
že**ní**ca	*you are of that kind*	že**ní**cabi	*you all are of that kind*
žéca	*she/he is of a certain kind*	žéca**bi**	*they are of that kind*

To indicate tribal affiliation, use the verb *žecá* "she/he is of that kind" after the name of the tribe or nation you belong to.

Dágu žen**í**ca (he)?	*Of what (tribe, work, trade) are you?*
Wadópena že**má**ca no!	*I am of the Wadopena Tribe!*
Céǧa K'ína že**má**ca no!	*I am of the Carry The Kettle Tribe!*
Dágu žéca (he)?	*What (tribe, work, trade) is she/he?*
Wí̜yą né žéca he?	*This woman is of what kind?*
Dágu žéca**bi** (he)?	*What (tribe, work, trade) are they?*
Žen**í**ca he?	*Are you of that (kind, tribe)?*
Že'**ú̜**cabi no!	*We are of that kind!*

Besides the word *tiwáhe* "family," there are others nouns which refer to different sizes of human groupings. *Oyáde* "tribe, nation" can be heard in ceremonial contexts such as when referring to the *kúši wanáǧi oyáde* "Grandmother Spirit Nation" or the *íyą oyáde* "Stone Nation."

Transitive Verb Inflections: *-ci-* "I on you" and *-maya-* "you on me"

The last inflections to be studied are the *I on you* set. To indicate an action of a first person singular on a second person, the form *-ci-* is used. Basically, *-ci-* indicates that the first person (*I*) is the subject and that the second person (*you*) is the object. However, the relation *you* (subject) on *me* (object) is indicated by two elements: *-ma-* (Class 4) + *-ya-* (Class 1), as in *mayák'u* "you give it to me." As seen in Chapter 8, *-ma-* is the stative Class 4 marker for first person, while *-ya-* is the Class 1 marker for second person. In sum, person markers of Class 4 indicate either the subject of intransitive stative verbs (**ma**stústa "I'm tired") or the object of transitive verbs (**ma**k'ú "she/he gave it to me"). Here is the morpheme analysis for a few verbs.

te__ȟína – *she/he cherishes him/her/it* (Class 1)

> te**cí**ȟina   *I cherish you*
> te**máya**ȟina   *you cherish me*

na__h̆'ų – *she/he hears, listens to him/her/it* (Class 1)

> nacíh̆'ų   *I hear you, listen to you*
> namáyah̆'ų   *you hear me, listen to me*

snoh__yá – *she/he knows him/her/it* (Class 1)

> snohcíya   *I know you*
> snohmáyaya   *you know me*

Verbs of classes 2 and 3 undergo sound changes which have to be memorized. For example, *wąyága* "she/he sees him/her/it" is a Y-stem verb that requires a change of *-y-* to *-mn-* (1SG subject) or *-y-* to *-n-* (2SG subject) when inflected with I↔you forms. Thus, for this inflection there are two markers indicating the first or second persons.

wą__yága – *she/he sees him/her/it* (Class 2)

>	wącímnaga	*I see you*	{wą-	cí-	mn-	aga}
			SEE-	1SUBJECT/ 2OBJECT-	1SG-	SEE
>	wąmáyanaga	*you see me*	{wą-	má-	ya-	n-	aga}
			SEE-	1OBJECT-	2SUBJECT-	2SG-	SEE

This first verb is very frequent since it is used in greetings: *Dąyą́ wącímnaga no!* "It's good to see you!"; *Aké wącímnagįkte no!* "I'll see you again!" Verbs of Class 3 that have a *y* or a *w* follow the same pattern as verbs of Class 2. They change *-w-* or *-y-* to *-m-* (1SG subject) or *-w-* or *-y-* to *-n-* (2SG subject) when inflected with I↔you forms.

į__yúǧa – *she/he asks him/her something* (Class 3)

>	įcímųǧa	*I ask you s/t*	{į-	cí-	m-	ųǧa}
			ASK-	1SUBJECT/ 2OBJECT-	1SG-	ASK
>	įmáyanųǧa	*you ask me s/t*	{į-	má-	ya-	n-	ųǧa}
			ASK-	1OBJECT-	2SUBJECT-	2SG-	ASK

The verb *k'ú* "she/he gives it to him/her/it" also undergoes a sound change but only for the *I on you* form. More precisely, the sound *k* of the stem changes to *c*: thus *ci-* + *-k'ú-* = *ci-c'ú* "I give it to you." This change does not apply to the *you on I* form.

__k'ú – *she/he gives it to him/her/it* (Class 1)

> cic'ú   *I give it to you*   sound change
> mayák'u   *you give it to me*   no sound change

Miní **cic'**úkta.	*I'll give you water.*
Mázaska **mayák'**ukta he?	*Are you going to give me money?*
Iná tí ektá a**máya'**ikta.	*You will take me to mom's place!* (a'í – *she/he takes him/her/it there*)
Ecágen **mayá**nušikne no!	*You always make me angry!*
Miyé i̧**mú̧ǧ**akta.	*I'll ask for it myself.*
"Dóki ní̧kta (he)?" i̧**mú̧ǧ**a.	*I asked him, "Where are you going?"*

Aspectual Markers

The grammatical category of tense relates generally to three different eras: past, present, and future. We already know that Nakoda, unlike English, does not have obligatory markers of tense. One can express that something happened in the past with adverbs like *waná̧gaš* "long time ago," but there are no such markers of past tense as that of English *-ed*. However, Nakoda marks modality (if a sentence is a declaration or an order, or if it is uncertain, or known by hearsay, etc.) as well as aspect. Aspect is a grammatical notion that relates to the inner temporal organization of a situation (Trask, 1993). For example, in English the neutral, progressive, or perfective aspects are expressed with auxiliaries and inflections like *-ed* and *-ing*.

Tense	Aspect	Examples
present	neutral	She **writes** a letter.
past	neutral	She **wrote** a letter.
future	neutral	She **will write** a letter.
present	progressive	She **is writing** a letter.
past	progressive	She **was writing** a letter.
future	progressive	She **will be writing** a letter.
present	perfective	She **has slept** all day.
past	perfective	She **had slept** a lot already when I came in.
future	perfective	She **will have slept** if you get there late.

Nakoda marks different types of aspects on the verb, but not tenses. In other words, for Nakoda speakers it does not matter *when something happened* (past/present/future tenses), but *if it usually happens* (habitual aspect), *if it is happening over and over again* (durative aspect), or *if it will potentially happen* (*-kta*). In this section we will study two types of aspectual markers: enclitics (an element that attaches on a verb but carries no accent), and particles (which are independent words).

-s'a – *habitual aspect*

In Chapter 10 we saw that the enclitic *-s'a-* meant "agent, one who does X" and that this element could also be used on verbs to indicate that an action is done continuously (i.e., one does it all the time). It should be remembered here that this enclitic implies some temporal boundedness. For example, although *he dances all the time* could mean that he literally does not ever stop dancing, we know that, in reality, that person has to stop in order to eat and sleep. This is what is meant by "temporal boundedness." This enclitic is translated with *usually*, *habitually*, and *all the time*. Moreover, it always follows the plural *-bi* and the negative *-šį* and provokes ablaut.

wacíbi	*they dance*	>	wacíbi**s'a**	*they dance all the time*
maníbi	*they walk*	>	maníbi**s'a**	*they walk all the time*
wódabi	*they eat*	>	wódabi**s'a**	*they eat all the time*

Mitúgaši, adé įš žeyábi**s'a**.	*My grandfather and my dad habitually said that.*
Ecágen žécųbi**s'a** he?	*Do they always do it as such?*
Wįcá né yaté**s'a**.	*This man drinks all the time.*
Wanágaš mitúgaši onówą nená nową́**s'a**.	*Long ago my grandfather used to sing these songs.*
Mikúši žeyé**s'a**.	*My grandmother always says that.*

The habitual *-s'a-* can also occur on stative verbs to indicate that an entity has a permanent quality. It is used in superlative constructions such as *the tallest man*.

cą́ ptéjena**s'a**	*the shortest tree*
wįcá ptéjena**s'a**	*the shortest man*

Note that taken out of context one cannot tell if the word is a noun (*i'és'a* "a talker, a blabbermouth") or a verb (*i'és'a* "she/he talks all the time"), since they have the same form.

-GA- – *durative aspect*

This enclitic indicates that a repetitive or continuous action is done over a stretch of time with no marked temporal boundaries. It is often translated with the *-ing* (progressive aspect) form of a verb (i.e., *He works* versus *He is working*) or with the auxiliary verb *keep* (i.e., *i'á* "she/he talks to him/her" versus *i'á**ga*** "she/he keeps talking to him/her"), or even with *all the time*, *over and over again*.

Dágu dókanų? Wabási**ga**.	*What are you up to? I've been driving all this time.*
Dágu dókų? Įštíma**ga**!	*What is he up to? He's fast asleep!*
"Hukwá!" eyá**ga**.	*He kept on saying "Hukwa!"*
"Teȟíya mągé no!" eyá**ga**.	*He kept on saying "I'm (sitting) in a bad situation!"*
Šųktógeja žé gú**ga**.	*The wolf kept coming back.*
Dágu dókanų**ga**?	*What have you been doing (for all this time)?*
Táȟca owánįkta**ga** no!	*I looked for a deer for a long time.*
Žécen žé yągá**ga**bi.	*So then they sat for a while.*

JÉ – *always*; **ECÁGEN** – *always, often*

The modality particle *jé* is used to indicate that something occurs habitually. It carries its own accent. Some speakers say it indicates "past tense" because habits can only be built up with past experiences. It usually occurs at the end of a sentence. The aspectual adverb *ecágen* means that something happens "often, always." It is formed from *ecá* "she/he/it is thus" (Class 4) + *-gen* "in the manner of."

Ahópa gicí ma'ų́nibi **jé**.	We always walk with respect.
Iná į́š adé nakón-i'abi **jé**.	My mother and my father always spoke Nakoda.
Mitúgaši wanágaš i'á cén nawáȟ'ų **jé**.	I heard my grandfather speak it thus long ago.
Mitášųga gicí iwá'a **jé**.	I always talk with my horse.
Ába háda įštíma **jé**.	He always slept during the daytime.
Ecágen híbi.	He came often.
Ecágen záptą apá háda hí.	He usually comes at five. (lit., when it hits five)
Ecágen žécųbis'a he?	Do they do that all the time?
Ecágen įštíma.	He's always sleeping.

Chapter 12 Exercises

EXERCISE 1

Translate the following sentences into Nakoda.

1. My father is of the Wadopena tribe. _____

2. I know you guys, you all live in Carry The Kettle. _____

3. Hi my friend! Come and eat with me. _____

4. Do you know me? _____

5. He kept on doing it. _____

6. They kept on dancing. _____

7. Give it to me now! _____

8. Do you often come here? _____

9. Do you all love me? _____

EXERCISE 2

Fill in the **I ↔ you** forms for the following transitive verbs (e.g., *I ask you, you ask me*)

	I on you (SG), future	you (PL) on me, negative
-teȟina- – *love*		
-snohya- – *know*		
-k'u- – *give*		
-wok'u- – *feed*		
-naȟ'ų- – *hear*		
-wąyaga- – *see*		

EXERCISE 3

Match the following Nakoda words with their English translation.

Téhąn Nakóda	Iȟáktųwąna	minítąga	wiwí	wakpá	owóšma
I'åšija	wasú hiȟą́	naȟ'ų́	ptéǧa	ocáguȟe	oná
gú	Gisų́na	Maȟpíyato	Wašíju	ošíjeja	amáȟpiya
mąkázi	ą́ba ú	Šahíya	Sihásaba	maȟpíyato	Wašíju sába

Black person, African _____ Stoney Nakoda _____

white person _____ Dakota _____

Yanktonai Dakota _____ Chinese _____

Cree _____ slough _____

sand _____ thicket, thick bush _____

she/he comes back _____ gravel road _____

lake _____ river _____

Blackfoot	_____	Chippewa, German	_____
Arapaho	_____	it is a blue sky	_____
it is dawn	_____	it is a storm	_____
it is cloudy	_____	it is hailing	_____
prairie fire	_____	she/he hears it	_____

EXERCISE 4

Translate these sentences into Nakoda and add the correct aspectual enclitics (*-s'a, -ga*) on the verbs.

1. These dogs are habitually angry. _____
2. They kept on talking to him. _____
3. They often sleep here. _____
4. They habitually eat there on Fridays. _____
5. What have they been doing for all this time? _____
6. I'm often tired now. _____

CHAPTER 13

Objectives

VOCABULARY

- Horse vocabulary
- Words related to hunting activities

GRAMMAR

- Linkers: *cén, nécen, žécen, ecén*
- Sentences with *štén* "if, when" and *hą́da(hą)* "whenever"
- Inflections of transitive verbs: *-wįca-* third person plural object

Dialogues

1. Mázaska óda wįcáwak'u.
   Dágucen wįcáyak'u (he)?
   Omágiyabi hą́da mázaska wįcáwak'u.
   Mį́š edáhą wacíge no!

   I gave them a lot of money.
   Why did you give it to them?
   Whenever they help me, I give them money.
   I want some too!

2. Šų́gatąga nitáwabi he?
   Hą́, mitášųga wikcémnabi, šųkwíyena, šų̨ḣpéna įš wįcámnuha. Dąyą́ iyáksamwįcawakiya no! Šųknį́deska gá wąnága he? Agą́n-nągikteḣtįyą he?
   Hą́!
   Ak'į́ sába žé ecų́ wo!

   Do you own horses?
   Yes, I have ten horses (my horses are ten), a mare and a colt too. I train them well. Do you see that Appaloosa over there? Would you like to ride it?
   Yes!
   Use that black saddle!

3. Háu koná! Dokén ya'ú?
   Dąyą́ wa'ų́ no! Hąyákena taȟcíjana iyúhana wąwícamnaga.
   Duktén nážįbi-c'ehą (he)?
   Wakpá kiyą́na nážįbi. Aházi háda yatkábi.

   Aké nená onébi yacíga he?
   Hą́, waná ųgíyįkte no! Táȟca wążí ktébi ųcígįkte no!

   Hello friend! How is it going?
   I'm doing well! Early this morning I saw a herd of deer.
   Where were they standing?
   They were standing near the river. When it is dusk, they drink.
   Do you want to go look for them again?
   Yes, let's go now. We (two) want to kill a deer.

Vocabulary

TYPES OF HORSES

šųgána	*old horse*	šųksába	*black horse*
šųȟpéna	*colt*	šųkwágįc'į	*pack horse*
šųkhíto	*blue horse*	šųkwícaȟtiyąna	*old stallion*
šųkknékeǧa	*pinto*	šųkwíyena	*mare*
šųknídeska	*Appaloosa*	šųk'ápeskana	*palomino*

HORSE EQUIPMENT

ak'į́	*saddle*	mąs'ípaȟte	*bridle and bit*
ak'įmaheda	*saddle blanket*	šųksíhamaza	*horseshoe*
ak'į́ha	*saddle bag*	šųkšpáya	*horse brand*
įká	*reins*	šųktáwap'i	*collar*
įpáȟte	*bridle*	šųk'íjapšįde	*horse whip*

WORDS RELATED TO HUNTING

caȟnísaba	*gunpowder*	ptecónica	*dry buffalo meat*
cótąga	*gun*	ptehá	*buffalo hide*
įwáyage	*gunsight*	sú	*seed, bullet, pellet*
owícanebi	*hunter*	tatágabina	*buffalo herd*

The verbs describing horse activities are also numerous. We give here the main ones, along with their conjugation and some sentences.

agą́n-yąga – *she/he rides a horse* (Class 3)

agą́n-mą̨ga	*I ride a horse*	agą́n-yągikta	*she/he will ride a horse*
agą́n-nąga	*you ride a horse*	agą́n-yągabį̨kteší	*they will not ride a horse*
agą́n-ųyągabi	*we ride a horse*		

iyáksamkiya – *she/he trains it* (Class 1)

iyáksamwakiya	*I train it*	iyáksamkiyį̨kta	*she/he will train it*
iyáksamyakiya	*you train it*	iyáksamkiyabį̨kteší	*they will not train it*
iyáksamųkiyabi	*we train it*		

oné – *she/he is looking for him/her/it* (Class 1)

owáne	*I look for him/her/it*	oníkta	*she/he will look for him/her/it*
oyáne	*you look for him/her/it*	oníkteší	*they will not look for him*
o'ų́nebi	*we look for him/her/it*		

wók'u – *she/he feeds him/her/it* (Class 1)

wówak'u	*I feed him/her/it*	wók'ukta	*she/he will feed him*
wóyak'u	*you feed him/her/it*	wók'ubį̨kteší	*they will not feed him*
wó'ųk'ubi	*we feed him/her/it*		

Agą́n-yągabi no!	*Ride the horse!*
Šųkšká **agą́n-mą̨gikta** no!	*I will ride a white horse!*
Mitášųga miyéȟ **iyáksamwakiya**.	*I train my horse myself (specifically).*
Mína wążí **oné**.	*He is looking for a particular knife.*
Táȟca **owánįkte** no!	*I'll look for a deer.*
Owáne né.	*I looked for it.*
Oyánįkta he?	*Will you look for it?*
Táȟca **o'ų́nįktaga**.	*We kept looking for a deer.*
Hąyákeji šúgatąga žé **wówak'ukta**.	*Tomorrow, I will feed that horse.*
Šúgatąga nená **wówįcak'u**.	*She/he feeds those horses.*

In the past and still to this day, hunting, fishing, and berry-picking sustained the Nakoda and all Indigenous people of the Americas. These activities are often discussed in daily life, and we present two of the most common verbs pertaining to hunting activities here.

iyámekiya – *she/he goes hunting* (Class 1)

iyáme**wa**kiya	*I go hunting*	iyámekiyi̜**kta**	*she/he will go hunting*
iyáme**ya**kiya	*you go hunting*	iyámekiyabi̜**kteši̜**	*they will not go hunting.*
iyáme**u̜**kiya**bi**	*we go hunting*		

kté – *she/he kills him/her/it* (Class 1)

wakté	*I kill it*	kté**kta**	*she/he will kill him/her/it*
yakté	*you kill it*	kte**bi̜ši̜**	*they will not kill him/her/it*
u̜kté**bi**	*we kill him/her/it*		

Hąyákeji štén **iyámeyakiyi̜kteši̜** no!	*When it was morning you did not go hunting!*
Ktékta!	*He will kill it!*
Madó žé wašíju **kté**.	*The bear killed the white person.*
Né miyé **wakté** né.	*I'm the one who killed it.*
Tá wąží **ktébi**.	*They killed a moose.*

Linkers: *cén, nécen, žécen, ecén*

In the preceding chapters we studied the structure of simple sentences containing one verb. In this chapter we survey ways to link two clauses (or short sentences containing one inflected verb each) together, as in:

> *He opened the door **and then** he saw the burglar.*
> *She is old **and because of that** she has problems remembering people.*
> *It is raining, **and therefore** I'm staying inside today.*
> *I think she likes me, **and thus** I'll ask her out tonight.*

Altough there are many ways to connect clauses together in Nakoda, by far the most common linker or conjunction is the particle *cén* "therefore, because, and then." It is extremely versatile and can be used in different contexts and serves different functions.

CÉN – *because, after x-ing*

Cén can be translated as a linker between a cause (*because I'm going to bed*) and a consequence (*I'll brush my teeth*), and in this case *cén* follows the cause. However, it can also serve as a **sequence marker**, as in *after having done this, I'll do that* or *after running for an hour, I'll rest*, and in this case, it follows the first clause. Note that oftentimes both translations are possible:

Wįcábi hokúwa iyáyabi žená [hąhébi **cén**], kníbi.	*Those men who went fishing came back home [**because** it was night].*
Šúga žená [miní cįgábi **cén**], kníbi.	*Those dogs came home [**because** they wanted water].*
[Šúga síja žé wąyága **cén**], napá.	*He fled [because he saw that bad dog.]* *[**After** seeing that bad dog,] he fled.*
[Mįštímįkta **cén**], hí wakpážaža.	*[**As** I intend to (go to) sleep], I brush my teeth.*

CÉN – *thus, as such, in a way, then*

Cén can link two independent clauses together or function as a manner adverb, or even to mark emphasis:

Ába né nína wašté **cén** hokúwa ųyábi.	*It's a nice day today, thus we go fishing.*
Mitúgaši wanágaš i'á **cén** nawáȟ'ų jé.	*I always heard my grandfather speak as such long ago.*
Dágu wak'ú **cén** įš? Dágu mnuhéšį.	*What can I give then? I have nothing.*

Note that there is an adverbial suffix *-cen/-ken* "in a way, manner" that is homophonous with the particle *cén*. It occurs on manner adverbs which can also link sentences together. Basically, manner adverbs formed with *-ken* are parallel to a set of intransitive verbs built on the demonstratives, as indicated in the following table:

Demonstratives	Intransitive Verbs/Adverbs	Manner adverbs
né – *this*	nécedu – *it is like this; like this*	nécen – *in this way*
žé – *that*	žécedu – *it is like that; like that*	žécen – *in that way, then, so*
gá – *that yonder*	gácedu – *it is in such a way; in such a way*	gáken – *in such a way*
é – *she/he/it is so*	ecédu – *it is, it happens so; as such*	ecén – *in the original way, and, thus*

As indicated in the preceding table, manner adverbs can also be used to coordinate two sentences together, as in *She fell asleep **and** left the lights on*. *Žécen* and *ecén* are often used for that particular function.

NÉ- – *this*

Nécedu otí̜ga.	*This must be the way. It must be like this.* (verb)
Nécen ecámu̜.	*I do it this way. This is how I do it.*
Waná̜gaš **nécen** eyábi.	*This is what was said long ago. Long ago they said it in this way.*
Nécen epá jé.	*This is the way I always say it.*

ŽÉ- – *that* (often used for future reference)

Žéceduši̜ ecú̜.	*He is not doing that right.* (adverb)
Žécedu ecú̜.	*He is doing it right.* (adverb)
Žécen eyábi.	*It is said in that way.*
Nakón-i'abi̜kta **žécen**, **žécen** u̜cí̜gabi.	*They will speak Nakoda then (in the future), and so this is what we want.*

É- – *in the original way, and, thus*

Tawáci̜ **ecéduš**i̜.	*She/he is stupid.* (verb) (lit., his/her mind is not right)
Hokšína žé tawáci̜ **ecéduš**i̜.	*That boy is stupid.* (verb)
Ecéduši̜ ecú̜.	*He is not doing it right.* (adverb) (lit., he is doing it the wrong way)
Mí̜š **emácedu**!	*I'm like this too!* (verb)
Ecén i̜š wacéwagiya no.	*I pray in this way too.*
"Dóha̜ni i̜škádeši̜ wo!" emágiya **ecén**.	*Never play with it! He told me thus.*
Wí̜ya̜ žé hí, **ecén** éyagu.	*The woman came and took it.*

Complex Sentences with the Conditionals *štén* "if, when" and *há̜da(ha̜)* "whenever"

In English, there are complex sentences expressing a condition and a consequence, as in *If I don't wear my coat, I'll catch a cold* or *If I eat early, I'll visit my friends*. The condition is encoded by *if*, which is placed before the first verb, while the consequence is expressed by *will* or *'ll* (future action) and appears after the second verb. We will say that the "if-clause" is subordinate and the "will-clause" is the main clause, as in:

[**If** I buy a horse],   you**'ll** teach me how to ride.
[SUBORDINATE CLAUSE]   MAIN CLAUSE

The subordinate clause appears between brackets since it is optional and does not express a complete idea, while the main clause does express a complete idea. In other words, the main clause could be used alone, as in *You'll teach me how to ride*, while this is not the case for the subordinate clause, *If I buy a horse*.

In Nakoda, conditional sentences are formed by using the word *štén* "if, when," which is placed after the verb of the subordinate clause. The general template for conditional sentences is the following:

OBJECT	+ (SUBJECT)	+ VERB_{SUBORDINATE}	+ ŠTÉN	+ VERB_{MAIN}
Wíyą žé		teyáȟina	**štén**	hįknáya wo!
[woman that		you.love.her	if]	marry.her imperative.sg

If you love that woman, marry her!

Įníduka **štén**, wóda wó! — *If you are hungry, then eat!*
Huhúžubina wa'í **štén**, timáwanįkta. — *When I get to Regina, I will visit people.*

It is important to note that *štén* also means "when" and can express 1) the idea of a *potential* action that will happen in the future; or 2) the idea of a *punctual* action:

When you come to the city, bring your children with you. (potential action)
When it is Friday, I play bingo. (punctual action)

The sentence template for this use of *štén* is exactly the same as shown above, except that *štén* in the sense of "when" (punctual) appears after nouns expressing days of the week (e.g., *on Sundays*) or temporal adverbs (e.g., *in the morning*), as well as after the verb of a subordinate clause. Here are a few examples to illustrate the "when" meaning of *štén*:

1. **Štén** "when" (punctual or potential action + *-kta*) in subordinate clause:

    Įnį́bi ųgáǧabi **štén**, miní odá ųcígabi no! — *When we make a sweat lodge, we want a lot of water.* (punctual)
    Ábawaką ehą́'i **štén**, micį́kši tawíju gicí timáni ų́bįkta. — *When it is [reaches] Sunday, my son and his wife are coming to visit.* (potential)

2. **Štén** "when" (punctual or potential action + *-kta*) after days of the week or temporal adverbs. It is often translated by "in, at, on, next":

    Hąyákena **štén**, aǧúyabisaga edáhą wacíga. — *In the morning, I want some toast.*
    Wiyódahą **štén**, aǧúyabi nągú wahą́bi ųyúdabįkta. — *At noon, we will eat bannock/bread and soup.*
    Ábawaką gicúni **štén**, owáyawa mnį́kta. — *On Monday, I will go to school.*
    Ábawaką **štén**, wa'úkta. — *I will come on Sunday.*

Finally, besides *štén* there is another word, *hądahą ~ hąda* "whenever," that is used in complex sentences to express a regularly occurring action, as in the following English examples:

> ***Whenever*** *she comes to visit me, we have a good chat.*
> ***Whenever*** *it's cold, I wear my duffled boots.*

3. **Hąda(hą)** "whenever" occurs in the same place as *štén* "if, when," that is, before the verb of the main clause or the time adverb. It is often translated by *whenever*, but is also translated by *when* or by a preposition—*on*, *in*, etc. This adverb indicates that something happens continuously, that is, on a regular basis, or that a condition has to be met (*if there is a storm*) in order for a consequence to occur (*I'll stay inside*).

> Ąba yužáža **hądahą**, wamnúžaža hįkna wacówa'ųba.
> *On Saturdays I wash all my stuff and do some baking.*

> Ąba įzáptą **hądahą**, tanó yúdabišį.
> *Whenever it is Friday, they don't eat meat.*

> Ošíjeja tągán **hądahą**, timáhen wa'ų́ jé.
> *Whenever there is a storm outside, I always stay inside.*

> Doháni wáhįhą **hąda**, tągán škádabi waštéwana.
> *When it snows, I like to play outside.*

> Wįcá matéjana **hąda**, hą'ų́manibi-c'ehą.
> *When I was a young man, we would walk around at night.*

Inflections of Transitive Verbs: *-wįca-* (Third Person Plural Object)

In Chapter 8 we studied the transitive inflections with a singular third person object and noted that it was expressed by a zero prefix (Ø), as in *wak'ú* "I give it to him." The internal analysis of this verb is as follows:

OBJECT	+	SUBJECT	+	VERB STEM
Ø-		wa-		k'ú

wak'ú – *I give it to him/her*

When the object is a third person plural, the prefix -wįca- is used and placed before the subject marker. Thus, if you want to say that you gave it to them, you add -wįca- in the object slot, as in:

OBJECT	+	SUBJECT	+	VERB STEM
wįca-		wa-		k'ú

wįcáwak'u – *I give it to them*

However, there is a small quirk with these forms. When the subject is "1PL" (we) and the object "3PL" (them), the order is SUBJECT + OBJECT and not OBJECT + SUBJECT like the other verbs seen above.

SUBJECT	+	OBJECT	+	VERB STEM
ųgi-		**wįca-**		k'u

ųgíwįcak'u – *we give it to them*

This special form of *k'ú* is underlined in the following table, along with other verb paradigms.

	-k'u- – to give it to him/her/it (Class 1)		**-wąyaga- – to see him/her/it (Class 2)**	
1SG	**wįcá**wak'u	I give it to them	wą**wįcam**naga	I see them
2SG	**wįcá**yak'u	you give it to them	wą**wįcan**aga	you see them
3SG	**wįcá**k'u	he gives it to them	wą**wįca**yaga	she/he sees them
1PL	<u>**ųgíwįca**k'u**bi**</u>	we give it to them	wą**wįca**'ųyaga**bi**	we see them
2PL	**wįcá**yak'u**bi**	you all give it to them	wą**wįcan**aga**bi**	you all see them
3PL	**wįcá**k'u**bi**	they give it to them	wą**wįca**yaga**bi**	they see them

	-snohya- – to know him/her/it (Class 1)		**-ųspekiya- – to teach him/her/it (Class 1)**	
1SG	snoh**wįca**waya	I know them	ųspé**wįca**wakiya	I teach them
2SG	snoh**wįca**yaya	you know them	ųspé**wįca**yakiya	you teach them
3SG	snoh**wįcá**ya	she/he knows them	ųspé**wįca**kiya	she/he teaches them
1PL	snoh**wįca**'ųyabi	we know them	ųspé**wįca**'ųkiya**bi**	we teach them
2PL	snoh**wįca**ya**bi**	you all know them	ųspé**wįca**yakiya**bi**	you all teach them
3PL	snoh**wįca**ya**bi**	they know them	ųspé**wįca**kiya**bi**	they teach them

Dágu **wicáyak'úbi** (he)?	*What did you give them?*
Mázaska óda **wicáwak'ú**.	*I gave them a lot of money.*
Hąhébi wanáǧi **wowícak'u**.	*She/he feeds the Night Spirits.*
Hąhébi wanáǧi **wowícak'ubi**	*Night Spirits Feeding ceremony*
Šúgatągabi nená **wąwícanaga**.	*Did you see those horses?*
Iyúhana gakí šóšobina **wąwícayaga**.	*He saw a whole bunch of mules yonder.*
Iyúhana **snohwícayabi**.	*They know them all.*
Šúgatąga **ųspéwicakiyebįšį** no!	*They didn't teach the horses!*
Šúgabi yámni **wicá'ųyuhabi** no!	*We have three dogs!*
Mikúši ąbahotųna agénųba **wicáyuha**.	*My grandmother has twelve chickens.*
Nągáhą né duwéni šúgatąga **ųwicábasibišį**.	*Nowadays none of us drives horse teams.*
Gitézi óda **wicáyuha**.	*She has a bunch of brats.*

Chapter 13 Exercises

EXERCISE 1
Translate the following sentences into Nakoda.

1. Those horses saw you. _____
2. The man trained many horses. _____
3. We gave them a lot of money. _____
4. If you come here, then you'll ride a horse. _____
5. Whenever it rains, I play inside with my younger sister. _____
6. My grandfather went hunting and he killed two deer and a duck. _____
7. If it rains, they will not go hunting. _____
8. Come again next Wednesday! _____
9. Whenever I have money, I give them some of it. _____
10. I'm pleased whenever I see the horses. _____

EXERCISE 2
Complete the following verb paradigms.

	wok'ú	kté	k'ú
I on them			
you on them, FUT			
he on them			
he on them, FUT/NEG			
we on you, NEG			
they on us, NEG			

EXERCISE 3
Translate the following story into English.

> Hąyákeja štén iyámewakiyįkta.
> Táȟca owánįkte no!
> Wąží wąmnága hą́da, waktékte no!
> Duwé iyúhana tanó cic'úbįkte no!
> Midáguyabi į́pibi hą́da wašté įštímabįkte no!

_____

_____

_____

_____

_____

_____

EXERCISE 4
Match the following Nakoda words with their English translation.

iyámeyakiya   agą́n-yągikteší   ak'į́ha   įką́
caȟnísaba   ptecónica   agą́n-mąga   šųknį́deska
cótąga   ptehá   šųkhį́to   šųksába
owį́canebi   sú   šųkšpáya   šųksíhamaza
įwą́yage   tatą́gašina   šųkknékneǧa   šųkwį́caȟtįyaną
šųgána   ak'į́   šųkwíyena   taȟcá

horse brand _____   deer _____

old stallion _____   mare _____

pinto _____   horseshoe _____

reins _____   black horse _____

Appaloosa _____   blue horse _____

saddle bag _____   gunsight _____

old horse _____   buffalo meat _____

seed, bullet, pellet _____   gun _____

gunpowder _____   I ride a horse _____

buffalo hide _____   you went hunting _____

buffalo robe _____   hunter _____

she/he will not _____   saddle _____
ride a horse

EXERCISE 5

Look at the horse vocabulary section at the beginning of this chapter. Analyze these words and give a literal translation by removing the root *šųk-* and finding the correct suffixes in the glossary. For example, *šųksába* > *šųk-* "horse" + *sába* "black."

CHAPTER 14

Objectives

VOCABULARY

- More transitive and intransitive verbs
- More adverbs and question words
- Expressing doubt, certainty, reliability, ability, obligation

GRAMMAR

- *Gicí* "with someone"; *óm* "with them"
- Reciprocal *-gici-* "action on one another"
- Modality particles
- Specific, unspecific objects

Dialogues

1. Šúgataga waží gakí nážį.
   Waktá! Nína šikná otí'įga! Niyúde no! Omáyagahniǧa he?
   Hą́! Waná ųkní duká!

   There is a big dog standing over there.
   Beware! He seems very angry! He'll eat you! Do you understand me?
   Okay! We (two) should go home now.

2. Žé nayáȟ'ų he?
   Hą́! Gakí ot'į́ apá stéya.
   Hukwáá́! Mitą́kši žewágiyįkta cén tagán škáda!

   Did you hear that?
   Yes! It seems like it is thundering over there.
   Oh! I'll tell that to my (male) younger sister because she is playing outside!

3. Duwé gicí yahí?
   Micíja gicí wahí. Įjámna štén nén ųgíštima epcá. O'įštima tíbi wąží iyéwaya duká no!

   Gakí owóde tíbi gakná yuką́.

4. Mitą́kši! Dágu awácąni (he)?
   Dágucen yacéya (he)?
   Hokšína wąží awácąmi. Ȟtánihą iyáya cén nągáhą cądémasija.
   Waná aházi no! Yakní wo!
   Hiyá! Omáwanįkta.

Who did you arrive with?
I came here with my child. Because there is a blizzard, I guess we (two) will sleep here tonight. I have to find a hotel!
There is one over there, beside the restaurant.

Little sister! What do you have on your mind?
Why are you crying?
I have a boy on my mind. He left yesterday, and this is why I'm sad now.
It is dusk already! Come home!
No! I'll go for a walk.

Vocabulary

agú	*she/he brings it back* (Class 1)
apá	*she/he hits, knocks him/her/it* (Class 1)
a'í	*she/he brings him/her/it there* (Class 1)
cądésija	*she/he is sad* (Class 4)
dágucen	*why* (ADV)
hústaga	*she/he/it is lean, skinny* (Class 4)
iyéska	*she/he interprets* (Class 1)
iyéya	*she/he finds him/her/it* (Class 1)
ijáhi	*it is mixed together with* (Class 4)
išną́na	1) *alone* (ADV); 2) *she/he is alone* (Class 3)
oǧúǧa	*she/he wakes up* (Class 4)
ománi	*she/he travels, goes for a walk outside* (Class 1)
o'įštima tíbi	*hotel* (N)
šikná	*she/he is mad, angry* (Class 1)
téhąduwa ~ téhąn	*a long distance, far* (ADV)
ús	*using it, because of* (POST)
wacį́	*mind, plan, goodwill* (N)
yuką́	*she/he/it exists* (VI)

Verbs that express processes involving the mind such as *thinking, pondering, wondering, remembering, forgetting* and *understanding* are numerous in Nakoda. Below are conjugations for the four most common ones, along with examples:

iyúkcą – *she/he thinks about him/her/it (Class 2)*

imnúkcą	I think about him/her/it	iyúkcąkta	she/he will think him/her/it
inúkcą	you think about him/her/it	iyúkcąbįkteši	they will not think about it
ųgíyukcąbi	we think about him/her/it		

wíyukcą – *she/he is thinking about things (Class 2)*

wímnukcą	I think about things	wíyukcąkta	she/he thinks about things
wínukcą	you think about things	wíyukcąbįkteši	they will think about things
wí'ųyukcąbi	we think about things		

giksúya – *she/he remembers him/her/it (irregular, similar to Class 1)*

wéksuya	I remember him	giksúyikta	she/he will remember him
yéksuya	you remember him	giksúyibįkteši	they will not remember him
ųgíksuyabi	we remember him		

ogáȟniǧa – *she/he understands him/her/it (Class 1)*

owágaȟniǧa	I understand him/her/it	ogáȟniǧakta	she/he will understand him
oyágaȟniǧa	you understand him	ogáȟniǧabįkteši	they will not understand him
ųgógaȟniǧabi	we understand him		

Dóken wínukcą (he)?	What are you thinking about?
Mary aké **iyúkcą** "Dágu aké ecámųkta?"	Mary thought, "What will I do next?"
Bağé nécen **wíyukcą** bo!	(all of you) Think in this way collectively!
	(bağé – together, bunched up, as a group)
Nągáhą né wáhįhąkta **inúkcą** he?	Do you think it will snow today?
Nakón-wįco'i'e **agíktųžabi**.	They forgot about the Nakoda language.
Wanúȟ **ųgíksuyabikteši** cá.	Maybe we won't remember it.
Mihúgagebi **wicágiksuyabi**.	My parents remember them.
Niyé **mayéksuya** he?	As for you, do you remember me?
ąbédu **wéksuya**	Memorial Day
Nakón-i'abi jónanaȟ **ogáȟniǧa**.	He understands very little Nakoda.
Nakón-i'abi gitána **owágaȟniǧa** duká iwá'eši.	I barely understand Nakoda, but I don't speak it.

Some phrases used to express mental behaviors are built with the noun *wací* "mind," which can be possessed using the prefix *-ta-*, as in *mitáwacį* "my mind," *nitáwacį* "your mind."

Tawácį dąyą́šį.	*He is mentally disabled.* (lit., His mind is not well.)
Tawácį ús iyéskabi.	*They converse using their mind.*
Tawácį ecédušį no!	*He is stupid!* (lit., His mind is not right) (ecédu – it is right, the correct way [vs])

Gicí "with someone"; *óm* "with them"

To indicate that a person is doing an activity with somebody else, as in the English sentence *I'll play with Charles*, the postposition *gicí* "with" is used. *Gicí* occurs before the verb, but after the noun it refers to (hence the label "postposition"). However, it should be kept in mind that the preceding noun is often deleted, resulting in the apparition of *gicí* at the beginning of a sentence. A locational adverb, such as *nén* "here," can also intervene between *gicí* and the verb.

Gicí škáda.	*She/he plays with him/her.*
Gicí wanówą.	*I sing with him/her.*
Gicí wawáci.	*I dance with him/her.*
Gicí én wa'ų́šį.	*I wasn't there with her.*
Mitákona **gicí** waškáda.	*I play with my friend.*
Mitáwįju **gicí** nén wahí.	*I arrived here with my wife.*
Duwé **gicí** yahí?	*Who did you arrive with?*
Nisų́ga duwé **gicí** škáda?	*Whom is your little brother playing with?*
James cihį́tku **gicí** kní.	*James came home with his son.*
Ȟuȟnáȟyabi, asą́bi **gicí** opétųbi céyaga.	*They should buy coffee with milk.*

The postposition *gicí* can also link two nouns and mean "accompanied with":

Ȟuȟnáȟyabi **gicí** asą́bi mak'ú.	*Give me coffee with milk.*
Škoškóbena **gicí** ijáhi.	*It's mixed with bananas.*

Finally, the postposition *óm* means that one is doing an activity with more that one person.

Micį́jabi **óm** nén wahí.	*I arrived here with my children.*
Óm mawáni.	*I'm walking with them.*
James cihį́tkubi **óm** kní.	*James came home with his sons.*

Reciprocal *-gici-/-ci-* "action done to one another"

Besides the postpostion *gicí* "with him/her/it," there is a verbal affix that is very similar in meaning and form— *-gici-* (or its short variant *-ci-*)—but which indicates that an "action is done to one another" and not "with another one." The verb is always transitive (subject+object) but the resulting derived verb is intransitive (subject only). Moreover, since the action is done by more than two people, the subject of a reciprocal verb is always plural. The singular version of a reciprocal would be expressed with the reflexive *I wash myself, he washes himself*, etc. As can be seen here, the short variant *-ci-* occurs when the stem starts with *k*:

long	i) wąyága	*she/he sees him/her/it*	>	wągíciknagabi	*they see each other*
short	ii) kíza	*she/he fights him/her*	>	gicízabi	*they fight one another*

kíza – *she/he fights him/her/it*

ųkíciza	*we two fought each other*	kicízabi	*they fought each other*
ųkícizabi	*we all fought one another*		

ógiya – *she/he helps him/her* (Class 1)

ųgógiciya	*we two helped each other*	ógiciyabi	*they helped each other*
ųgógiciyabi	*we helped one other*		

wąyága – *she/he sees him/her/it* (change of *y* to *kn*, Class 2)

wą'ųgiciknaga	*we two see each other*	wągíciknagabi	*they see each other*
wą'ųgiciknagabi	*we all see one another*		

giksúya – *she/he remembers him/her/it* (irregular, like a Class 1)

ųgíciksuya	*we two remember each other*	gicíksuyabi	*they remember each other*
ųgíciksuyabi	*we all remember one another*		

Wįcá žé Kelly dagúya.	*That man is related to Kelly.*
Dagúgiciyabi.	*They are related to one another.*
Dagú'ųgiciyabi.	*We are related to one another.*
Cųwįtkubi awógiciknagabis'a.	*Her daughters habitually gossip about one another.*
Misúga iyópegiciyabi.	*My younger brothers are arguing with one another.* (*iyópeya* – *she/he scolds, quarrels, argues with him/her* [Class 1])
Nakón-wįcašta ecágen ógiciyabi.	*Nakoda people often help one another.*
Owá ógiciyabi.	*They all cooperate.*
Wanágaš košká wašté'ųgicinabi.	*Long ago a boy and I liked one another.*
Mihúgagebi awágiciknagabi.	*My parents care for one another.*

Note that when *-gici-* follows an unvoiced consonant (like *k*) the form is *-kici-* as with *snokyá*: *Eyáš snokkíciyabi* "They know one another quite well."

Modality Particles

Modality particles are small words that express the speaker's commitment and knowledge about the truth value of his/her sentence, that is, whether she/he is certain or not about what is said, or if she/he was told about it, but also social obligation and ability. Note that most modality particles occur systematically after the verb.*

1. **Duká** expresses an obligation or the duty to do something. It often occurs after the verb.

Táȟca owánįkta **duká** no!	*I had to look for a deer!*
Úkteši̋ **duká**.	*She/he should not have come.*
Úkta **duká**.	*She/he should have come.*
Žécų **duká** no!	*She/he should do that!*
Žécų **duká** wo!	*You should do that!*
Nína nišį́tų cén aktága **duká** wo!	*You're very fat; thus, you should run!*
Niyé nihústaga óda wóda **duká** wo!	*As for you, you're skinny; you should eat more!*

    Note that *duká* also functions as a conjunction with the meaning "but."

Mihų́ owáyawa žéci amá'įkta, **duká** aké cída knį́kta.	*My mother will take me over there to school, but she will go home again.*

    Some speakers from Carry The Kettle use *céyaga* instead, but both seem to have the same meaning.

Ú **céyaga**!	*He should come.*
Ú **céyagįšį**!	*He should not come.*
Iyúha žén ųyą́bi **céyaga**.	*We must go there together.*
Wanágaš ecámų **céyaga**.	*I should have done that long ago.*
Wanágaš ejíyabi **céyaga**.	*They should have said it to her long ago.*

2. **Otį́ga** expresses a sound guess based on mental inference or some knowledge of the state of affairs.

Úkta **otį́ga**.	*It seems like he will come.*
Úkteši̋ **otį́ga**.	*It seems that he will not come.*
Šikná **otį́ga**.	*She/he seems angry.*

---

* This section is based partly on Linda Cumberland's doctoral thesis *A Grammar of Assiniboine: A Language of the Northern Plains* (2005: 313–343).

Some speakers use *stéya* "it seems like" instead:

Šikná **stéya** no!	She/he seems angry!
Aké osní no, wáhįhąkta **stéya** no!	It is cold again; it seems it will snow.
Ąbá né Huhúžubina ektá imnámnįkta. Mağážukte **stéya** no!	I am going to go to Regina today. It seems like it's going to rain!
Ąbá né nína maštá, amáȟpiya **stéya**.	It's very hot today, but it seems like it's cloudy.
Ecágen žéci ų́bi **stéya**.	It seems they are always over there.

3. **Hųštá** expresses an opinion based on secondhand narrative or on hearsay. Oftentimes the verb *eyábi* "they said" is used instead:

Wažíyadahą ektá nína wáhįhą **hųštá**.	It is said that it is snowing very hard in the north.
Wįcá né yatkés'a wána tawíju apá **hųštá** no!	It is said that this man drinks a lot and that now he hit his wife!
Wanágaš nécen **eyábi** no!	This is what they said long ago!
Úkta **hųštá**.	It is said he would come.

4. **Ųkášį** "if only, I wish" expresses the fact that an event is unexpected, contrary to facts or desires, as in *I wish he'd done it* (but the facts tell me he did not).

Mázaska mnuhá **ųkášį** no!	If only I had money!
Mağážu **ųkášį** no!	If only it rained!
Ą́ba wašté **ųkášį**.	If only it was a nice day.\ I wish it was a nice day.
Huhúžubina ocágu wašté **ųkášį**.	If only Regina roads were good (but they are not).

Specific, Unspecific Objects

In English, to convey the idea that one wants a given type of car or pencil or drink, the definite article *the* is used, but if any car will do then the indefinite article *a* is used. One can also omit the indefinite article and still get the indefinite meaning, especially for mass nouns.

Specific	**Unspecific**
I want that car.	I want a car.
I want the car you mentioned.	I want love not friendship!
I want one all-dressed pizza.	I want a drink.

Notice that the use of a number such as *one* also indicates specificity in English. The marking of specificity works in a similar way in Nakoda. There are three general ways to indicate this:

1. Demonstrative *žé* (plus intensifier, specifier *-ȟ*)

Mína **žé** ayágu wo!	*You bring that knife.* (discussed about earlier on)
Mína**ȟ** nuhá he?	*Do you have the (specific) knife?*
Ocáguȟ **žé**'e.	*That's exactly the road.*

2. No demonstratives at all (unspecific)

Mína agú wo!	*Bring a knife.*
Mína owánįkta.	*I am looking for a knife.*
Mína nuhá he?	*Do you have a knife?*
Mína mak'úkta no!	*He will give me a knife!*

3. Number *wążí* "one, a" (unspecific)

Ába né iná pasú agástaga **wążí** co'úba.	*Today mother is roasting a turkey.*
Wįcíjana gá búza **wążí** k'úbi.	*They gave that girl over there a cat.*
Škoškóbena **wążí** yúda.	*He is eating a banana.*
Wamní **wążí** wąmnága.	*I see an eagle.*
Búza zí **wążí** mnuhá.	*I have a brown cat.*

Interjections

Interjections like *Mom! Hey! Shut up! Beware!*, etc., are words used to warn, salute, or call out to someone. Usually interjections are short and cannot be analyzed internally.

Ahé!	(expression of humility used at the beginning of prayers or songs)
Dágeyešį!	*Shh! Shut up! Don't talk!*
Dágunišį!	*Nothing at all!*
Eyáš aké!	*Not again!*
Hą́ jé!	*Yes, okay, mmh!*
Hą́ jé žécen!	*Yes, okay, so!*
Hinága!	*Wait!*
Hiyá	*No!*
Hį́į́!	*Oh my!* (women's expression of surprise)
Hukwá!	*Not interested!*
Hukwá waná he?	*What's happening now?*
nų́ške…	*uh…* (when a speaker is thinking about what to say)
Wągá!	*as if (it was true)*
Waná hinága!	*Wait now!*
Waktá!	*Beware!*

Dágeyešį! Dáguškina žé gídąh įštíma'.	Shhh! The baby is finally sleeping.
Hįį! Naháh yazą́bi.	Gee! They are still sick!
Hįįįį! Ába nén osní.	Oh my! It is cold today!
Dagų́ dókanų? **Dágunišį!**	What are you doing? Nothing at all!
Waktá šiwákna!	Beware, I'm angry!
Waštéyana he? **Hiyá!**	Do you like this? No!
Waná hinága! Togáhe mas'áwapa.	Wait now! First, I will phone him.

Other words that differ according to the gender of the speaker include the interjections *hukwáá* "For heaven's sake!" or "Oh my God!," which are used by male speakers to indicate surprise. Positive interjections like *hók* "yes (male speaker)" have a gender-neutral counterpart *hą́* "yes." Finally, expressions like *Háu koná!* "Hello, friend!," were traditionally used between male speakers but are genderless today.

Chapter 14 Exercises

EXERCISE 1

Translate the following sentences into Nakoda.

1. What are they thinking about? _____
2. I have this girl on my mind. _____
3. He understands English. _____
4. I don't understand you. _____
5. The boys don't understand them. _____
6. My daughter will understand that lady. _____
7. I guess it'll rain. _____
8. He has to do it. _____
9. We should do that now! _____
10. It is said that he did not do it. _____
11. I wish I understood Chinese. _____
12. Do you have the money? _____

13. That's the man (I'm talking about). _____
14. Where is the car? _____
15. Give me a smoke! _____
16. I guess he has a car. _____
17. Wow! I saw two wolves! _____
18. Wait! I'll do it myself. _____
19. Beware! He is coming here! _____
20. Oh my! This horse is big. _____
21. I ate with them. _____
22. Sometimes I sleep with my children. _____

EXERCISE 2
Complete the following paradigms.

	ogáȟniǧa	iyúkcą
I on them, FUT		
they on me, NEG		
he on him, FUT/NEG		
they on you, FUT/NEG		
you all on me, FUT/NEG		
I on you		
they on us, FUT/NEG		

EXERCISE 3

Match the following Nakoda sentences with their translation.

1. Wįcíjana žé gicí waškáda.   _____ He is standing with the horses!

2. Taspą́ wążí yúda.   _____ I arrived there with my son.

3. Šúga gicí škáda.   _____ I'll dance with her.

4. Mitímno gicí wanówįkta.   _____ We were not here with her.

5. Gicí wawácįkta.   _____ Who did you arrive with?

6. Micį́kši gicí wa'í.   _____ He is eating an apple.

7. Wacíbiȟ žé'e.   _____ That's exactly the dance.

8. Tašúgabi óm náži.   _____ I'll sing with her oldest brother.

9. Duwé gicí yahí?   _____ I want that fork.

10. Nisúga duwé gicí škáda?   _____ Whom is your little brother playing with?

11. Cųwį́tku gicí kní.   _____ He came home with his daughter.

12. Gicí én ų'ų́bišį.   _____ She/he is playing with a dog.

13. Įcápe žé wacíga.   _____ You play with this girl.

CHAPTER 15

Objectives

VOCABULARY

- More transitive verbs
- Forming complex nouns for tools and places

GRAMMAR

- Instrumentals *ya-, ga-, na-, ba-, yu-, wo-*
- Indefinite prefix *wa-*
- Locatives *a-, o-, į-*
- Nominalizing ablaut and zero nominalization

Dialogues

1. Bang! Dókų (he)?
   Dágunišį! Įdú tadé tiyóba žé natága.
   Iyáya hį́kna tiyóba, įwáknage į́š waštéya natága wo!

   Bang! What happened?
   Nothing! It's just the wind that closed the door shut.
   Go and shut the door and the windows properly!

2. Hįį́į! Dágu dókanų?
   Į́yą wąmnága hį́kna nawápsija cén sipátąga ksumáye no!
   Aké ecų́šį!

   Oh my! What happened to you?
   I saw a stone and I kicked it and this is why my big toe is hurting now!
   Don't do it again!

3. Macádeskuya, néci ú wo!
   Tecíȟina cén nína yut'ícízįkte no!
   Waná hinága! Togáhe dáguškina awámnaga.
   Há, téhą yągábi wacígišį no!

   My sweetheart, come here! I will squeeze you real tight because I love you very much.
   Wait now! First, I'll take a peek at the baby.
   Okay! I don't want to wait too long!

4. Ȟtánihą iyámewakiya hįkna táȟca wąmnága.
   Žé yakté-c'ehą he?
   Há! Awáota hįkna gakí wot'á.

   Yesterday I went hunting and I saw a deer.
   Did you kill it?
   Yes! I shot it and it died over there in the distance.

Instrumentals

In English, to express the idea that someone is doing something with an instrument (e.g., with a saw or hammer) or a body part (e.g., with one's teeth or feet), or simply that natural forces are acting upon something one uses prepositional phrases or verbs that express a movement of the body, or of a tool, as in:

> He hit him **with a bat**.
> I poked the fire **with a stick**.
> The elephant **crushed** the dumb tourist. (body weight)
> I **jerked** it back and forth until it snapped. (hand movement)
> She cut it **with a jigsaw**.
> I opened that beer bottle **with my teeth**.

In Nakoda, the idea of using an instrument or a body part to perform an action is expressed with instrumentals prefixes. These elements are attached to verbal roots that cannot be used alone. In order to have a general idea of instrumental formation look at the following table which displays all the instrumentals attached to a single root *-ksa* "to cut." Note that most instrumental verbs belong to Class 1 and 2.[*]

Instrumental	Example
ya- – with the mouth, teeth; by speech	**yaksá** – she/he bites it off (Class 2)
ga- – with striking, sharp blow; force of the wind	**gaksá** – she/he cuts it with a tool (Class 1)
na- – action of the foot, leg; internal force, by itself	**naksá** – she/he breaks it forcefully (Class 1)
ba- – by pushing, poking	**baksá** – she/he breaks it by sitting on it, by pushing (Class 1)
yu- – by pulling, action of the hand, general causation	**yuksá** – she/he cuts it by hand (e.g., with scissors) (Class 2)
wo-, mo-, bo- – action from a distance, by shooting, pointed object, force of wind, water, accidental collision	**woksá** – she/he breaks his/her word, betrays **boksá** – she/he breaks it by pushing with an instrument (e.g., with a truck) (Class 1)

---

[*] This section is based on Cumberland (2005:227–231).

1. **Ya-** "with the mouth, teeth; by speech." These verbs are all of Class 2, as *mnašpé*, etc.

yat'á	*she/he kills it by biting, by inhaling or ingesting poison*
yaȟnéja	*she/he tears it with the teeth*
yašpá	*she/he breaks, cracks it open with the teeth (e.g., a peanut)*
yašíkna	*she/he angers him/her verbally*

2. **Ga-** "by striking, with a sharp blow; force of the wind." These verbs are all of Class 1 and require prefixes, as in *wagát'a*.

gat'á	*she/he kills someone by striking (e.g., as with a club)*
gaȟnéja	*she/he tears it by pressure, rips it open with its weight*
gaȟnóga	*she/he makes a hole by striking with an instrument*
gapésto	*she/he sharpens a point with an instrument*

3. **Na-** "action of the foot, leg; internal force, by itself." These verbs are all of Class 1 and require infixes, as in *nawát'a, nawáȟnoga, nawášpe*, etc.

nat'á	*she/he kicks someone to death*
naȟnóga	*she/he makes a hole by kicking*
našpá	*she/he opens up forcefully with the foot*
natága	*she/he closes it, by pushing or by force (e.g., wind closes a door)*
napsíja	*she/he kicks it*
nazúda	*she/he wears it down*

4. **Ba-** "by pushing, poking." These verbs are all of Class 1 and require prefixes, as in *wabát'a, wabáȟneja, wabákca*, etc.

bat'á	*she/he/it crushes someone to death*
baȟnéja	*she/he punctures it (e.g., with a sharp tool)*
baȟnóga	*she/he makes a hole with a sharp tool, to pierce*
bašpá	*she/he opens with a sharp tool*
bakcá	*she/he combs it*

5. **Yu-** "by pulling, action of the hand, general causation." These verbs are all of Class 2, as in ***mnušpé***, etc.

yubéhą	*she/he twists it*
yužáža	*she/he washes it by scrubbing*
yut'á	*she/he kills someone by strangulation*
yuȟnéja	*she/he tears it with the hand*
yuȟnóga	*she/he makes a hole in it with an instrument or with the hand*
yut'įza	*she/he tightens it up by stretching, pulls it up tight*
yušíkna	*she/he angers him/her by poking, teasing*
yušpá	*she/he opens up*
yuȟíja	*she/he wakens someone by pulling*

6. **Wo- ~ Bo- ~ Mo-** "action performed in a distance, by shooting, pointed object, force of wind, water, accidental collision"

wot'á	*she/he/it dies in a distance*
wosíja	*she/he breaks it (by throwing)*
boȟnóga	*she/he makes a hole by pressing on it*
bošpá	*she/he knocks it open with force, pressure*
modą́	*she/he bumps against someone (Class 1)*

Indefinite Prefix *wa-*

In English, to express the idea that the object of a verb is indefinite in quality or number, one uses the nouns *things*, *stuff* or *something*, or drops the indefinite article *a*. Even though there are often no changes in the verb form between the transitive (*I'm reading a book on astronomy*) and the intransitive forms (*I'm reading*), some verbs have an intransitive counterpart such as *I bought it* vs *I shopped*.

Definite (transitive)	**Indefinite (intransitive)**
I'll buy it.	I'll go shopping.
I'll think about it.	I'm thinking here!
I'll read it.	I'll read.
I'll play with it.	I'll play.

In Nakoda, to express an indefinite object add the prefix *wa-* "indefinite object, things, people" (or the short variant *w-* when the stem starts in a vowel) to a transitive verb. The derived verb becomes intransitive as indicated in the following examples. Note that the point of insertion in the indefinite object verb is the same as the transitive verb: *opétų > opéwatų* "I buy it"; *wópetų > wópewatų* "I buy stuff."

Transitive verbs		Intransitive indefinite object verbs	
bamnáya	she/he irons it	**wa**bámnaya	she/he iron clothes
capá	she/he stabs him/her/it	**wa**cápa	she/he stabs
co'úba	she/he roasts it, fries it	**wa**có'ųba	she/he is baking, bakes stuff
oné	she/he looks for him/her/it	**w**óne	she/he is looking for something
opétų	she/he buys it	**w**ópetų	she/he buys stuff, shops
oyága	she/he tells, announces it	**w**óknaga	she/he tells his/her own story, discusses it (possessive verb -k-)
padá	she/he butchers it	**wa**páda	she/he does butchering, butchers meat
snokyá ~ snohyá	she/he knows him/her/it	**wa**snókya ~ **wa**snóhya	she/he is smart, knowledgeable
špáyą	she/he cooks it	**wa**špáyą	she/he is cooking
úšina	she/he pities him/her/it	**wa'**úšina	she/he pities people, is kind to people
yawá	she/he counts it, reads it	**wa**yáwa	she/he reads
yužáža	she/he washes it	**wa**yúžaža	she/he washes things

Ą́ba yužáža hádahą **wamnúžaža** hį́kna **wacówa'ųba**.	On Saturdays I do some washing and baking.
Pté páda.	He is butchering a female buffalo.
Nągáhą **wawápadįkta**.	Now I'll do some butchering.
Wįcá žé **wacó'ųbabi** ogíhišį.	This man can't cook.
Wópetų nábįkta štén mázaska dóna yacígabi (he)?	How much money will you all want, when you all go shopping?
Wįcá né **wasnóhya** duká cihį́tku **wasnóhyešį**.	This man is knowledgeable, but his son is ignorant.
Pežítoyeh hí štén aké nén, ti'ų́manibįkta kó **wó'ųknagabi** no!	When the green arrives here again, we will visit and tell stories!
Mi'áde **wašpáyes'a** žéca no!	My father is a chef.

Locatives *a-*, *o-*, *į-*

Nakoda has three prefixes called "locatives" that are added to a word to indicate a general location. In some cases these prefixes are used to derive a noun indicating a location (e.g., *church*, *circus*) or a thing (e.g., *ladder*) from a verb. Locative prefixes are placed before the prefix *wa-* "indefinite object" and can transform an intransitive verb into a transitive one. In other words some locatives may add an object to an intransitive verb.

1. A- "in, on, on purpose; about someone, with someone (add an object)"

   bapsų́ she/he pours liquid out (manually)
   > a**bápsų** she/he pours liquid in

   nową́ she/he sings (VI)
   > a**nówą** she/he sings for or over someone who is ill (VT)

	wąyága	*she/he sees him/her/it* (VT)	
	> **a**wáyaga	*she/he looks after him/her/it* (VT)	
	> **a**wáyages'a	*guard, bodyguard* (N)	

	wóda	*she/he eats* (VI)	
	> **a**wódabi	*table* (N)	

As mentioned above, the locative prefix *a-* can also be used to derive transitive verbs of "taking," "bringing," or even "collective group action."

í   *she/he arrives there* (VI)
> **a**'í   *she/he takes him/her/it there* (VT)
Gakí **a**máya'i.   *Take me over there!*

hí   *she/he arrives here* (VI)
> **a**hi   *she/he brings him/her/it here* (VT)
Awícayahįkte no!   *You will bring them back (here)!*
> **a**hí   *they come here as a group* (collective group action, does not require *-bi* "plural")
Né hékta nén aškán Įháktuwąbi nén **a**hí no!   *Back in the recent past the Sioux came here.*

gu   *she/he comes back* (VI)
> **a**gú   *she/he brings him/her/it back* (VT)
Cá edáhą nén **a**gú wo!   *Bring some wood here!*
Wóyude **a**wágu.   *I brought food.*

wąyága   *she/he sees him/her/it* (VT)
> **a**wáyaga   *she/he looks after him/her/it* (VT) (i.e., takes care)

2. **O-** "inside, in, into, nouns of a place, outside"

basísa   *she/he sews it* (VT)
> **o**básisa   *she/he sews it on* (VT)

bazó   *she/he shows it* (VT)
> **wa**bázo   *she/he shows things* (VI)
> **o**wábazo   *circus* (N)

įknúžaža   *she/he washes him/herself* (VR)
> **o**'įknužaža   *bathroom* (N)

maní   *she/he walks* (VI)
> **o**máni   *she/he walks outside, is taking a walk, is travelling*

oksú	*she/he plants it* (VT)	
	> **wó**kšu	*she/he plants things* (VI)
	> **ow**ókšubi	*garden* (N)
	én **ow**ókšubi	*in the garden*
opétų	*she/he buys it* (VT)	
	> **wó**petų	*she/he buys stuff, shops* (VI)
	> **ow**ópetų tíbi	*store* (N)
wacégiya	*she/he prays* (VI)	
	> **o**wácegiya tíbi	*church* (N)
	Ába waká žehą́ **o**wácegiya žecí wa'í.	*I went to church on Sunday.*
wóda	*she/he eats* (VI)	
	> **o**wóde tíbi	*restaurant* (N)
yawa	*she/he counts* (VT)	
	> **wa**yáwa	*she/he reads* (VI)
	> **ow**áyawa tíbi	*school* (N)
yúda	*she/he eats it* (VT-Y)	
	> **wó**yude	*food* (N) (w(a)- *indefinite* + -o- *locative*)

3. **Į-** "in relation to, with, in contact with." In many cases it indicates an instrument or a tool related to the base verb. Note that many show nominalizing ablaut (or meaningful vowel change *a > e*).

ani	*she/he climbs* (VI)	
	> **į**'áni	*ladder* (N)
bamnáya	*she/he irons it* (VT)	
	> **wa**bámnaya	*she/he irons clothes* (VI)
	> **įwá**bamnaya	*iron* (N)
basísa	*she/he sews it* (VT)	
	> **į**básis**e**	*needle* (N)
mohtága	*she/he bumps into it accidentally* (VT)	
	> **į**móhtag**e**	*bumper* (N)
okmá	*she/he writes it* (VT)	
	> **wa**'ókma	*she/he writes things* (VI)
	> **įwá**'okma	*pencil* (N) (*also* įwó'okma)

tokšú	*she/he hauls him/her/it* (vt)	
	> **wa**tókšu	*she/he hauls something* (vi)
	> **i̧wá**tokšu	*truck* (n) (lit., a thing used to haul things in)
wu̧gá	*she/he lies down* (vi-n)	
	> **i̧**wúga	*she/he goes to bed*
		she/he lies down in bed (vi-n)
yušpá	*she/he opens it by pulling* (vt-y)	
	> **i̧**yúšp**e**	*key* (n) (lit., a thing that opens things)
capá	*she/he stabs him/her/it* (vt)	
	> **i̧**cápa	*she/he stabs, forks with it* (vi)
	> **i̧**cáp**e**	*fork* (n) (lit., a thing one stabs with)
yuksá	*she/he cuts it manually* (e.g., with a saw) (vt)	
	> **ca̧**yúksa	*she/he cuts wood* (vt)
	> **i̧cá̧**yuks**e**	*saw* (n)

Nominalizing Ablaut and Zero Nominalization

In Nakoda, one can form new nouns by adding suffixes such as *-na* "diminutive" or *-s'a* "habitual agent." However, there are two other ways to do so, namely, *vowel change* (or nominalizing ablaut) and *zero nominalization*. We have encountered vowel change (i.e., ablaut) in previous sections.

In Chapter 3 we saw that ablauting was a sound-changing process that affected some of the final vowels of some verb stems. For instance, "verbal ablaut" is triggered when the enclitic *-kta* "potential/future" is attached to the root *yúda* "she/he eats it" > *yúdi̧kta* "she/he will/ intend to eat it." However, verbal ablauting carries no meaning in itself. This is different from "nominalizing ablaut," which is also a case of vowel change, but this one changes the meaning of the word.

Nominalizing ablaut is not triggered by a suffix (unlike verbal ablaut), and it is used to derive nouns from verbs, which indicate the function of an object. The tricky thing here is that nominalizing ablaut is unpredictable since not all ablauting verbal stems change their final vowel to *e*, and this is why we consider nominalizing ablaut and zero nominalization as complementary word formation processes. Zero nominalization operates on verbal roots that do not ablaut, while nominalizing ablaut operates on those verb roots that change their final vowel to *e*.

1. **Nominalizing Ablaut** is a change of a vowel into *e* that creates nouns from verbs. It often occurs with į- "instrument, thing used to" as noted above.

    basísa   *she/he sews it* (VT)
        > **į̇básise**   *needle* (N) (į- "instrument")

    capá   *she/he stabs him/her/it* (VT)
        > **į̇cápa**   *she/he stabs, forks with it* (VI)
        > **į̇cápe**   *fork* (N) (į- "instrument")

    giknų́ga   *she/he dives in water, like a bird* (VI)
        > **giknų́ge**   *Mormon* (N) (lit., the diver, in reference to their baptism custom)

    mohtága   *she/he bumps accidentally into someone* (VT)
        > **į̇móhtąge**   *bumper* (N) (į- "instrument")

    nųwą́   *she/he swims* (VI)
        > **onų́we**   *swimming hole, bathtub* (N) (o- "location")

    škáda   *she/he plays* (VI)
        > **oškáde**   *picnic* (N)

    yuksá   *she/he cuts it with a sharp tool* (VT) + nominalizing ablaut
        > **cąyúksa**   *she chops wood* (VI)
        > **į̇cáyukse**   *saw* (N) (į- "instrument")

2. **Zero Nominalization** derives a verb into a noun but without a change in the shape of the word. This parallels the difference in English between *a good read* (noun) and *I read* (verb). In Nakoda, for example, a word like *waką́sija* can mean either "evil spirit" (N) or "she/he is evil spirited" (VS), as indicated by the possibility of inflecting the latter *wamákąsija* "I am evil spirited" or inserting the former in an NP *waką́sija né* "this evil spirit."

    cą́ + iyúpi   *tree* (N) + *she/he jumps* (VI)
        > **cą́'íyupi**   *monkey* (N)

    įštá + gitų́   *eye* + *she/he wears it* (VI)
        > **įštágitų**   *glasses* (N)

    į'áni   *she/he climbs on it* (VT)
        > **į'áni**   *ladder* (N)

k'į́	*she/he carries it on the back* (VT)	
	> ak'į́	*she/he carries it on the back* (VT) (*a-* "locative, with purpose")
	> ak'į́	*saddle* (N)
maskádo	*she/he pounds metal* (VT)	
	> maskádo	*blacksmith* (N)
pté + kúwa	*cow, cattle* (N) + *she/he chases it, pursues it* (VT)	
	> ptekúwa	*rancher* (N)
ti	*she/he dwells* (VI)	
	> tí	*dwelling, house* (N) (besides *tíbi*)
zibéna	*it is thin* (VS)	
	> zizíbena	*it is very thin* (VS)
	> zizíbena	*thin cloth* (N)

Chapter 15 Exercises

EXERCISE 1

In this chapter we became familiar with three types of prefixes that are used to form complex words. Here are some words built on the roots *-žužu-* "take off," *-mu-* "sound," and *-žaža-* "wash," which illustrate the productivity and complexity of Nakoda word formation. Look at the following series of derived words and try to separate the prefixes and suffixes (if any) and find the meaning of the other derived words. You will have to use a dictionary or the English/Nakoda lexicon found at the end of this book.

1. yužúžu; gažúžu; bažúžu.

2. namú; gamú; wagámu; gamúbi; įjámu; múwąga

3. yužáža; įyúžaža; kpažáža; hi'įkpažaža; owáyužažabi; ą́ba owáyužažabi

EXERCISE 2

Find a Nakoda dictionary and select ten words that have one of the locatives *a-*, *o-*, and *į-* (10 in total). Try to find the verb from which they are derived as well as their literal meaning.

EXERCISE 3

Conjugate the following verbs, with the appropriate modality suffixes or particles.

	yuksá	wópetų
I, FUT/NEG		
you, might		
he, FUT, habitually		
we, FUT/NEG		
you all, should		
they, kept on		

EXERCISE 4

Translate this short story into English, then change it into the "we" form.

Wanágašehą omáka agénapcuwąga wikcémna šákpe sám šaknóǧa'ehą. Wįcá matéjana hą́da, há ųmánibi-c'ehą. Į́yą wąmnága žehą́ hį́k nawápsija cén sipátąga ksumáya, sipátąga ksumáya hą́da, mawánišį no! Į́yą aké nawápsiješį no!

Free translation

_____

_____

_____

_____

_____

_____

"We" form translation

_____

_____

_____

_____

_____

_____

CHAPTER 16

Objectives

VOCABULARY

- More common objects
- Animals, birds and fish
- Plants and fruits

GRAMMAR

- Reduplication
- Compounding
- Causatives *-ya* and *-kiya*
- Aspectual auxiliary verbs
- Modal verbs

Dialogues

1. Nisúga dágu dóku?
   Nakón-i'abi uspé, nakón-okmabi nína wayúpi áya.
   Duwé né uspékiya? Wa'úspekiya táwa žé dóken egíyabi?
   Duwéni! Wa'úspekiya yuhéšį no!
   Hįį! Miyé dóken nakón-i'abi snohwáyešį!
   Wanúh uspénikiyabi žé cįgíkte no!

   What is your (male) younger brother up to?
   He is learning the Nakoda language and he's getting very good at writing it.
   Who is teaching him? What is the name of his teacher?
   Nobody! He does not have a teacher!
   Wow! As for myself I don't know how to speak Nakoda!
   Maybe he'll want to teach it to you!

2. Wanáğaš asábi wíkni, asábi súda íš ğáğabi.
Há, nąğáhą dágu iyúhana wópetų tíbi én opé'utųbi, žécen mázaska ğáğabi a'úyabi.

Long ago, they made butter and cheese too.
Yes, and nowadays we buy everything from the store, and that is why we have to keep on making money.

3. Mi'áde naháh ğánaši, duká waná paháskaskana yuhá.
Há ğána áya duká naháh wawášte.
Snohwáya, nécen wíyabi eyábi.

My father is not old yet, but he has white hair already.
Yes, he is getting old, but he is still good-looking.
I know this is what the women say.

Vocabulary

REDUPLICATED WORDS FOR ANIMALS

bispízena	*mouse*	homnáska	*gold-eye fish*
cağádodona	*woodpecker*	tugígina	*snail*
cąkáhuknekneğana	*chipmunk*	wamnúška hišmášmą	*caterpillar*
hiháhąna	*pigmy owl*	wamnúška pašáša	*red ant*
hiháwapapana	*barking owl*	wamnúška sapsábena	*cricket*

COMPOUNDS

ağúyabisu	*wheat kernel*	pežíȟoda	*sage*
cąská	*white poplar*	tapškáda	*she/he plays baseball (Class 1)*
Cąğúsam wicá	*American*	taspą ğí hišmá	*peach*
gugúša ší	*bacon*	taspą pestóstona	*pear*
hąhébi wódabi	*supper*	tuȟmáğa cesní	*honey*
hąyákena wódabi	*breakfast*	wakátąga cihíktu	*Jesus*
hicáhu	*cattail stalk*	wakmúhazaskuya	*sweetcorn*
wicánuȟnuğena	*pumpkin*	waȟpé tága	*cabbage*
ištágitų	*glasses*	wiyódahą wódabi	*dinner*

ASPECTUAL AUXILIARY VERBS

áya	1) *she/he/it is becoming (Class 4)*; 2) *she/he is continuously doing (Class 2)*
ų́	*she/he does continuously, goes around (Class 1)*
yągá ~ yįgá	1) *she/he sits and does continuously*; 2) *she/he is (Class 3)*

MODAL VERBS

cįgá	*she/he wants to* (Class 1)
wayúpi	*she/he is skilled at* (Class 2, Y-stem)
ogíhi	*she/he is able to* (Class 1)
wašténa	*she/he likes it* (Class 1)
snokyá ~ snohya	*she/he knows how* (Class 1)
šką́	*she/he tries to* (Class 1)
ší	*she/he asks/tells/orders someone* (Class 1)

Reduplication

The label "reduplication" refers to the process of doubling one of the syllables of a word or a full word, as in the case of these fictive examples: *tikini > titikini*; *kojit > kojijit*. English shows reduplication in *chiffchaff, jibber jabber, mishmash, mumbo-jumbo,* but these examples are in restricted number and the meaning of English reduplication remains obscure. In Nakoda, reduplication is very frequent and adds a specific meaning to a word. Before presenting the different meanings, one has to know that part of a syllable, a full syllable, or even a full word can be reduplicated in Nakoda. The latter is much less frequent.

PARTIAL SYLLABLE REDUPLICATION

hoǧą́	*fish*	>	hoǧą́ǧąna	*minnow* (N)
pahásaba	*black hair*	>	pahásapsaba	*she/he has black hair* (VS)

FULL WORD REDUPLICATION

hú	*leg, stem*	>	**huhú**	*bones* (N)
cą́	*wood, tree*	>	**cącą́**na	*drumstick* (N) (*-na* "diminutive")

The meaning of reduplication can be broken down as follows:

1. Plurality of inanimate things/objects. Usually the verb undergoes reduplication:

Pąǧí šašá žená éyagu!	*Take those red potatoes.* (VS)
pahá**sapsab**a	*she/he has black hair* (VS)
pahá**skaska**na	*she/he has white hair* (VS)
wįcáȟniȟni	*smallpox* (N)
įštá **tąktág**a	*big eyes* (N)

2. Intensification of a state, event or process. It is translated as "very, much":

búza **skaskáska**na	*pure white kitten* (N) (compare *búza skána* "white cat" (N) (not reduplicated)
Nínaȟ **osnísni**	*It's very cold outside.* (VIMP) (+ *-ȟ* "intensifier")
Šųktógeja nų́ba **tąktą́ga**bi.	*The two wolves were very big.* (VS)
wa**má**wašte	*I am good, good looking.* (VS)
cuwį́knąga šašábi	*Royal Canadian Mountain Police* (N) (lit., red coats)

3. Small size of an entity, or lesser degree of intensity:

cącą́na	*drumstick* (N)
hoǧą́ǧąna	*minnow* (N)
cąšáša	*red willow* (N)
honáǧina**toto**bi	*blue fly* (N)
totóna	*it is light blue* (VS)
šašána	*it is orange* (VS)
dáguškiškina	*doll* (N)

4. Iterativity, that is, a repetitive action:

mąkóšką**šką**	*earthquake* (N) (lit., earth that shakes)
wamą́ka**šką**šką́bi	*animals* (N) (lit., those that move on earth)
Cą́ wagáksaksa.	*I chop wood constantly.*
Žé ecų́cųna.	*He did that over and over again.*

Compounding

A compound is a single word made of two words. Compounds are stored as such in the speaker's mind, although they are made of two distinct words. Here are a few compounds in English. Note that verbs, adjectives, prepositions and nouns can be put together to form a new word.

NOUN + NOUN	*baseball, housewife, wallpaper*
ADJECTIVE + NOUN	*blackboard*
VERB + NOUN	*breakwater*
PREPOSITION + NOUN	*underworld*
ADJECTIVE + ADJECTIVE	*blue-green*

Nakoda has all sorts of compounds that combine verbs, nouns, adverbs, and postpositions. There exists a distinction between *lexical compounds,* which are single words made of two words "welded" together, and *syntactic compounds,* which are less tightly bound. Lexical compounds are written as one word with or without a hyphen and bear only one accent. On the other hand, syntactic compounds are more loosely attached and bear two accents: a primary; and a secondary, which is marked on the second word.

Compounds are especially common with words denoting modern things, and as a general rule if an object has been known for a long time, it will be labelled with a lexical compound. Consequently, syntactic compounds often express modern things that are relatively alien to traditional Nakoda culture. However, there are exceptions, since one can hear both *šúga tága* (a syntactic compound written as *šúgatąga*) and *šųktága* "horse" (lexical compound). Here is an overview of the types of compounds found in Nakoda.

NOUN + NOUN	tašáge	*ruminant hoof*
NOUN + STATIVE VERB	cąšáša	*red willow*
	cąníska	*cigarette*
NOUN + POSTPOSITION	timáhen	*inside a dwelling*
	cą'ágąn	*chair*
VERB + VERB	įkník yá	*she/he goes to observe* (Class 2)
VERB + NOUN	owácegiya tíbi	*church*
ADVERB + VERB	dąyá ų́	*she/he is well* (Class 1)
POSTPOSTION + VERB	agą́n wókmabi	*desk*

We have already encountered both types of compounds in the preceeding chapters. Here are some very common ones.

aǧúyabi	*bannock, bread* (N)
aǧúyabisu	*wheat kernel* (N) (bread + seed)
aǧúyabiskuya	*cake, cookie* (N) (lit., bread + it is sweet)
aǧúyabisaga	*toast* (N) (lit., bread + it is dry)
aǧúyabi šnoyábi	*fried bannock* (N)
asą́bi	*milk* (N)
asą́bi wį́kni	*butter* (N)
asą́bi súda	*cheese* (N)
bizéna	*gopher* (N)
bistága	*prairie dog* (N) (lit., gopher + it is big)
gugúša	*pig* (N)
gugúša šį́	*bacon* (N)
hųská	*pants, leggings* (N)
hųskáto	*jeans, denims* (N)

iná	*mother*
iná maká	*Mother Earth* (N)
įkmų́	*lynx* (N)
įkmų́tąga	*mountain lion* (N)
máza	*iron* (N)
mázagiyą	*airplane* (N) (lit., iron + it flies)
mázakada	*hot metal* (N) (lit., iron + it is hot)
mázaska	*money* (N)
mázaska hągé	*fifty cents* (N) (lit., iron + it is white + half)
mázaska tíbi	*bank* (N)
mázasni	*cold metal* (N)
mázaša	*penny* (N)
mázawada	*train* (N)
máza'i	*gun muzzle* (N)
máza'ocągu	*train track* (N)
wįcá	*man* (N) (means *human* in compounds)
wįcáho	*human voice* (N)
wįcáho éyagu	*voice recorder* (N)
wįcáwaką	*Holy man* (N)
wįcóni	*human life* (*oní* "life")
owį́canebi	*hunter* (N) (from *oné* "she/he looks for it")

Causatives *-ya* and *-kiya*

The causative suffixes *-ya* and *-kiya* roughly mean "to cause X to be, or become Y." They are equivalent to the English sentences:

I made him do it.
I turned it into a complete joke.
I made him become famous.
I caused it to collapse.

The most important thing to remember with causative suffixes is that they add an object to a stative verb (*be full, be pleased, learn on one's own*, etc.), making it transitive (*to fill him, to please him, to teach him*, etc.). This is shown in the next table where three intransitive verbs are derived into their causative versions. Note that the point of insertion of the person markers in the causative verb (Class 1) differs from that of the simple intransitive verb (Class 4).

Intransitive (Class 4)					
įpi	she/he is full, sated	iyógipi	she/he is pleased	ųspé	she/he learns on his/her own
įmápi	I am full, sated	iyómagipi	I am pleased	ųmáspe	I learn on my own
įnípi	you are full, sated	iyónigipi	you are pleased	ųníspe	you learn on your own

Causative (Class 1)					
-ya				**-kiya**	
įpiya	she/he sated him/her	iyógipiya	she/he pleases him/her	ųspékiya	she/he teaches him/her
įpíwaya	I sated him/her	iyógipiwaya	I please him/her	ųspéwakiya	I teach him/her
įpíyaya	you sated him/her	iyógipiyaya	you please him/her	ųspéyakiya	you teach him/her

Dayą́ẖ įpíciya!	I filled you really well.
Midáguyabi įpíyabi.	My relatives sated him.
Nén yahí hádahą iyógipimayaya jé.	You always make me happy whenever you come here.
Né duwé ųspénijiya (he)?*	Do you have someone to teach you?
Šų́gatąga ųspéwįcakiyabįšį no!	They didn't teach the horses!
Ecágen miyé ecúmakiya.	She always makes me do it by myself.
Iyógapte ecúmakiya.	She makes me do the dishes.

As you can see from the preceding table, the person markers of Class 1 are always inserted right before the causative suffixes *-ya* and *-kiya*. Here are a few words derived from causative stems:

ȟuȟnáǧa	it is burned (Class 1)
ȟuȟnáȟ-ya	she/he burns it (Class 1)
ȟuȟnáȟ-ya-bi	coffee (N) (*-ya* "cause to" + *-bi* "noun")
piná	she/he is thankful (Class 4)
piná-ya	she/he makes him/her be thankful (Class 1)
pinámaya-ya	I thank you! (lit., you made me thankful, you pleased me)
stustá	she/he is tired (Class 4)
stustá-ya	she/he tires him/her (Class 1)
stusté-ma-ya-ya	you are tiring me
Stusté-ci-ya he?	Am I tiring you?

---

* Here the *k* of the causative suffix *-kiya* softens to *j* when preceded by *i*. The same happens with the verb *egíya* "she/he tells him/her," as in *Dóken eníjiyabi?* "What is your name?" versus *Bill emágiyabi.* "I am called Bill."

šá	*it is red*
ša-gí-**ya**	*she/he reddens his/her own (Class 1)*
í-šagi-**ya**	*lipstick* (N) *(zero nominalization; í "mouth")*
špą́	*it is cooked (Class 4)*
špą-yą́	*she/he cooks it (Class 1)*
wa-špą́-yą	*she/he is cooking (Class 1)*
ųspé	*she/he learns on his/her own (Class 4)*
ųspé-**kiya**	*she/he teaches him/her (Class 1)*
wa-'ųspe-**kiya**	*teacher* (N) *(wa- "indefinite object")*
wa-'ųspe	*(short form)*
wa'ųspe-wįca-**kiya**	*male teacher* (N)
wa'ųspe-wįyą-**kiya**	*female teacher* (N)

Many kinship verbs that follow the pattern "I have him as a friend" are made using *-ya*, which functions as a "relational" element, as in the following four examples.

cįjá	*child* (N)
cįjá-**ya**	*she/he adopts him/her as a child (Class 1)*
Jana cįjá-wa-**ya**.	*I adopted Jana.*
dágu	*thing, something* (N)
dagú-**ya**	*she/he has him/her as a relative (Class 1)*
dagú-wa-**ya**	*I am related to him/her*
hįkną́	*husband* (N)
hįkną́-**ya**	*she/he married him/her (Class 1)*
hįkną́-wa-**ya**	*I married him/her*
hįkną́-ci-**ya**	*I married you*
koná	*friend* (N)
koná-**ya**	*she/he has him/her as a friend*
	she/he is friends with him/her (Class 1)
koná-wa-**ya**	*I am related to him/her*
koná-wįca-ya-**ya**	*you are related to them*

Beware not to confuse the causative *-ya* with the homophonous but distinct suffix *–ya*, which derives adverbs from verbs: *teȟíya* "with difficulty," *įkcéya* "in a common way, commonly," *waką́ya* "in a holy manner."

Aspectual Auxiliary Verbs

Aspectual enclitics were explained in Chapter 12. In this chapter we will learn how to use the auxiliary verbs that express aspect, like *starting to, becoming, gradually becoming, continue doing*. In English, auxiliary verbs like *be* or *have* can be used alone but only if they function as the main verb, like *I am* (i.e., I exist), *I have a truck*. Otherwise, auxiliaries cannot be used alone *I am sick > *I am; I will have to work > *I will have*. Just like English, Nakoda auxiliaries cannot be used alone, as they must be preceded by a verbal complement. In sentences with a verbal auxiliary and a verbal complement the word order is as follows:

SUBJECT	+	VERB_{COMPLEMENT}	+	VERB_{AUXILIARY}
waȟpé		šá		áya
leaves		be.red		they.are.getting

The leaves are getting red.

Some speakers inflect the auxiliary verb and others the complement verb. Here are some of the most common auxiliary verbs.

1. **Áya** "becoming, continue doing." The inceptive (to become) as well as the continuous aspects are expressed with two homophonous auxiliary verbs *áya*. These auxiliaries are placed after a verb complement and carry the person and modality markers, exactly like the English "to be," as in:

    He **is**_{AUX} *coming*_{COMPL}   I **am**_{AUX} *leaving*_{COMPL}

    a. Stative auxiliary **áya** – *becoming, getting, turning* (NV-conjugation, Class 4):

    | Yazą́ a**má**ya! | I'm starting to be sick! |
    | A'ókpaza **áya**. | It's getting dark. |
    | Aȟázi **áya**. | It's becoming dusk. |
    | Ą́ba ú **áya**. | It's starting to be morning. |
    | Osní **áya**. | It's getting cold. |

    Some verbs require that the verbal complement be inflected for person, such as *miní įt'á áya* "she/he is thirsty," *miní mat'á áya* "I am thirsty" (lit., I am starting to die for water). However, some verbs present variations since some speakers inflect the verbal complement instead of the auxiliary (underlined), as in:

    | Skúya óda núda štén **ní**šįtų áyįkta. | If you eat too many sweets, then you'll get fat. |
    | **Ma**stústa áya! | I'm getting tired! |

    b. Active auxiliary **áya** – *continuously doing* (Y-stem, Class 2):

    | Šų́ga žé búza žé kuwá **áya**. | The dog is constantly chasing the cat. |
    | Cą́ gaksáksa **ámna**. | I constantly chop wood. |

2. **Ų́** – *continuously doing, go about* (regular stem, Class 1). This verb can be translated with the progressive form *-ing* although it often implies the idea of a movement.

Tugášina ceyá wa'**ų́** no!	*Grandfather, I'm constantly crying!*
Giksúya wa'**ų́** no!	*I am remembering!*
Mitúgašibi dóken i'ábi žé įyúkcą wa'**ų́**.	*I'm thinking of how my grandfathers spoke.*

3. **Yągá ~ Yįgá** – 1) *do continuously*; 2) *to be* (Class 3). Speakers often translate this auxiliary verb with "sit," but in many cases it means "to do something continuously (while sitting or not)" but also "to be (in such a condition)." The suffix *-bi* "to" is not required on the main verb.

Iná mitą́kši į́š gicí i'á **mągá** jé.	*I always sit and discuss (continuously) with both my mom and aunt.*
Įštímaši **yįgá**.	*He is sleepless.*
Iyódąga **mągá** cén.	*I've been sitting down for some time.* (lit., sit + continuous + *cén*)
Téhą **mągá**.	*I've been sitting for a long time.*

Note that the third person is often pronounced *yįgá* (the *y* changes *ą* into *į*) while the first person is *mągá* and the second person is *nągá* as expected.

Modality Verbs

In the preceding chapters we looked at the structure of sentences containing only one verb. In Chapter 13 we started studying complex sentences containing two verbs: *If you **come** to my place, then we'll **look** at it*. In this chapter we will further study complex sentences, and especially those containing what is known as "modality verbs". These verbs mark the speaker's degree of certainty about what he is saying, his/her feelings about an action/state, but also the obligation, permission or ability to do something (Cumberland, 2005:393).

Modality verbs, like the aspectual auxiliary verbs seen in the previous section, play the role of the *main verb* and come last in a sentence, while the complement verb comes first. The modality verb bears the person and number markings (although some verbal complements also have person/number markers). Many modality verbs require the suffix *-bi* "to" on the verbal complement.

SUBJECT	+	VERB_{COMPLEMENT}	+	VERB_{MODAL}
Bobby		įštíma**bi**		cíga.
bobby		sleep.**to**		he.wants

Bobby wants to sleep.

VERB_COMPLEMENT	+	VERB_MODAL
Basí**bi**		wa**mn**úpi.
drive.**to**		I.am.skilled

I'm skilled at driving.

1. **Cįgá** "want to do something" (regular stem, Class 1) requires the suffix *-bi* "to" on the verbal complement:*

Eyá**bi** wacígešį.	*I don't want to say it.*
Eyá**bi** cįgábišį.	*They don't want to say it.*
Téhą yįgá**bi** wacígešį.	*I don't want to wait/sit too long.*
Ú**bi** cįgá.	*He wants to come.*
Iyécįgayena né basí**bi** wacíge no!	*I want to drive this car!*
Ecú**bi** wacíga.	*I want to do it.*
Žécų**bi** ųcígešį.	*We (two) don't want to do that.*
Wašpáyes'a žéca**bi** wacíga.	*I want to be a chef.*
Táȟca kté**bi** wacíga.	*I want to kill a deer.*

2. **Wayúpi** "skilled at" (Y-stem, Class 2) requires the suffix *-bi* "to" on the verbal complement:

Gicíza**bi** wayúpi.	*He is skilled at fighting.*
Gicíza**bi** wamnúpi.	*I'm skilled at fighting.*
Gicíza**bi** wanúpi?	*Are you skilled at fighting?*
Nína basí**bi** wayúpi.	*She/he is good at driving.*
Šų́gatąga gá nína iyópsija**bi** wayúpi.	*That horse over there is very skilled at jumping.*

3. **Ogíhi** "able to" (regular stem, Class 1) does not require the suffix *-bi* "to" on the verbal complement. Some speakers inflect the verbal complement instead of the modality verb, or even both of them:

Maní ogíhi**bi**šį.	*They cannot walk.*
Ecų́ ogíhi gaca!	*As if he was capable of doing it!*
Ecų́**bi** ogíhi gaca!	*As if they were capable of doing it!* (3PL is marked on the verbal complement)
Naȟ'ų́ owágihi.	*I can hear it.*
Ecámų owágihišį.	*I cannot do it.* (person/number marked on both verbs)
Dágu ecų́ né wašté ecų́ ogíhi.	*She/he can do things well.*
Dágu ecų́ né wašté ecámų owágihi.	*I can do things well.*

Don't confuse this auxiliary verb with its intransitive negative counterpart *ogíhišį* "she/he is weak," which requires no complement: *Waná owágihišį* "Now, I'm weak."

---

* It should be kept in mind, however, that some semi-speakers do not use/recognize the suffix *-bi* "to" at all, as in *Dágu yatką́ yacígabi?* "What do you all want to drink?"

4. **Wašténa** "like to" (Class 1) requires the suffix *-bi* "to" on the verbal complement:

Téhą yįgá**bi** waȟtéwanešį no!	*I don't like to sit/wait too long!*
Tíde yįgá**bi** waštéwana.	*I like to sit at home.*
Ománi ų́**bi** waštéwana.	*I like to walk around.* (lit., I like to be walking about)
Wáȟįhą háda, tągán škáda**bi** waštéwana.	*Whenever it snows, I like to play outside.*

5. **Snokyá ~ Snohyá** "know how" (Class 1, regular stem) requires the suffix *-bi* "to" on the verbal complement:

Dóken ecų́**bi** snokwáyešį.	*I don't know how to do it.*
Dáguškina i'á**bi** snohyá.	*The baby knows how to talk.*
Wanágaš wací**bi** snokwáya.	*I knew how to dance long ago.*
Wanágaš wací**bi** žehą́ snokwáya.	*I knew then how to dance long ago.*

6. **Šką́** "try to" (Class 1, regular stem) requires the suffix *-kta* "future, hypothetical event" on the verbal complement:

Waná i'á**kta** šką́.	*He is trying to talk.*
Waná nakón-i'a**kta** wašką́.	*I'm trying to talk Nakoda.*
Makízi**kta** šką́.	*He tried to fight me.*
Giksúyį**kta** šką́!	*Try to remember it!*

Chapter 16 Exercises

EXERCISE 1

Translate into English the following sentences.

1. Ȟtánihą cą ųgáksaksabi. _____

2. Wáhįhą áya. _____

3. Nína osní áya. _____

4. Eyábi yacígišį he? _____

5. Hokšíbina žená eyábi cįgábišį. _____

6. Gicízabi wanúpibi? _____

7. Nína nowąbi wamnúpi. _____

8. Šúga né iyópsijabi wayúpi. _____

9. Dáguškina i'ábi snohyéšį. _____

10. Wanágaš nakón-i'abi snokwáya. _____

11. Ųgíye wašpáyąbi waȟté'ųnibišį no! _____

EXERCISE 2

Build the causative or relational version of the following words and indicate their meaning.

| aházi | hįkną | ípi | piná |

| dagúya | įbíǧa | iyógipi | špą́ |

| síja | cįjá | šá | stustá |

EXERCISE 3
Fill in the following verb paradigms.

	nową...wayúpi	nakón-i'abi...ogíhi
1SG FUT		
1SG FUT/NEG		
2SG NEG		
3SG FUT/NEG		
1PL FUT		
1PL FUT/NEG		
2PL FUT		
3PL FUT/NEG		

EXERCISE 4

Check for the following words in the lexicon or a dictionary of Nakoda, analyze them and give a literal translation.

young man	oil lantern
cannibal (man eater)	killer
war bonnet with trailer	it's hailing
from inside (indoors)	bronco
mare	old stallion
buffalo meat	fire keeper
clock	island in the middle of a lake
tree dweller (dwarf)	prairie dog
February	from across the border
wheat kernel	language, word

EXERCISE 5

Look at the reduplicated nouns and the compounds in the vocabulary section at the beginning of this chapter and try to analyze the words used in these complex words. For the reduplicated nouns you will need to figure out what is being reduplicated.

CHAPTER 17

Objectives

VOCABULARY

- Winter clothing
- Keeping something, cooking, cleaning, and washing oneself

GRAMMAR

- Reflexive *-i'ci- / -ik-* "to act upon oneself"
- Possessive *-gi- / -k-* "to act upon one's own thing (possession or person)"
- Dative *-gi-* "to act to, for, upon somebody else"
- Benefactive *-giji-* "to act for the benefit of somebody else"
- Summary

Dialogues

1. Mihų́ snohyáya he?
    Hiyá, duktén náži?
    Gakí, sąksája tó wąží ų́. Wíyą gá ašón'įc'iya.

    Há! Waná wąmnága. Nína téjanahtiyą!

    Do you know my mother?
    No! Where is she standing?
    Over there, she is wearing a blue dress.
    It's the woman yonder smudging herself.
    Yes! I see her now. She is very young!

2. Iná! Tągán osní he?
Híį! Tągán nína osní. Hayábi cóza žéca gic'ų́!

Há! Nąbíkpa, cuwíknąga įš nitáwa wąmnágešį. Duktén yągábi (he)?
Gakí hąyákena nená mnužáža.

Mother! Is it cold outside?
Oh my! It is very cold outside. Wear your warm clothes!

Okay! I don't see my mittens and my warm coat. Where are they sitting?
Over there. I washed them this morning.

3. Ȟtánihą mitúgaši timáwagini.
Dóken šką́ (he)?
Waná nína gána hį́kna maní ogíhįšį no!
Waná cųwį́tku wacį́giya.

Yesterday I visited my grandfather.
How was he feeling?
He is very old, and he cannot walk anymore!
He depends on his daughter now.

4. Duwé búza žé knuhá (he)?
Miyéȟ, né mitáwa no!
Duwé búza žé opénijitų (he)?
Inána opémajitų no.

Who is keeping that cat?
Myself specifically, it's mine!
Who bought you that cat?
My aunt bought me this cat.

Vocabulary

cąšíhąba	rubber boots	nąbíkpa	gloves
céğa	pail	owá	all
cóza	she/he/it is warm	oyák'u	socks, stockings
cuwį́knąga	coat, shirt	sąksája	dress
hayábi	clothes	šináğaȟci	shawl
iyéya	she/he finds him/her/it (Class 1)	wéhą	last spring
kté	she/he/it kills him/her/it (Class 1)	wówaši hayábi	working clothes; coveralls

Reflexive *-įc'i-/-įk-* "to act upon oneself"

The prefix *-įc'i-* indicates that the subject of the verb is acting upon him or herself. Thus, the subject is both the agent and the object of an action. We already know that with the transitive verb *teȟína* "she/he loves him/her" the point of insertion is after the first syllable *te* as indicated in the following example:

    teȟína   *she/he loves him/her*
        > te-**wá**-ȟina   *I love him/her*

    teȟína   *she/he loves him/her*
        > te-**yá**-ȟina   *you love him/her*

The reflexive *-įc'i-* "to act upon oneself" is inserted in each verb's point of insertion. Here, the subject markers of Class 3, *-m-* "I" and *-n-* "you," are required (as seen in Chapter 5).

    tehína   *she/he loves him/her*
        > te-**m**-**įc'i**-hina   *I love myself*
        > te-**n**-**įc'i**-hina   *you love yourself*

When *-įc'i-* is added to a stem that starts with a *y*, as with *yužáža* "she/he washes it by scrubbing," *-įc'i-* is truncated to *-įk-* and the *y* of the stem changes to *n*.

    -įk- + **-yužáža**   *oneself + she/he washes it by scrubbing* (Class 2)
        > **m-įk-n**úžaža   *I wash myself* (Class 3)

    -įk- + **-yužúžu**   *oneself + she/he takes it apart, to strip him/her/it off* (Class 2)
        > **įk-n**úžužu   *she/he undresses him/herself* (Class 3)

Below you will find verbs from Classes 1, 2, and 3 marked with the reflexive *-įc'i-* or *-įk-*. It is very important to note that when you insert *-įc'i-* in a Y-stem (Class 2), *y* becomes *n* and *c* becomes *k*. Thus, *wayága* "she/he sees him/her/it" becomes *wą'įknaga*. Note that all the resulting reflexive verbs belong to Class 3, whatever the verb class of the stem may be, as shown by the person markers *-m-* (1SG) and *-n-* (2SG).

tehína – *she/he loves him/her/it* (Class 1)

tem**į́c'i**hina	*I love myself*	te'**į́c'i**hin**į**kta	*she/he will love him/herself*
ten**į́c'i**hina	*you love yourself*	te'**į́c'i**hina**b**ikteš**į**	*they will not love themselves*
te'**ų́gįc'i**hinabi	*we love ourselves*		

wayága – *she/he sees him/her/it* (Class 2)

wa**mį́k**naga	*I see myself*	wą**'į́k**nag**į**kta	*she/he will see him/herself*
wa**nį́k**naga	*you see yourself*	wą**'į́k**naga**b**ikteš**į**	*they will not see themselves*
wą**'ų́gįk**nagabi	*we see ourselves*		

wašpáya – *she/he cooks it* (Class 1)

wašpá**mįc'i**ya	*I cook for myself*	wašpá**'įc'i**y**į**kta	*she/he will cook for him/herself*
wašpá**nįc'i**ya	*you cook for yourself*	wašpá**'įc'i**ya**b**ikteš**į**	*they will not cook for themselves*
wašpá**'ųgįc'i**ya	*we cook for ourselves*		

yužáža – *she/he washes him/her/it* (Class 3)

mi̦knúžaža	*I wash myself*	**i̦**knúžaža**kta**	*she/he will wash her/himself*
ni̦knúžaža	*you wash yourself*	**i̦**knúžaža**kteši̦**	*they will not wash themselves*
ųgí̦knužaža**bi**	*we wash ourselves*		

Iyuhána dąyą́ wódabi, nína įpí'**ic'i**yabi.	*They all ate well and sated themselves.*
Ašón**mi̦c'i**yi̦kte no!	*I'll smudge myself!*
Waȟpé ús a'**í̦k**naȟpabi.	*They covered themselves using leaves.*
Mnihé **ic'í**ya	*She has courage in herself.*
Wanágaš minékši **ic'í**kte.	*Long ago my uncle (mother's brother) killed himself.*
I̦knúžaža wo!	*Wash yourself. / Go take a bath!*
Hinága! **Mi̦**knúžužu!	*Wait! I'm undressing myself!*
Awą́**mi̦c'i̦**knaga!	*I care for myself!*

Possessive -gi-/-k- "to act on one's own"

In English, the following sentences can be very ambiguous especially when taken out of context:

He is keeping his cat.
He likes his car.
She loves her boyfriend.
He hit his dog.

The last sentence can mean that a man is either hitting his own dog or another person's dog. Nakoda avoids such ambiguities by using a prefix *-gi-* (or its short form *-k-*) to form verbs called "possessive verbs," labelled vpos in the lexicon. When added onto a verb, *-gi-/-k-* means that an action is done to someone's own thing (possession or person). There are three important details to remember here: i) Class 2 verbs change their *y* to *n* when preceded by *k-*, thus, the sequence *k+y* becomes *kn*; ii) the derived possessive verb belongs to Class 1; and iii) with first and second persons the markers undergo the following changes: *wa-* + *-gi-* gives *we-* while *ya-* + *-gi-* gives *ye-*.

gi- + ec'ų́	*one's own* + *she/he does it* (Class 3)	
> **gi**c'ų́	*she/he wears his/her own thing*	
	(lit., *she/he does his/her own thing*) (Irregular)	
> **wé**c'ų	*I wear it**	

---

* The noun *gisų́* "Asian person" follows the same pattern. It is derived from the noun *sų́* "braid," which becomes *gisų́* "she/he braids him/herself" (lit., she/he braids his/her own). Thus, the first and second persons are *wésų* "I braid myself" and *yésų* "you braid yourself."

k- + yuhá	one's own + she/he has it (Class 2)	
> **kn**uhá	she/he has, keeps his/her own thing (Class 1)	
> wa**kn**úha	I keep my own thing	

k- + yužáža	one's own + she/he washes it by scrubbing (Class 2)	
> **kn**užáža	she/he washes his/her own thing (Class 1)	
> wa**kn**úžaža	I wash my own thing	

k- + bakcá   one's own + she/he combs it (Class 1)
    > **k**pakcá   she/he combs his/her own hair (Class 1)
        (b changes to p when preceeded by k)
    > wa**k**pákca   I comb my own (e.g., hair)

k- + eh*ą́*'i   one's own + she/he/it reaches it (Class 1)
    > ehą́**ki**   she/he reaches an age, is of a certain age (Class 1)
    Waníyedu dóba ehą́waki.   I am four years old.

ų́ – *she/he wears it* (Class 3)

wéc'ų	I put on my own (irregular)	**gic'ų́kta**	she/he will put on his own
yéc'ų	you put on your own	**gic'ų́bįkteší**	they will not put on their own
ųgíc'ųbi	we put on our own		

yuhá – *she/he has it* (Class 2)

wa**kn**úha	I have mine (Class 3)	**kn**uhį́kta	she/he will have his/hers
ya**kn**úha	you have yours	**kn**uhábįkteší	they will not have theirs
ų**kn**úha**bi**	we have ours		

Wówaši hayábi **wéc'ų**.	I put on my coveralls.
Cąšíhąba **wéc'ų**.	I put on my rubber boots.
Wapáha **yéc'ų**.	You put on your hat.
Hayábi **gic'ų́**!	Put your clothes on!
Gugúša šįtų́ né knuhábi.	They kept their fat pig.
Céğa žé waknúha.	I have my pail with me.
I'íjuna wąží yaknúha he?	Do you have your spoon with you?
Šųkcíjana né ųknúha.	We (two) kept this puppy of ours.
Cuwíknąga cóza žecá yaknúhabi he?	Do you all have warm coats with you?
Nąbíkpa yaknúha he?	Do you have your mitts with you?
Wįcíjana gá búza knuhéšį.	That little girl over there is not carrying her cat.
Idé knužáža!	Wash your face!
Cuwíknąga knužáža wo!	Wash your shirt!
Pahá wakpákca.	I comb my hair.

Šúga iyéwagiya.	I found my own dog. (iyéya – she/he finds him/her/it)
Micį́kši wacį́wagiya.	I depend on my son. (wacį́ya – she/he depends on him/her/it)
Jane cįhį́tku pahá **kn**uksá.	Jane cut her son's hair.
Micų́kši **k**pási.	My daughter is driving her own (vehicle). (basí – she/he drives it)

Dative *-gi-* "to act to, for, of somebody else"

The dative prefix *-gi-* indicates that an action is directed to or intended for somebody else. This prefix can be translated by an English verb + "to, for, from, because of."

He speaks to me.
I killed the moose for him.
I asked her for it.
They stole it from me.

Note that the base verb can be of Class 1 or 2, but the resulting dative verb (labeled simply VT in the lexicon) belongs to Class 1.

gi- + eyá	to, for, of + she/he says it (irregular verb)	
	> e**g**íya	she/he says it to him/her (Class 1)
	> ewá**g**iya	I say it to him/her
gi- + bazó	to, for, of + she/he shows it (Class 1)	
	> **gi**bázo	she/he shows it to him/her (Class 1)
	> wa**gí**bazo	I show it to him/her
gi- + yawá	to, for, of + she/he counts, reads (Class 2)	
	> **gi**yáwa	she/he reads it to him/her (Class 1)
	> wa**gí**yawa	I read it to him/her
gi- + apé	to, for, of + she/he is waiting (Class 1)	
	> a**g**ípe	she/he waits for him (Class 1)
	> iyá**g**ipe	she/he waits for him/her to come (Class 1)
	> iyáwa**g**ipe	I wait for him/her to come
gi- + wašténa	to, for, of + she/he likes him/her/it (Class 1)	
	> wašté**g**ina	she/he is pleased with him/her/it (Class 1)
	> wašté wa**g**ina	I am pleased with him/her/it
gi- + timáni	to, for, of + she/he visits (Class 1)	
	> timá**g**ini	she/he visits someone, one's relative (Class 1)

bazó – *she/he shows it* (Class 1)

wagíbazo	*I show it to him/her*	**mijí**bazo ~ **magí**bazo	*she/he shows it to me*
yagíbazo	*you showed it to him/her*	**nijí**bazo ~ **nigí**bazo	*she/he shows it to you*
gibázo	*she/he shows it to him/her*		
ų̄gíbazo**bi**	*we show it to him/her* (Class 1) or *she/he shows it to us*		
yagíbazo**bi**	*you all showed it to him/her*	**nijí**bazo**bi**	*she/he shows it to you all*
wį̄cágibazo	*she/he shows it to them*	**gi**bázo**bi**	*they show it to him/her*
cigíbazo	*I show it to you*	**mayági**bazo	*you show it to me*

eyá – *she/he says it* (irregular verb)

ewágiya	*I say it to him/her*	**emági**ya	*she/he says it to me*
eyágiya	*you say it to him/her*	**enígi**ya	*she/he says it to you*
egíya	*she/he says it to him/her* (Class 1)		
ų̄gégiya**bi**	*we say it to him/her* or *she/he says it to us*		
eyágiya**bi**	*you all say it to him/her*	**enígi**ya**bi**	*she/he says it to you all*
ewį̄cagiya	*she/he says it to them*	**egí**ya**bi**	*they say it to him/her*
ecíjiya	*I say it to you*	**emáyagi**ya	*you say it to me*

John nécen emá**gi**ya, "Yatkéšį̄ wo!"	*This is what John told me, "Don't drink!"*
Kelly emá**gi**yabi.	*They call me Kelly.*
Nitúgaši **gi**bázo!	*Show it to your grandfather!*
Iyúhaȟ wį̄cá**gi**bazobi.	*They showed it to every single one of them.*
Nén iyáwa**gi**pe.	*I wait for him to come here.*
Iyúhana nén iyá**gi**pebi.	*Everybody waited here for him/her to come.*
Owá! Iyáma**gi**pe!	*Everyone! Wait for me to come!*
Yaúbi hą́dahą̄ waštéwa**gi**na jé.	*Whenever you all come, I always like it.*
Cą̄dé ksuwá**gi**ya.	*I am heartbroken because of her.*
	(ksuyá – *she/he/it hurts him/her/it*)
Dóhą̄ni mitúgaši timáya**gi**nįkta?	*When will you visit my grandfather?*
Wéhą̄ timáwį̄ca**gi**ni.	*She/he visited them last spring.*
Wazíyam nína wáhįhą̄ e**gí**yabi.	*They say it's snowing in the north.*
Žécen emá**gi**ya kó!	*That's what she said to me, that's it.*
"Tída gú!" ecíjiya!	*"Come home!" I said to you!*

Benefactive -giji- "to act for the benefit of somebody else"

Benefactive verbs indicate that an action is undertaken for the "benefit" or honour of somebody else. These verbs have two objects, a direct object (a thing₁) and an indirect object (the beneficiary₂) as can be seen in the following English examples:

> I picked it₁ up from the ground for him₂.
> She sang (a song₁) in his₂ honour.
> I bought you₂ a coat₁.
> Tell us₂ the story₁ of how you met mom.

The Nakoda benefactive marker is *-giji-*. This prefix is different from the postposition *gicí* "with" although they sound alike. The benefactive *-giji-* attracts the accent on its first syllable *gi* and undergoes the following changes, which makes the resulting verb irregular:

wa-	1SG, SUBJECT	+	-gíji-	BENEFACTIVE	→	**wéji-**
ya-	2SG, SUBJECT	+	-gíji-	BENEFACTIVE	→	**yéji-**
ma-	1SG, OBJECT	+	-gíji-	BENEFACTIVE	→	**míji-**
ni-	2SG, OBJECT	+	-gíji-	BENEFACTIVE	→	**níji-**

In the verbs *owícawejimnaga* "I told it on their behalf" (stem *oyága*) and *opégijitų* "she bought it for him" (stem *opétų*), the subject and object positions are the same as in a simple transitive verb. The only difference is that *-giji-* (or *-ji-*) is added after the subject prefix. There is no marker or slot for the direct object in these verbs. Here is the prefix order for this type of verb. It is the same as for the dative verb. Note that some speakers nasalize *mi-* and *ni-* into *mį-* and *nį-*.

STEM	+	INDIRECT OBJECT	+	SUBJECT	+	BENEFACTIVE	+	VERB STEM
o		wįca		we		ji		mnaga
		them		I				

I told it on their behalf.

STEM	+	INDIRECT OBJECT	+	SUBJECT	+	BENEFACTIVE	+	VERB STEM
opé		Ø		Ø		giji		tų
		him		she				

She bought it for him.

Here are more benefactive verbs along with the intransitive verbs they are derived from. Note that the benefactive verbs are of Class 1.

-gíji- + nową́		*for the benefit of + she/he sings* (Class 1)
	> **gíji**nową	*she/he sings for him/her, in his/her honour* (Class 1)
	> **míji**nową	*she/he sang for me*

-gíji- + yawá		*for the benefit of + she/he counts, reads* (Class 2)
	> **gíji**yawa	*she/he reads for him/her* (Class 1)
	> **níji**yawa	*she/he reads it to you*

-gíji- + iyéska		*for the benefit of + she/he converses, translates* (Class 2)
	> iyé**giji**ska	*she/he translates for him/her*
	> iyéwį̇ca**giji**ska	*she/he translates for them*

-gíji- + įyų́ǧa		*for the benefit of + she/he asks him/her* (Class 3)
	> į**gíji**yųǧa	*she/he asks him/her for him/her* (Class 1)
	> į**míji**yųǧa	*she/he asks me for him*

-gíji- + gáǧa		*for the benefit of + she/he makes it* (Class 1)
	> **gí**jaǧa	*she/he makes it for him/her*
		(contraction of *gíjigaǧa* > *gíjaǧa*) (Class 1)
	> **wé**jaǧa	*I make it for him/her*

Here are the conjugation tables for two benefactive verbs of classes 1 and 2, along with the forms for both the subject and object markers of the first and second persons.

nową́ – *she/he sings* (Class 1)

wéjinową	*I sing for him/her*	**míji**nową	*she/he sings for me*
yéjinową	*you sing for him/her*	**níji**nową	*she/he sings for you*
gíjinową	*she/he sings for him/her*		
ųgíjinowąbi	*we sing for him/her, in his/her honour* or *she/he sing for us, in our honour*		
yéjinowąbi	*you all sing for him/her*	**níji**nowąbi	*she/he sings for you all*
wį̇cágijinową	*she/he sings for them*	**gíji**nowąbi	*they sing for him/her*
cijínową	*I sing for you*	**mayé**jinową	*you sing for me*

oyága – *she/he tells it* (Class 2)

o**wé**jimnaga	*I tell it for him/her*	o**míji**yaga	*she/he tells it for me*
o**yé**jinaga	*you tell it for him/her*	o**níji**yaga	*she/he tells it for you*
o**gíji**yaga	*she/he tells it for him/her*		
ųgógijiyagabi	*we tell it for him/her* or *she/he tells it for us*		
o**yé**jinaga	*you all tell it for him/her*	o**níji**nowąbi	*she/he tells it for you all*
o**wį̇ca**gijiyaga	*she/he tells it for them*	o**gíji**yagabi	*they tell it for him/her*
o**cíji**mnaga	*I tell it for you*	o**mayeji**nága	*you tell it for me*

Mikúši **gíji**nową.	*She sang in my grandmother's honour.*
Cijábi wįcá**gi**jağa bo!	*You all make it for the children!*
Wašáša hąwí štén mi'áde iyécįgayena opé**miji**tųkta.	*Next July my father will buy me a car.*
Waná wé**ji**basi.	*I'm driving for her now.*
Iná wó'ų**giji**špi.	*We two pick berries for mother.*
Wíyą žé wįcíjana šųkcíjana wąží opé**giji**tų.	*That woman bought a puppy for the girl.*
Há, žé owé**ji**mnaga!	*Yes, I told him that!*
Žé'ųs owé**ji**mnaga.	*That is why I told him that.*
Žé'ųs owícawe**ji**mnagįkta.	*That is why I'll tell them that.*
Mikúši owé**ji**ne.	*I hunt for my grandmother. (lit., look for it)*
Pağų́da wįcáwe**ji**ağa.	*I made ducks (e.g., wooden ducks) for them.*
Žé yé**ji**ağa he?	*Did you make that for him?*
Įyémi**ji**nųğa he?	*Did you ask it to her for me?*
Wįkóške žé įcí**ji**mųğa.	*I asked that girl for you.*

Summary

Simple transitive verb	Possessive verb -gi-/-k-	Dative verb -gi-	Benefactive verb -giji-/-ji-
yuhá	**k**nuhá *she/he has, keeps his/her own thing*	—	—
ų́	**gi**c'ų́ *she/he wears his/her own thing*	—	—
bazó	—	**gi**bázo *she/he shows it to him/her*	**gíji**bazo *she/he shows it for him/her*
wašténa	—	waštéwa**gi**na *I am pleased with him/her/it*	—
onóda	—	o**gí**noda *she/he borrows it from him/her*	o**gíji**noda *she/he borrows it for him/her*
gáğa	—	—	**gíji**ağa *she/he made it for him/her*

Chapter 17 Exercises

EXERCISE 1

Translate the following sentences into Nakoda.

1. Yesterday my younger brother sang for/in honour of my grandfather.

   _____

   _____

2. They know that I care for myself.

   _____

   _____

3. In the morning I comb my hair and I brush my teeth.

   _____

   _____

4. My grandfather is 89 years old.

   _____

   _____

5. I read a Nakoda language book to my son.

   _____

   _____

6. Will you keep making it for me?

   _____

   _____

7. Are you pleased with it?

_____

_____

8. Tomorrow we will visit our grandmother.

_____

_____

9. I said to him, "Don't come here!"

_____

_____

10. My uncle wore a war bonnet with a trailer.

_____

_____

11. They don't wear work boots habitually.

_____

_____

12. Last Friday, my cousin committed suicide.

_____

_____

13. On Sundays I habitually cook for myself.

_____

_____

EXERCISE 2
Provide the dative and benefactive forms for the following verbs.

	bazó	wašténa	eyá
dative, you > him			
dative, you > him, FUT			
dative, you all > me, NEG			
dative, you > us, FUT			
benefactive, you > him			
benefactive, you > they, FUT			
benefactive, I > you			
benefactive, I > them, FUT/NEG			

EXERCISE 3
Match the correct Nakoda verb with its English translation.

1. iwícagijiyuǧa   _____ I sing for you
2. waʼíknagabi   _____ I wash myself
3. uknúhabi   _____ you smudge yourself
4. miknúžaža   _____ she asked them for him
5. emágiya   _____ they see themselves
6. ašónnic'iya   _____ he told it to me
7. timáʼugini   _____ we keep our own
8. cijínową   _____ we (two) visit him

EXERCISE 4

Match the Nakoda words with their English translation.

cąšíhąba	oyák'ų	awágu	tída	tawáci̧	hįháhąna
hayábi	šinágaȟci	anípabi	dágucen	dágeyešį	pežíȟoda
gic'ų́bįkktešį	nų́	omá'ųnibi	iyéwaya	taspą́ pestóstona	wamnúpi
nąbį́kpa	nįknúžaža	cądé'ųsijabi	yuką́	cąská	ogíhešį
įwábamnaya	moȟtága	įcápe	įmóȟtage	basísa	onų́we
a'ų́yabi	duká	cągádodona	nayápsija		

_____ I found it   _____ sage

_____ sock   _____ she/he is not able to

_____ iron   _____ she/he bumps into him/her

_____ she/he sews it   _____ bumper

_____ Shh! Shut up!   _____ I am skilled at

_____ pigmy owl   _____ his/her mind

_____ home   _____ poplar

_____ why   _____ you wear it

_____ fork   _____ swimming pool

_____ gloves   _____ shawl

_____ clothes   _____ rubber boots

_____ pear   _____ they will not put it on

_____ I bring it   _____ you wash yourself

_____ they hit you   _____ we are sad

_____ we travel   _____ it exists

_____ but   _____ we keep on…

_____ woodpecker   _____ you kick it

CHAPTER 18

Objectives

GRAMMAR

- Reading, analyzing texts, writing translations
- Searching for and analyzing unknown words

Dialectal Differences

As in many other languages we find some dialectal differences in Nakoda. Roughly put, there is a dialectal boundary between two sets of communities. The differences are mostly lexical and phonological in nature, with some differences in the usage of some male enclitics.

Differences	Western Communities: Carry The Kettle, Mosquito/Grizzly Bear Head/Leanman		Eastern Communities: Pheasant Rump, White Bear, Oceanman
interrogative enclitic *he*	both genders use *he*		only male speakers use *he*
Black person; African	hásaba		wašíjusaba
seven	iyúšna		šagówį
cane	sakné		sakyé
switch of *kt > tk*	cqtkúša	*robin*	cqktúša
	-tka ~ -kta	*potential/future*	-kta
switch of *tk > kt*	ziktábina	*bird*	zitkána
	aktúgu'ɏyabi	*our father*	atkúgu'ɏyabi
	įktú	*to be lit*	įtkú
	cqm'úzįkta	*wild onion, onion*	cqm'úzįtka
	yaktą́	*to drink*	yatką́
difference of *k/h*	snokyá	*to know him/her/it*	snohyá
syllable switch	škaška	*to be crooked, curved*	kšikšá

Chapter 18 Exercises

For the exercises in this last chapter you will work on five texts. Your task is to read them aloud and complete the specific instructions that follow each text. Search for the words you are not familiar with in the lexicon at the end of this book or in a Nakoda dictionary.

TEXT 1

Né wótijağa ğáğa mitúgaši
(Story written by Elder Armand McArthur.)

Iyópiya wa'ú̧! Omáka da̧yá̧ yuhá. Téha̧ wacímnageši̧ wanáğaš Šiyónide ektá wa'í. Wašíju Wa̧ží wótijağa ğáğa žéci wa'í. Žehá̧ tijáȟ wanówa̧. Wašíju Wa̧ží owágiya mitúgaši. Wašíju Wa̧ží wanáğaš waníja. Né tíbi ektá téha̧ žéci wa'ú̧ši̧. Wéksuya né da̧yá̧ wo'ú̧knagabi aké wa'ówabi wa̧ží mak'ú.

Taháši, á̧ba da̧yá̧ yuhá.

Wi̧cášta Há̧ska žé cažé mitáwa.

1. Read the text aloud very slowly and concentrate on the stress pattern.

2. Below each word, indicate the word class (verb, noun, adverb, pronoun, particle, demonstrative, postposition or enclitic).

3. Write a free translation of this text.

_____
_____
_____
_____
_____
_____
_____

4. Now locate all the verbs that describe human activities in the 1SG and create a new translation, changing the 1SG to 1PL inflections. Thus, a sentence like *Tá wążí **wakté*** "I killed a moose" would become *Tá wążí **ųktébi*** "We killed a moose." Remember that in order to correctly change the inflections of the verbs, you need to know the class of each verb.

_____

_____

_____

_____

_____

_____

_____

5. Read your 1PL version aloud.

TEXT 2

Wašpáyąbi

The original version of this story was written by Elder Herb Walker (taken from Schudel, 1999:234). Schudel's orthography has been changed to that of Fort Belknap used in this book. Note that in Carry The Kettle the potential/future *-kta* is sometimes pronounced *–tka*.

Nągáhą né wašpáyąbi hą́da océti né dohága kádatka žehą́n eknébi, iyécįga nąkáda.

Dágu špą́yąbi jé hąwí-gağabi wįyúbi žécen iyécįga įną́žį.

O'aškan į́š né cą́ ų́s océti kangíyabi.

Océti mą́za káda štén, céğa okná miní įbíȟyabi, hį́k waȟpé gáğabi.

Péda né sní áya hą́da cą́ a'ópeyabi. Aké péda né ną'į́ktųya.

Žéca ų́s cągáksaksa óda timáhen giknágabi.

Mnógedu tí okáda hą́da, tągán wašpáyąbi.

Cą́ ų́s wašpáyąbi né į́š nągáhą mą́za kanyábi ų́s wašpáyabi né ijítoką.

Cą́ ų́s wašpáyąbi né jé nína wašté.

Héktac'ehą į́yą néca gamímeya eknébi.

Žén cą́ ų́s wašpáyąbi.

Cą́ įkpá néca gapéstobi hį́k tanó įcápabi hį́k péda į'ágam yúza tanó jé špąyą́bi.

1. Read the text aloud very slowly and concentrate on the stress pattern.

2. Below each word, indicate the word class (verb, noun, adverb, pronoun, particle, demonstrative, postposition or enclitic).

3. Write a free translation of this text.

_____

_____

_____

_____

_____

_____

_____

_____

4. Now locate all the verbs that describe human activities in the 3PL and create a new translation, changing the 3PL to 1SG inflections. Thus, a sentence like *Tá wążí ktébi* "They killed a moose" would become *Tá wążí wakté* "I killed a moose." Remember that in order to correctly change the inflections of the verbs, you need to know the class of each verb.

_____

_____

_____

_____

_____

_____

_____

5. Read your 1SG version aloud.

TEXT 3

Mniwája agásampadahą ųhíbi-c'ehą

This story was told by Elder Wilma Kennedy from Carry The Kettle in December 2017. The conjunction **hą'ų́ka** (*and then*) is used to link two clauses or to end a sentence in stories.

1. "Wanágaš én, néci ųhíbi, mniwája agásampadahą ųhíbic'ehą" eyá.

2. "Žéci ųk'ų́bi, žéci waná dágu, dágu nówa ųyúhabišį cén waná ųg'ų́šibįkta," eyá.

3. "Žécen, watápe nówa iyápe yą́bi nówa, makóce wą́ží iyéyabi cén.

4. Én makóce gácedu wógųyena" gáya, yįgáhą gáhąn.

5. Dágu nówa, wóskuya kó, óda cén, dágu nówa įš, ų́s dąyą́ ų́bįkte nówa iyéyabi cén.

6. Híbi hą́'ųka dókiyam padáhą makóce, dókiyam mniwája agásam.

7. Žécen wįcáȟtįyą gáyabi cén, "Owá néci híbi hą́'ųka, miní né, miní agásam, owá néci, makóce nén iyógipiya tíbihą."

8. "Ába knábi cįgábi cén, owá knábįktešį šką́bi hą́'ųka iyáyabi" gáya.

9. Dókiyodahą híbi žé, žécedu iyúhana miní hą́'ųka, nená makóce wídagen yįgé žé, iyúhana mnimáhen iyáyahą cén.

10. "Dóken tiyám kíbi žécen, waná gáhąn néci, néci ų́bi" gáya.

11. "Žéci, žehą́dahą, néci ųg'ų́bi ųká" eyá.

1. Read the text aloud very slowly and concentrate on the stress pattern.

2. Below each word, indicate the part of speech (verb, noun, adverb, pronoun, particle, demonstrative, postposition or enclitic). For each verb indicate the verb class.

3. Write a free translation of this text.

TEXT 4

Įkusana hįk šųkcúkʼana

The original version of this legend was written by Elder Herb Walker (taken from Schudel, 1999:126). Schudel's orthography has been changed to that of Fort Belknap used in this book, and the spelling of many words has been corrected (e.g., *ga ye ja* > *gaéca* "and then").

1. Owóknage wąží žeyábi no!
   _____

2. Įkusana né pteptéğana dóna én opíʼįcʼiya.
   _____

3. Ąbédu wąží omnáye én šųkcúkʼana wąží akípa.
   _____

4. Įkusana né žeyá, "Háu koná, né maštíjatąga wąží knapá yaʼų́.
   _____

5. Maštíjatąga nená niná núzahąbi no!
   _____

6. Dóken né núza he?"
   _____

7. Šųkcúkʼana né žeyá, "Né cejá mąhą́skaska cén tehíšįyąh éwaknaga".
   _____

8. Žécen įkusana né žeyá, "Mįš́ įknúhanah wąžíh mnukábįktac!"
   _____

9. Gáken šųkcúkʼana įhábi noʼų́s kó aptą́yą.
   _____

10. Įkusana né šųkcúkʼana žé įyúğa, "Dágucen né nína įyáha he?"
    _____

11. Šųkcúkʼana né žeyá, "Né niğé mąká yusnóhą yaʼų́, dóken wąží nukábįkta (he)?"
    _____

210 NAKÓN-IʼA WO! | BEGINNING NAKODA

12. Gáken į́kusana šųkcúk'ana né žégiya.

13. "Žé né wįjáyakac, aktágabi nína ninúzahą, mį́š né miní én nųwą́bi wamnúpi c" eyá.

14. "Né dágu wąží įmnúkcąc."

15. "Né ptéğa nén a'ókšą ųgáktagįkta, duwé togáheya nén kní štén maštį́jatąga né éknaguktac!"

16. Gáken šųkcúk'ana né žéya "žé'įš įdúȟ ohíwayįktac" eyá.

17. Gáken į́kusana né žeyá, "dókedu cén eyáš ųgíyayįktac!" eyá.

18. "Hų́n," šųkcúk'ana né "hų́n," eyá.

19. Gáken šųkcúk'ana né miní a'ókšą aktága, į́kusana né'įš miní én nųwą́.

20. Šųkcúk'ana né yucápcabadugen aktága.

21. Gáken dóhądu ȟtįyą ga'éca tógadam édųwą ga'éca.

22. Gakí togádam į́kusana waná hiyáya.

23. Gáken šųkcúk'ana né, į́kusana kapá iyáyįkta cén kapéya aktága.

24. Dónaȟ žécų duká į́kusana né įdúȟ togádam wąyága.

25. Ahágeȟ édųwą gá įkusana gakí héktam padáhą ų́.

26. Gáken šųkcúk'ana né akéš owáštenagen aktága.

27. Maštíjatąga žé awáciyągen.

28. Gaháduȟtįyą ga'éca duktén maštíjatąga éknagabi cén dágunišį.

29. Gáken šųkcúk'ana né miní įt'á áya cén, miní én įnážį ga'éca dágu wąyága.

30. Gakí wągám édųwą ga'éca.

31. Žéci cą agám įkusana né a'ana wążí gicí wóknaga, dóken wódabi.

32. Gáken šųkcúk'ana né žeyá, "Há koná mį́š edáhą mąk'ú bo!"

33. Gáken įkusana né waná ípi cén, wóyapte žená kún yušná.

34. Gáken šųkcúk'ana né'įš iyógipiya wóda.

35. Žécų hį́k iyúhana nína įgíȟabi no!

1. Read the text aloud very slowly and concentrate on the stress pattern.

2. Write a free translation of each line in the space provided.

3. Answer the following five questions about the story:

    a. What did Coyote carry in his mouth?
    _____

    b. Why did Coyote laugh so hard?
    _____

    c. What is the contest set up by Mink?
    _____

    d. Why did Coyote slow down?
    _____

    e. Who ate the jack rabbit?
    _____

TEXT 5

Wacégiyabi

    Adé waką́tąga!

    Hó namáh̃'ų wo!

    {your name} emágiyabi!

    Adé waką́tąga, mitúgaši, mikúši!

    Ą́ba wašté né wópina wak'ú (no)!

    Adé waką́tąga!

    Midáguyabi iyúhana niyá-wašte wįcák'u-c'ehą, wópina tą́ga wak'ú (no)!

    Dágu iyúhana: miní, péda, mah̃píya íyą, makóce né į́š.

    Wamą́kašką́bi iyúhana: tatą́ga, pté, zitkána, hog̃ą́ į́š.

    Wópina tą́ga wak'ú (no)!

    Adé waką́tąga!

    Hó namáh̃'ų (wo)! Ų́šigiya nawáži̧ hį́kna wacéwagiya (no)!

    Ų́šímana (wo)! Pinámayaya (no)!

1. Read the text aloud very slowly and concentrate on the stress pattern.

2. Below each word, indicate the word class (verb, noun, adverb, pronoun, particle, demonstrative, postposition or enclitic).

3. Learn this prayer by heart and adjust the content as needed.

REFERENCES

Cumberland, Linda A. 2005. *A Grammar of Assiniboine: A Siouan Language of the Northern Plains*. PhD Thesis, Indiana University, Department of Anthropology.

Fourstar, Jerome. 1978. *Assiniboine Dictionary* (manuscript). Wolf Point, MT.

Parks, Douglas R. 2002. *English-Nakoda, Nakoda-English Student Dictionary*. Bloomington: Hoteja Project and Indiana University.

Schudel, Emily K. 1997. *Elicitation and Analysis of Nakoda Texts from Southern Saskatchewan*. Master's Thesis, University of Regina.

Trask, Larry. 1993. *A Dictionary of Grammatical Terms in Linguistics*. UK: Routledge.

APPENDIX 1
KINSHIP TABLE

In the following tables you will find the kinship terms for my, your, our and his/her forms. Of course, this list is far from being complete, but it will give you a broad idea of the words used since some local variants have also been included. Many of these terms are seldom used and oftentimes even fluent speakers have problems remembering them. This is especially true for relations outside the nuclear family (i.e., mother, father, brother, sister, grandmother and grandfather), and even more so for in-laws. (The term ego means "speaker" and is the point of reference for kinship systems.) The labels +1, +2 and –1, –2 indicate a generation or two above or below. The asterisk * is an expected form not provided by the language consultants.

EGO + 2 gen.	my	your	our	his/her
grandfather	mitúgaši (reference) ųká (address)	nitúgaši	ųgítukąkišitku	tugą́šicu tugą́šitku
grandmother	mikúši ųjí (address)	nikúši	ųgíkušitku	kušícu kúgišiktu

EGO + 1 gen.	my	your	our	his/her
father	adé (address) miyáde ~ mi'áde (reference)	niyáde	miyádebi aktúgu'ųyabi atkúgu'ųyabi	atkúgu atkúgubi
mother	iná (address) inábi (address) mihų́ (reference)	nihų́ nihų́bi	ųgínabi hų́gu'ųyabi	hų́gubi
father's brother	adéna	niyádena		
father's sister and mother's brother's wife	mitų́wi	nitų́wi		tųwícu
mother's brother and father's sister's husband	minékši	ninékši		nekšícu
mother's sister and father's brother's wife	inána	ni'ínana	ųgínanabi	
mother's sister's husband and father's sister's husband	adéna	niyádena		
father-in-law	mitúga mitúgą	nitúgą		tugą́gu
mother-in-law	mikų́	nikų́	ųgíkųbi	kų́gu

EGO is MALE	my	your	our	his/her
older brother and older male parallel cousin	micína	nicína		cįcúna
older sister and older female parallel cousin	mitágena	nitágena	ųgítągenabi	táguna
younger brother and younger male parallel cousin	misúga	nisúga		sųgágu
younger sister and younger female parallel cousin	mitákši	nitákši		tąkšíco
female cross-cousin	mihágaši	nihágaši		hągášico
male cross-cousin	mitáhąši	nitáhąši		tahášicu
wife	mitáwįju	nitáwįju		tawíju
brother-in-law	mitáhą	nitáhą		tąhącu
sister-in-law	mihágo	nihágo		hągágo

EGO is FEMALE	my	your	our	his/her
older brother	mitímno	nitímno	ųgítimno(gu)bi	timnógu
older sister and older female parallel cousin	micúna	nicúna		cúgųna
younger brother and younger male parallel cousin	misúga	nisúga		sųgágu
younger sister and younger female parallel cousin	mitą́	nitą́		tągágu
female cross-cousin	mišík'eši	nišík'eši	mišík'ešibi	šic'éšicu / šik'étku
male cross-cousin	mišícepąši	nišícepąši		šicépąšitku
husband	mihíkna	nihíkna	ųgíhįknągubi	hįknągu
co-wife	mitéya			
brother-in-law	mišíc'e	nišíc'e		šic'étku
sister-in-law	mišíjepą	nišíjepą		šijépągu

EGO – 1 gen.	my	your	our	his/her
son	micį́kši	nicį́kši		cįhį́tku
daughter	micų́kši	nicų́kši	ųgícųkši	cųwį́tku
nephew	mitų́ška	nitų́ška		tųškácu
niece (male speaker)	mitų́žą	nitų́žą		tųžą́co

EGO – 2 gen.	my	your	our	his/her
grandchild	mitákoža	nitákoža	ųgítakožabi ųgítagožakpagu	takóžakpagu

Other Terms	my	your	our	his/her
child	micį́jena	nicį́jena	micį́jabi	cįjéna
male friend of a man	mitákona	nitákona		takónagu
female friend of a man		nįší		šįtkúya

APPENDIX 1: KINSHIP TABLE

APPENDIX 2
GLOSSARY OF GRAMMATICAL TERMS

Ablaut = process whereby the final vowel of a stem changes its value. Usually it is an additional element that provokes the ablauting process. In the following examples, the suffix *-kta* "future, potential" provokes the ablaut of a preceding *a* into a nasal *į*, or *i* into *į*. The outcome of ablauting is often a nasal vowel.

| wóda | + | kta | > | wódįkta | *she/he will eat* |
| wací | + | kta | > | wacįkta | *she/he will dance* |

Note: In some Nakoda dictionaries or linguistic literature, the vowel that becomes ablauted is indicated with an uppercase. Thus, *wóda* "she/he eats" would be written *wódA*. The uppercase indicates that if the suffix *-kta* "potential, future" (or any other ablauting suffix) follows, the *A* changes for a nasal *į*.

Active/Stative = refers to the distinction between actions like *to think, live, take it* and states like *to be nice, black, sad*.

Agent = is the person doing the action of a transitive verb (i.e., an action verb that implies a transfer of force), as in ***I*** *called them,* ***you*** *kicked him,* ***she*** *fed me*.

Benefactive = indicates that an action is undertaken for the "benefit" or honour of somebody else.

Conjugation = refers to the set of persons (6 in total), number (singular, dual, and plural), and mood inflections that can be found on a verb.

Dative = indicates that an action is directed to or intended for somebody else.

Derivation, to derive = refers to a word formation process whereby some elements are added on a root to specify its meaning, as in *race > racer* "the one who races" or *do it >* ***re****do it*.

Discontinuous stem = refers to stems that are split into two parts, usually a small one at the beginning and another one towards the end; e.g., the verb *maní* "she/he walks" splits in two and an infix is inserted, as in *ma-**wá**-ni* "I walk," *ma-**yá**-ni* "you walk."

Enclitics = are elements that attach rather loosely at the end of verbs and nouns, like *-s'a* "habitual," as in *wódes'a* "an eater," or *-kta* "future/potential," as in *wódįkta* "she/he will eat."

Inflection, to inflect = refers to the addition of elements on the verb that indicate person, number, tense, and mood. In English, there are very few inflections left except for the *-s* in *he reads*, which indicates third person singular, indicative mood.

Interjection = refers to short words (*Hey! Watch out! Ouch!*) that are used to call out or warn people. They keep the channel of communication open.

Morpheme = is the smallest unit of meaning (e.g., in *cat-s* you can separate *-s* and it means "more than one," thus we will say that *-s* is a morpheme and *cat-* a stem; in the Nakoda noun *búzabi* "cats" the part *-bi* is a morpheme that means "more than one").

Object = the person or thing upon whom or which an action is done (*he kicked **me**, she killed **the ducks***).

Possessive = applies to verb morphology and means that an action is done to someone's own thing. On a noun it refers to the possessor markers.

Reduplication = is the doubling of one syllable of a verb usually to express plurality (*šá* "it is red" becomes *šašá* "they are red").

Reflexive = indicates that the subject of the verb is acting upon him or herself. Thus, the subject is both the agent and the object of an action. In English, the reflexive is expressed by the pronouns + *-self, -selves*.

Stem = is the base of a word that expresses a lexical idea like *sleep, eat, run, man, dog*, etc. In Nakoda, the third person singular, like *wóda* "she/he/it eats" is used as the citation form of a verb and also expresses an order: "Eat!"

Subject = is the person doing the action in an intransitive verb (*I sleep, **they** are running*); in a transitive verb the subject is the agent (***he** kicked the ball*).

Transitive/Intransitive = a distinction that applies to verbs: a) intransitive verbs have only a subject (*I am sleeping, I ran*) while transitive verbs imply a transfer of force between an agent/subject and an object (*I shot the puck, you dunked the ball*).

APPENDIX 3
VERB CLASSES

	CLASS 1 Regular stems *wa-ya-*		CLASS 2 Y-stems *mn-n-* (delete the *y* = point of insertion)	
	make it *(prefix)*	**walk** *(infix)*	**drink** *(prefix)*	**sit down** *(infix)*
I	**wa**gáğa	ma**wá**ni	**mn**atką́	i**mn**ódąga
you	**ya**gáğa	ma**yá**ni	**n**atką́	i**n**ódąga
she/he	gáğa	maní	yatką́	iyódąga
we	**ų**gáğa**bi**	ma'**ų́**ni**bi**	**ų**yátką**bi**	**ų**gíyodągabi
	bakcá – *comb it* bazó – *show it* cįgá – *want it* hí – *arrive here* hiyú – *depart from there* í – *arrive there* kní – *return home* knuhá – *have one's own* kté – *kill it* k'ú – *give it* néža – *urinate* nową – *sing* opétų – *buy it* snóhą – *crawl* šką – *try, do, feel* tí – *live (in a place)* ú – *come here* ų́ – *be*	a_gú – *bring it* a_hópa – *respect it* a_pá – *hit it* a_ktága – *run* awášpą_ya – *cook* ehą́_ki – *reach it* e_gíya – *call it* iyé_ska – *converse, translate* iyáksam_kiya – *train it* iyáme_kiya – *hunt* iyé_ya – *find it* i_'á – *talk (to), speak (to)* ná_žį – *stand* o_gíhi – *be able* o_kmá – *write it* o_né – *look for it* opé_tų – *buy it* snoh_yá – *know it* ši_kná – *be angry* te_hína – *love it* wacé_giya – *pray* wadó_pa – *paddle* wa_cí – *dance* wó_da – *eat* wo_k'ú – *feed it*	yá – *go there* yawá – *count it* yúda – *eat it* yuhá – *have it* yužáža – *scrub it*	éyagu – *take it* iyáya – *depart* wayáwa – *read* wąyága – *see it* wayúpi – *be skilled* wa'áyaza – *bead*

ACTIVE VERBS

CLASS 3		CLASS 4		
Nasal markers *m-n-*		**Nasal+Vowel markers *ma-ni-***		
(delete the *y* or *w* = point of insertion)				
wear *(prefix)*	do it *(infix)*	be tired *(prefix)*	be full *(infix)*	
m**ų́**	ecá**m**ų	**ma**stústa	į́**ma**pi	**I**
nų́	ecá**n**ų	**ni**stústa	į́**ni**pi	**you**
ų́	ecų́	stustá	į́pi	**she/he**
ų'ų́bi	ecų́gųbi	ųstústa**bi**	ųgį́pi**bi**	**we**
įknúžaža – wash oneself	įwų́ga – go to bed	cesní – be pooping	á_ya – becoming, continuing
įštíma – sleep	įyų́ǧa – ask it	dąyą́ – be well	cądé_sija – be sad
yągá – be seated	dóka'_ų – do what	gána – be old	cądé_wašte – be kind
agą́n-yągá – ride a horse		háska – be tall	iyó_gipi – be pleased
		káda – be feverish, hot	Na_kóda – be Nakoda
		júsina – be small	ų_spé – be learning by oneself
		šįtų́ – be fat	wa_ką́ – be holy
		tą́ga – be big	wa_šíju – be White
		téjana – be young, new	žé_ca – be of a kind
		yazą́ – be sick	

ACTIVE VERBS	**STATIVE VERBS*** – "to be" verbs Also direct object of transitive verbs such as: **ma**k'ú – *she/he gives it to **me*** **ni**c'ú – *she/he gives it to **you***

* For a full explanation of stative verbs, see pages 59–64 and 84–85.

NAKODA/ENGLISH LEXICON

The following Nakóda/English lexicon is only a fraction of the totality of Nakoda words. It contains all the words presented in this document as well as those gathered during the fieldwork sessions. The abbreviations used are the following:

ADV = adverb
ART = article
AUX = auxiliary
CONJ = conjunction
CTK = Carry The Kettle
DEM = demonstrative
ENCL = enclitic
INTERJ = interjection
-IRR = irregular verb (similar to Class 1)
N = noun
-N = nasal conjugation (Class 3)
NUM = number

OM = Oceanman
PART = particle
PL = plural
POST = postposition
PR = Pheasant Rump
PRO = pronoun
QUANT = quantifier
VREC = reciprocal verb
SG = singular
SUF = suffix
VI = intransitive verb (Class 1)
VIMP = impersonal verb
VPOS = possessive verb

VR = reflexive verb (Class 3)
VS = stative verb (Class 4)
VT = transitive verb (Classes 1, 2, 3)
-Y = Y-stem conjugation (Class 2)
~ = local or dialectal variants of a word (one speaker)
; = sub-dialectal variant, not specifically intraspeaker variation (speakers from different regions)

Take note that in alphabetic ordering oral vowels (*a, e, i, o, u*) come before nasal ones (*ą, į, ų*), and that the glottal ' is treated as a consonant that comes after all other consonants. Finally, two-word compounds come after single words.

A

abá (QUANT) some (used with count nouns)
abáȟnan sąksája (N) silk dress
abámnu (VI) to burp
abápsų (VT) to sprinkle, water it
acóga (N) armpit
acú (VS) to be damp
adé (VOC) Father! (N) my father
adéna (N) my uncle (father's brother)
adéyabi (N) Indian agent
agáȟpa (VT) to cover him/her/it (e.g., with a blanket)
agána (VT) to fill, sprinkle something on it
ágasampadahą (ADV) from there across to here
agąn (POST) on top of it, on it
agąn-yąga (PR); **-yįga** (CTK) (VT-N) to ride a horse

agé- (PREF) on top (used with teen numerals)
    agéwąži "eleven" (NUM)
    agénųba "twelve"
    agéyamni "thirteen"
    agédoba "fourteen"
    agézaptą "fifteen"
    agéšakpe "sixteen"
    agéšagowį "seventeen"
    agéšaknoǧą "eighteen"
    agénapcuwąga "nineteen"
agénųba (N) dozen
agícida (N) uniform, soldier
agícida įtáca (N) policeman
agícida wi'óti hųgá (N) chief of the warrior lodge
agípe (VT) to wait for him/her/it
agísas (ADV) proudly
agísni (VT) to recover from it
agú (VT) to bring him/her/it back
aǧóbas'a (N) snorer
aǧúyabi (N) flour, bread
aǧúyabisaga (N) toast (lit., dry bread)
aǧúyabiskuya (N) cake, cookie (lit., sweet bread)
aǧúyabisu (N) wheat kernel
aǧúyabi baská (N) dough
aǧúyabi šnoyábi (N) fried bannock
aháge (ADV) last, last one; behind
ahą́ (VT) to step on it
ahą́zi (VIMP) to be dusk, dark; to be a dark evening
ahą́ziga (VIMP) to be kind of dark
ahą́zikiya (VT) to darken it
ahé (INTERJ) expression of humility used at the beginning of prayers or songs
ahí (VT, VI) 1) to arrive with him/her/it here; 2) to arrive here as a group
ahídųwą (VT) to look on, over him/her/it
ahógipa (VT) to respect, honour him/her/it
ahópa (VT) to respect, honour, revere him/her
aké (ADV) again
akí (ADV) both, equal, same
akída (VT) to watch, look at it
akínija (VT) to debate, argue about it
akípa (VT) to meet him/her
akíyecedu (ADV) alike
aknąk (POST) along
aknáya (VT) to follow him/her/it
aknáya (N) fool
aknáyąbi hąwí (N) April's fool
aknéška (N) salamander
akní (VT) to bring him/her/it home
aktášį (VT) to disown
ak'į́ (N) saddle
ak'į́ha (N) saddle bag
ak'į́maheda (N) saddle blanket
ak'į́pasu (N) saddlehorn
ak'į́tųga (VT) to saddle it
amáȟpiya (VIMP) to be cloudy (N) cloud
amáȟpiyato (VS) to be a blue sky
amį́knaga wacíbi (N) crow belt dance
amnágena (VIMP) to be still, peaceful
amnéza (VT) to check, examine, scrutinize him/her/it up
amníjiya (ADV) all over, all around
amógiyą ~ amúgiyą ~ įmúgiya (N) car
amógiyą hú nąpóbi (N) flat tire
anádą (VT) to raid an enemy
anáȟma (VT) to keep a secret
anáȟmaya (ADV) secretly
anápta (VT) she/he stops somebody or something
anówą (VI) to sing for or over someone
anówąbi (N) quarterly singing
apá (VT) to hit, knock him/her/it
apáȟta (VT) to tie it up on it
apápa (VT) to knock lightly on it
apéya (ADV) in a waiting manner
aptáyą (VS) to fall over, roll over, capsize, be upside down
asásya (VT) to be proud of him/her; to make him/her proud
asą́bi (N) milk
asą́bi súda (N) cheese
asą́bi wį́kni (N) butter
asní (VS) to recover from an illness
asníya (VT) to heal him/her/it
astústaga (VS) to be rather tired
aškán ~ o'áškan (ADV) recently, lately
ašón'įc'iya (VR) to smudge oneself
atkúguya; aktúguya (VT) to have him as a father

awácį (VT-N) to feel, think about, have it on one's mind
awácįyą (ADV) for the sake of it, in a contemplative manner
awácįyągen (ADV) wondering about it
awákąya (VT) to bless him/her/it
awánųka (ADV) accidentally
awášpąya (VI) to cook a feast
awáyaga (VT-Y) to look after him/her/it
awáyages'a (N) guard, bodyguard
awódabi (N) table
awógiciknagabi (VREC) to talk about one another
awóknaga (VT) to talk about it, discuss it
áya (VS-AUX) to become, turn into
áya (VI-Y) to do continuously
ayáskama (VI) to be stuck on it
ayúȟuga (N) crust
ayúpta (VT-Y) to answer him/her
ayúštą (VT-Y) to lose it
azé (N) breast, udder
azíȟya; azínya (VT) to smudge her/him/it
azį́'įc'iya (VR) to smudge oneself
a'ámna (VS) to be a moldy smell
á'ana (N) crow
a'ábayabi (N) a wake after a death
a'í (VT) to take it/him/her there
a'ínina (ADV) quietly
a'į́kboğa (N) sweet pine, Indian perfume, cedar
a'į́knaȟpa (VR) to cover oneself
a'į́kpapsų (N) perfume
a'ógadą (VT) to nail it
a'óȟązi (VIMP) to be cloudy, overcast
a'ókpaza'áya (VIMP) it is dark
a'ókšą (ADV) around something
a'ópeya (VT) to add on it
a'óta (VT) to shoot with a gun
a'óžąžą (VIMP) to be sunny, lightened up (N) light
a'óžąžą yuhá'ųbi (N) lantern
a'ú (VT) to bring him/her/it here

Ą

ą́ba (N) day
ąbáhotųna ~ ąbáhotų (N) chicken
ąbáhotųnamnoga (N) rooster
ąbaneyas'a (ADV) all day long
ąbawaką (N) Sunday
ąbawaką gicúni (N) Monday
ąbawaką tága (N) Christmas
ąba įdóba (N) Thursday
ąba įnúba (N) Tuesday
ąba įyámni (N) Wednesday
ąba įzáptą (N) Friday
ąba né ~ ąba nén (ADV) today
ąba ú (VIMP) to be dawn
ąba ú wįcáȟpi (N) morning star, Venus
ąba yužáža (N) Saturday
ąbédu (N) day
ąbédu wéksuya (N) Memorial Day
ąbéyas'a (ADV) all day long
ąbé'įštima (VI) to sleep during day time
ąmháska wí (N) February (from *ą́ba hą́ska wí*)
ąm'ósni (VIMP) to be a cold day (from *ą́ba osní*)
ąpšíja (VIMP) to be a gloomy day
ąpšíjeja (VIMP) to be a stormy day, a day with bad weather

B

bağé (ADV) together, bunched up, as a group
bahá (N) hill
bahótų (VT) to make a loud sound by pushing, rubbing
baȟnéja (VT) to puncture it (e.g., with a sharp tool)
baȟnóga (VT) to make a hole with a sharp tool, to pierce
bakcá (VT) to comb him/her/it
bakį́da (VT) to wipe it
baksá (VT) to break it with an instrument (e.g., with a chainsaw)
bakšíja (VT) to fold it
bamnáya (VT) to iron it
bamnúğa (VT) to make a crunching sound with the hands or tool
bapsų́ (VT) to pour out, spill a liquid
basí (VI) to drive
basnóhą (VT) to push it
bašpá (VT) to open it with a sharp tool
bat'á (VT) to crush him/her/it to death

bazó (VT) to show it
bažúžu (VT) to erase it
Bigána (N) Piegan
bispízena (N) mouse
bistága (N) prairie dog
bíško (N) nighthawk
bizéna (N) gopher
bizéna tága (N) groundhog
bo (ENCL) male imperative plural
bó (VI) to swell
boȟnóga (VT) to make a hole by pressing on it
boksá (VT) to break it by pushing with an instrument (e.g., with a truck)
bošpá (VT) to knock it open with force, pressure
bustágesa (N) type of spring bird
busyá (VT) to dry it
buščíjana (N) kitten
bušpá (VT) to pry it (e.g., with a bar)
búza (N) cat
búza (VS) to be dry
bu̧bú (VS) to crumble (as rotten wood, dried bannock)

C

c (ENCL) gender neutral declarative
ca (PART) such a person, such a kind
cá (PART) probably, must
cába (N) beaver
cabáȟmikma (N) wagon
cağúsija (N) tuberculosis
caȟnísaba (N) black gunpowder
caná (N) crotch (genital area)
capúga (N) mosquito
Capúga-Matópa-Hústaga (N) Mosquito/Bear Head/Leanman person or nation
catká (VS) to be left-handed
catkána (ADV) left side
cažé (N) name
cá̧ (N) tree, wood
ca̧báhotu̧na yucéya (N) guitar
ca̧bákmi̧kma (N) wagon, bicycle
ca̧báza (VI) to put up a fence
ca̧bázabi (N) fence

ca̧cá̧ (VS) to shiver
ca̧cá̧na (N) shivering
cá̧ceğa (N) wooden pail
cá̧ceğa awáyaga (N) drum keeper
ca̧dé (N) heart
ca̧déskúya (N) sweetheart, girlfriend
ca̧déwašte (VS) to be kind, good-hearted
ca̧dé i̧náži̧ (VS) to have a heart attack
ca̧gáȟage (N) trailer of a war bonnet
ca̧gáksaksa (VT) to chop wood into kindling
ca̧gámubi (N) log drum
ca̧gúsam (ADV) across the border (N) United States
Ca̧gúsam wi̧cá (N) American
ca̧gúsampadaha̧ (N) from across the border
ca̧ğáȟtu̧bi (N) beaver dam, bridge
cáha̧ba (N) shoes
cáha̧ba háske (N) cowboy boots
cáha̧ba i̧sámye (N) shoe polish
ca̧káhuknekneğana (N) chipmunk
ca̧m'úzi̧tka (PR, OM); **ca̧m'úzi̧kta** (CTK) (N) wild onion, onion
ca̧né (VI) to look for wood
ca̧ní (N) tobacco
ca̧ní súda (N) twisted tobacco
ca̧níska (N) cigarette
ca̧níya; ca̧ní̧ya̧ (VI) to pout, sulk
ca̧núba (N) pipe (VI) to smoke a pipe
ca̧núba i̧húca̧ (N) pipestem
ca̧núba oȟpága ecúbi (N) pipe ceremony
ca̧núba waká̧ (N) sacred pipe
ca̧pá (N) chokecherries, pin cherries
ca̧pásaba ha̧wí (N) August
ca̧pásusuna (N) pepper
ca̧ská (N) white poplar
ca̧šáša ~ ca̧šášana (N) red willow
ca̧šíha̧ba (N) rubber boots
ca̧ší̧ (N) resin, chewing gum
ca̧šká (N) hawk, chicken hawk
ca̧šmúyabi (N) sugar
ca̧šmúyabi pšu̧káka (N) candy
ca̧tkúša; makúša (N) robin
cá̧waka̧ (N) sun dance center pole, cross
ca̧wámnuška (N) wood tick

cąwóhą ~ cą'óhą (ADV) in a wooden area, in the brush
cąwópiye (N) storage box
cąwóšma (N) dense bush
cąyága (VI-Y) to moan
cąyák ų́ (VI) to agonize in pain
cą́ gahómni (N) stick used in a round dance
cą'ágą; cą'ágą yįgábi (N) chair
cą'ágą yįgábi wįcášta (N) chairman
cą'íyušnohą (N) sleigh
cą'óhą (ADV) in the forest
cą'ótina (N) tree dweller, dwarf
cą'ówiža ~ cą'ówiža (N) floor, mat
cé (N) penis
cégiya (VT) to bless him/her
céǧa (N) kettle, pail, pot
Céǧa K'ína (N) Carry The Kettle reservation
céǧa tága (N) pail
cehú (N) jaw
ceȟníbi (N) syphilis, sexual disease
cejá (N) thigh
cekpá (N) navel
cén (CONJ) then, so, thus
cesní (VI) to defecate (N) feces, dung
cesní oyátaga (VS) to be constipated
češkámaza (N) 1) council, alliance; 2) police
cetápą (N) man whole genitalia
cetí (VI) to build a fire, start a stove
céya (VI) to cry
céyaga (PART) should, must, ought to
ceyágadaga; cayágadaga (N) wild mint, peppermint
céyagįšį (PART) should not, must not
céya í (VI) to arrive there crying
ceyés'a (N) crybaby
ceží (N) 1) tongue; 2) gun trigger
cįcá (VS) to be curly
cįcúna (N) his older brother
    micína "my older brother"
    nicína "your older brother"
cįǧá (VT) to want him/her/it
cįhítku (N) his/her son
    micíkši "my son"
    nicíkši "your son"

cįhítkuya (PR, OM); cįhíktuya (CTK) (VT) to adopt a son
cijá (N) child
cijáya (VT) to adopt him/her as a child
cį́tka (PR, OM); cį́kta (CTK) (N) raisin
có (N) truth
cogádu (ADV) in the middle, center
cogáduȟ (ADV) right in the center
cogą́n (ADV) in the center
cogą́nwida (N) island in the middle of a lake
cóǧa (VS) to be honest
coȟwíjaka (VI) to tell the truth
coknága (N) breech cloth
cóna (POST) without, deprived of
coná (N) belief
coníca (N) dry meat
cos'į́c'iya (VR) to warm oneself
cótąga (N) gun
cóza (VS) to be warm (e.g., coat)
co'ų́ba (VT) to roast, to fry it
cucúšte (N) ribs
cuȟéwąga (VIMP) to be a hoar frost
cuna (ENCL) repetition
cusní (VIMP) to be chilly
cuwí (N) chest
cuwída (VS) to be cold, chilly (animate referent)
cuwį́knąga (N) coat, shirt
cuwį́knąga hą́ska (N) long coat, shirt
cuwį́knąga šašábi (N) Royal Canadian Mounted Police
cuwį́snohą (N) sleigh, sled
cúgųna (N) her older sister
    micų́na "my older sister"
    nicų́na "your older sister"
cųwį́tku (N) his/her daughter
    micų́kši "my daughter"
    nicų́kši "your daughter"
-c'ehą; -'ehą (ENCL) in the past, just then

D

dágeyešį (INTERJ) Shh! Shut up! Don't talk!
dágu (N) thing, something (PRO) what (QUANT) any, none
dágucen (ADV) why

dáguȟ (PRO) anything, something different
dagúmna (VI) to be a smelly thing
dáguni (PRO) none, nothing (objects)
dágunih̆ (PRO, ADV) nothing at all
dágunišį (VS) it is nothing (NUM) zero
dágunišįȟtįyą (VS) it is nothing at all
dáguškina (N) baby, infant, child
dáguškiškina (N) doll
dagúya (VT) to have him/her as a relative
dagúye (N) relative
dąyą́ (VS) to be well (ADV) well, fine
dąyágen (ADV) in a careful manner, carefully
dąyą́šį yįgá (N) death bed
dóba ~ dóm (NUM) four
dóbagiya (ADV) four by four
dóbana (NUM) only four
dógiš'ų (VI) to be weak from an illness
dógiš yįgá (VI-N) to be sitting dying; to be on one's death bed
dóhąc'ehą (ADV) when in the past (realized event)
dóhąda ~ dóhą (ADV) when in the future, later (potential, irrealized event)
dóhągeja (ADV) at what time
dóhąni (ADV) never
dókaš (ADV) maybe
dóka'ų; dókų (VI-N-IRR) to do what (*dókamų, dókanų, dókų*)
dókedu (VS) to be how it is, whatever happens
dókeja (VI) to be a matter
dóken (ADV) how
dóki (ADV) where, to where
dókiya (ADV) anywhere
dókiyadahą; dókidahą (ADV) where from
dókiyo (ADV) in which direction
dóna (ADV) some, how many
duȟáȟa (VS) to be dimpled
duká (CONJ) but (ENCL) supposedly, should
duktám (ADV) away from a place, somewhere
dukté (PRO) what, which
duktégakošta (PRO) any which one
duktén (ADV) where
duktén túbi (N) place of birth
duwé (PRO) who, anyone (VS) to be someone
duwégakošta (PRO) anybody

duwéȟ (PRO) whoever, somebody specifically
duwéni (PRO) nobody, no one
duwénišį (VS) to be nobody

E

é (VS) to be
ecá (VS) to be thus, to be of that kind
ecágen (ADV) constantly, always
ecákiya (VI) to think about it
ecámna (VI) to have a smell
ecá'ų; ecú (VT-N-IRR) to do it (*ecámų, ecánų, ecú*)
ecédu (VS) to be, to happen so
ecén (ADV) in the original way, and, thus, so
ecéya (VS) to be in such disposition
éceyen (ADV) only
ecį́ (VI) to wonder about it
ecúgabi (VS) to be lazy
edáhą (ADV) some of that (mass noun)
édunaȟ (ADV) close by, near
éduwą (VT) to look at it
egíya ~ ejíya (VT) to tell, call him/her/it
eháš (ADV, INTERJ) too much, exceedingly, more than one can handle (aggressive behavior)
ehą́ki (VI) 1) to reach or arrive at a certain point; 2) to be a certain age
ehą́'i (VI) to reach or arrive at a certain point
ejé'ena (ADV) or just, alone
éknaga (VT) to put it, place it down, to catch it
éknagu (VT) to take it back
ektá (ADV) at, to
ektášį (ADV) wrongly
én (ADV) here, in it
epcá; gepcá; gepcámį (PART) I think, it seems to me, apparently
éstena (ADV) early, soon, right away
eštá (CONJ) or, either
éti (VI) to camp
eyá (VI-IRR) to say it (*epá, ehá*)
éyabaha (N) hilltop announcer
éyagu (VT-Y) to take it
éyaš (CONJ) but, only, well, then (ADV) enough
eyés'a (N) chatterbox, blabbermouth

G

gá (DEM) that one over there
gábi (AUX) to be reluctant to, to hate doing
gaca (ENCL) as if
gacédu (VS) to be in such a way
gacén (ADV) about, approximately
gadódona (VT) to peck, shake it
gáǧa (VT) to make it
gaǧéǧe (VT) to sew it
gahą́du (VI) to be right there
gahágeȟi (ADV) that far, not so far off
gahóȟpa (VT) to cause someone to cough by hitting
gahómni (VT) to do a courting dance
gahómni wacíbi (N) round dance, courting dance
gaȟnéja (VT) to tear it by pressure, to rip open with one's weight
gaȟníha (VT) 1) to choose him/her/it; 2) to vote for him/her
gaȟnóga (VT) to make a hole by striking with an instrument
gaȟópa (N) canyon, ravine, valley
gáken (ADV) 1) in that way, in such a way; 2) immediately, right away
gakí (ADV) way over there, in a distant area
gakná (ADV) beside
gakní (VT) to bring back to him/her
gakókya (VT) to make a sound by hitting things together
gaksá (VT) to chop it off with a tool (e.g., hatchet)
gaksáksa (VT) to chop wood
gaktá (ADV) near that over there
gamímeya (ADV) in a circle
gamnéja (VT) to destroy it
gamnéza (VIMP) to be dawn
gamú (VT) to beat it, hit it (e.g., drum)
gamúbi (N) drum
gamúyabi (N) drumstick
gán (ADV) over there
ganá (DEM) those over there
gána; gą́na (VS) to be old
ganį́yą (ADV) direct
ganú (VT) to fan it
ganų́za (VIMP) to be windy

ganų́za tą́ga (VIMP) to be a gale wind
gapésto (VT) to shave, sharpen a point
gapsį́da (VT) to whip something
gaptúǧa (VT) to chip, crack it
gasní (VT) to put out with water, extinguish a fire by smothering, to cool it off (e.g., by shaking it)
gaškópa (VT) to bend it (i.e., permanently)
gašná (VT) to cut it with a tool (e.g., with scissors)
gašpá (VT) to open with an ax, tool
gašpábi (N) quarter (coin)
gašpábi okíse (N) dime (half a quarter)
gat'á (VT) to kill him/her/it by striking (e.g., as with a club)
gawós (PRO, DEM) those two yonder
gáya ~ gá ~ gáyabi (PART) they say, it is said
gazógic'ų (VI-IRR) to skate (*gazówec'ų, gazóyec'ų*)
gazógic'ų skáda (VI) to play hockey
gažó (VT) to whistle with it
gažóya (ADV) with a whistling sound
gažúžu (VT) to pay it off, pay for it (e.g., cheques, bills)
ga'éca (ADV) and then
ga'ų́spe (VT) to train an animal (with a tool, stick)
gibázo (VT) to show it to someone
gicí (POST) with another person or thing
gicí ecų́na (N) bet
gicí kpą́bi (N) twins
gicíkna'įškadabi (VI-REC) to tease one another
gicíksuyabi (VI-REC) to remember one another
gicíktena (VI-REC) to defeat one another
gicíza (VI-REC) to fight one another
gicó (VT-IRR) to invite, call him/her (*wéco, yéco*)
gicúni (VT-IRR) to quit an activity (*wécuni, yécuni*)
gic'ų (VPOS-IRR) to wear one's own thing (*wéc'ų, yéc'ų*)
gídąȟ (ADV) finally
gíjaǧa (VT-BEN) to make it for someone
gíjinową (VT-BEN) to sing for someone
gikmą́ (VT) to resemble him/her
gikną́; gikną́knąga (VT) to pamper, cuddle, sweet-talk to him/her/it
gikną́ga (VR) to save one's own, to cache for oneself
gikšúya (VT-IRR) to remember him/her/it (*wékšuya, yékšuya*)

giktá (VI-IRR) to get up (wékta, yékta)
gimą́mana; gimą́miną (N) butterfly, moth
giníhą (VI) to be afraid
giníja (PART) almost
gisníwįcayabi ecúbi (N) healing ceremony
gisníya (VT) to save or cure him/her from an illness
Gisúna (N) Asian
gisúna šúga (N) chow dog
gitána (ADV) a little bit, barely
gitézi (N) boy, lad, kids, brat (slang)
gitú (VPOS) to wear one's own over the shoulders
giyáwa (VT) to read to someone
gįyą́ (VI) to fly
gįyáyabi (N) airplane
gįyékiyabi (N) airplane, car (archaic)
góza (VI) to wave
gú (VI) to come back
gugúša (N) pig
gugúša šį (N) bacon
gúwa (INTERJ) Come!
gų́ (VT) to desire, wish for him/her/it

Ǧ

ǧí (VS) to be light yellow
ǧuǧúya (VT) to char, scorch it
ǧúmna (VI) to have a burnt smell
ǧuyá (VT) to brown, scorch it

H

há (N) skin, bag, any type of container (e.g., pouch, box)
hahána (VS) to be lively, excited
haȟníša (N) crybaby
haská(na) (N) white person
háu (INTERJ) hello
hayábi (N) clothes, costume, suit
hayábi owópetų (N) clothing store
há okmábi (N) birthmark, tattoo
hą́ (INTERJ) hello (ADV) yes
hą́ (VS) to be standing, be in place
hą́ba (N) moccasin
hą́ba ecúbi (N) moccasin game
hąbí (N) juice

hą́cogądu (ADV) midnight, middle of the night
háda (ADV) when (single occurrence)
hádahą (ADV) whenever (multiple occurrences)
hągágo (N) his sister-in-law
    mihágo "my sister-in-law"
    nihágo "your sister-in-law"
hągé (N) half
hąhébi (N) night
hąhébic'ehą (ADV) last night
hąhébi wanáǧi wówįcak'ubi (N) feed the night spirits ceremony
hąhébi wódabi (N) supper
hąhéyas'a (ADV) throughout the night, all night
hąkpáza (VIMP) it is evening, twilight
hąmáni (VI) to walk at night
hąnúni (VI) to get lost at night
háska (VS) to be long, tall
hąwácibi (N) women dance, night dance
hąwí (N) 1) moon, sun; 2) month
hąwígaǧabi (N) clock, timer
hąwísaba (N) lunar eclipse
hąwíyaba (N) moonlight
hąwí bapsú (N) wet moon, Cheshire moon (lit., moon pouring out)
hąwí cogą́du (N) half moon
hąwí hįnápa (N) sunrise
hąwí iyáya sába (N) eclipse (lit., sun turns black)
hąwí okíse (N) half moon
hąwí ozúna (N) full moon
hąwí togáhe oyášpe (N) quarter moon
hąwí ų́šį (VIMP) to be a night without a moon
hąwí waȟcá (N) sunflower
hąyáke (ADV) late morning
hąyákeji (ADV) tomorrow
hąyákena (ADV) morning
hąyákenaȟ (ADV) early morning
hąyákena cogą́du (ADV) mid-morning
hąyákena wódabi (N) breakfast
hąyákes'ą (ADV) throughout the morning, all morning
hą́'eyas'ą (ADV) throughout the night, all night
hą́'ųka (CONJ) and then (serves to link clauses or to end a sentence in storytelling)
he (PART) male interrogative

hé (N) horn
heȟága; heȟáge (N) elk
hékiška (N) mountain sheep, mountain goat
hékta (ADV) back then
héktam (ADV) behind
heyúką (VI) to have horns
hé'a (N) louse
hí (VI) to arrive here (N) tooth
hímaza (N) gold tooth
hinága (INTERJ) Wait!
hipépena (N) ant (lit., sharp teeth)
hiyá (ADV) no
hiyáya (VI-Y) to pass by
hiyú (VI) depart to come over here
hí įcáğa (VS) to be teething
hįcą́ (N) cattail
hįcą́hu (N) cattail stalk
hįhą́ (VIMP) to fall, come down
hįhą́ (N) 1) owl; 2) dove
hįhą́hana (N) pigmy owl
hįhą́są (N) snowy owl
hįhą́wapapana (N) barking owl
hįhą́ oȟnóga otís'a (N) burrowing owl (lit., hole dweller owl)
hįȟpáya (VI) to collapse, fall apart
híį (INTERJ) Oh my! (female speaker)
hį́kna; hį́k (CONJ) and
hįknágu (N) her husband
    mihį́kna "my husband"
    nihį́kna "your husband"
hįknátų (VT) to have a husband
hįknátųbi (N) marriage
hįknáya (VT) to marry him/her
hįnápa (VI) to appear
hįníga (VS) to be mean
hįšmą́ (VS) to have thick hair, fur
hó (N) voice (VS) to howl
hoğą́ (N) fish
hoğáğana (N) minnow
hoğámna (VI) to smell like fish
hoȟpá (VI) to cough
hoȟpí (N) nest
hók (ADV) yes (male speaker)
hokšína (N) boy

hokšína ohídi (N) superhero (lit., brave boy)
hokšíyuha (VI-Y) to give birth
hokún (ADV) down, below, downstairs
hokún daȟą́ (ADV) from below
hokún įjámna (VIMP) to be a ground blizzard
hokúwa (VI) to fish
homnáska (N) gold-eye fish
honáǧina ~ honáǧi (N) fly
honáǧinatotobi (N) blue fly
hopépe (N) perch, pike
hopútįȟį yuką́ (N) catfish
hotų́ (VI) to make a distinctive cry (e.g., any animal, coyote, bison, horse, etc.)
hotų́tų (VI) to neigh, to cackle
hú (N) leg, stem, stalk, wheel
húde (N) bottom of an object, basement, root
Hudéšana (N) Red Bottom Nakoda
huhú (N) bone, bones
Huhúžubina (N) Regina (place)
huȟnáǧa (VS) to be burnt
hukwáá; húk (INTERJ) male interjection for surprise, disinterest (e.g., For heaven's sake!; Oh my God! Ah! Not again!)
hústaga (VS) to be lean, skinny
huštéyagen (ADV) with a limp
hutká (N) root
hú mįmámina (N) wheel
hųgá (N) chief, king
hųgágebi (N) parents
hųgášicu (N) his/her female cousin
    mihų́gaši "my female cousin"
    nihų́gaši "your female cousin"
hųgóȟ'a (VS) to do a giveaway
hųgóȟ'abi (N) give away
húgu (N) his/her mother (reference)
    mihų́ "my mother"
    nihų́ "your mother"
húguya (VT) to have her as a mother
hųkwíyą; hųgáwį (N) queen
hų́n (ENCL) I wonder
hųská (N) pants, leggings
hųskána (N) stockings
hųskáto (Nn) jeans, denims
hųštá (PART) they say, it is said

Ȟ

-ȟ (SUF) intensifier, multiplier, adverbializer
-ȟtįyą (SUF) intensifier (desire, want, very)
ȟaȟá (VI) to be a liquid that flows
Ȟaȟátųwą (N) Gros Ventres, Atsina person or nation
ȟaȟúda (N) thread, rope
ȟeȟágana; ȟeȟágagana (N) spider
Ȟewáȟtųkta (N) Hidatsa
ȟeyám (ADV) in the back, behind
ȟmúyahą (VI) to be rumbling, buzzing (e.g., as a motor)
ȟní (VS) to have a sore
ȟníbi tága (N) cancer
ȟníya (VS) to have the chills
ȟnó (VI) to growl
ȟóda (VS) to be grey
ȟogá (N) badger
ȟpuȟpú (VS) to be scaly, rough, chapped
ȟtánihą (ADV) yesterday
ȟtayédu (ADV) evening
ȟubá wagíkna kagána (N) bat (mammal)
ȟubáhu (N) wing
ȟuȟnáȟya (VS) to burn, scorch
ȟuȟnáȟyabi ~ huȟnáȟyabi (N) coffee
ȟuȟnáȟyabi céǧa (N) coffee pot
ȟuȟúna (N) ghost, monster (i.e., invoked to scare kids)
ȟųwį́ (VS) to be rotten
ȟ'ą́ (VS) to behave, act

I

í (N) mouth
í (VI) to arrive there
íbutaga (VT) to kiss him/her/it
iná (VOC) Mother! (N) my mother (also *mi'ína*)
inána (N) my aunt (mother's sister)
Iná maká (N) Mother Earth
Iná waką́ (N) Holy Mary
inína (ADV) quietly
íšagiya (N) lipstick
ítutu (VS) to have a slobbering mouth
íyabiza (VT-Y) to smooch him/her, to kiss producing a loud sound
iyágipe (VT) to wait for him/her
iyáȟpaya (VT) to grab it with force
iyáksamkiya (VT) to train it (e.g., horse)
iyám (ADV) against, along
iyáme í (VI) to be gone hunting
iyáme iyáya (VI-Y) to go hunting
iyáni (VT) to climb on it
iyáya (VS-AUX) to gradually become
iyáya (VI-Y) to leave, set to go
iyážo (N) whistle, eagle bone whistle
iyážok'įbi (N) whistle carrier
iyá'ųba (VT) to accuse, blame him/her
iyécįga (ADV) on its own
iyécįgayena; iyécįga(na); iyécįgena (N) car
iyégijiska (VT) to translate for him/her
iyégiya (VPOS) to find one's own
iyéȟ (PRO) he himself, she herself, they themselves
iyéȟabi (PRO) they themselves
iyéska (VI) to interpret, converse
iyéska; iyéskabi (N) interpreter, announcer
iyéš (PRO) him/her (as opposed to somebody else, e.g., it/they on the other hand)
iyéya (VT) to find it
iyódąga (VI-Y) to sit down
iyódiyegiya (VI) to be miserable
iyógapte; ogápte (N) plate, dish, shell, dipper
iyógapte škóba (N) bowl
iyógaptopi (N) cupboard
iyógipišį (VT) to be displeased about him/her/it
iyógipiya (VT) to make him/her happy
iyók'įba (N) cradleboard
iyópegiciyabi (VREC) to berate, reprove, attack one another verbally
iyópeya (VT) to scold, reprove him/her
iyópiya (VS) to be happy, pleased, merry
iyópsija (VI) to jump
iyóptayą (ADV) towards
iyúhana; iyúha (ADV) all, all of them
iyútą (VT-Y) to try it, to try it on (e.g., clothes, task)
izį́mna (VI) to have a burnt smell
izį́tkiya (VI) to burn incense for a ritual, a smudge
i'á; iyá (VI, VT) to talk, speak; to talk, speak to him/her/it

i'ábi (N) rumors
I'ášijana; I'ášija; I'ásija (N) Chippewa, Saulteaux, German, Ukrainian, French

Į

į́ (VT) to wear it on the shoulder
įbáhį (N) pillow
įbásise (N) needle
įbíǧa (VI) to boil
įbíȟya (VT) to boil it
įcáǧa (VS) to grow up
įcápa (VT) to pierce, stab it
įcápe (N) fork
įcáyukse (N) saw
įcéte (N) rim
įc'íknaya (VR) to fool oneself
įc'íyuǧa (VR) to ask for oneself
įdáziba (N) bow
įdé (N) face
įdéȟnoga (N) pumpkin
įdé'įbakįda (N) towel
įdóba (NUM) fourth
įdómni (VS) to be dizzy
įdú (ADV) only, just, simply
įdúgam (ADV) backwards, leaning back
įdúka (VS) to be hungry
įdúya (ADV) for no reason, for nothing
įdú wiǧá hąwí (N) May
įgámu (N) drumstick
įgázo (N) skate
įhágam (ADV) after
įhágapa (VS) to be younger than
Įháktųwąna (N) Sioux (Dakota)
į́hokun (ADV) underneath something
įhų́ (INTERJ) exclamation of surprise
įȟá (VT, VI) to laugh at, to laugh
įȟá'įc'iya; įȟé'įc'iya (VR) to smile, grin, laugh at oneself
įȟpégiciyabi (VI-RECIP) to divorce from one another
įȟpéya (VT) 1) to discard, throw him/her/it away; 2) to leave him/her/it behind, alone; 3) to banish him/her
įjáhiya (VT) to blend it, mix it together
įjáȟabe (N) whip
įjáȟabe wįca (N) whipman
įjáȟtąge (N) tattooing, vaccination needle
įjámna (VIMP) to be a blizzard
įjánu (N) fan
įjáše (N) button
įjáška (VT) to tie with, to tie a knot, to tie it on
įjášna (N) scissors
įjída (ADV) above
įjídoba (NUM) fourth
įjíma (ADV) next time
įjínapcuwąga (NUM) ninth
įjínažį (VI) to stand above
įjíšaknoǧą (NUM) eighth
įjíšakpe (NUM) sixth
įjítoką (ADV) different when compared to
įjíwikcemna (NUM) tenth
įjíwikcemna šákpe (NUM) sixtieth
įjíyuha (ADV) entire, whole thing
įjí'agezaptą (NUM) fifteenth
įjú (VOC) Grandmother
įjú (VI) to smoke
įką́ (N) reins
įkcé (ADV) common
įkcéya (ADV) in a common way
įkcé wįcášta (N) Indigenous person
įkcé zizíbena (N) cotton
įkíya (VT) to make him/her wear it on the shoulders
įkmų́ (N) lynx
įkmų́na (N) bobcat
įkmų́tąga (N) mountain lion
įkníya (VT) to come to observe, to investigate it
įknúdašį (VI) to disrespect oneself, to be stupid
įknúhana (ADV) suddenly
įknúhąhana (ADV) occasionally, one of these days
įknúkcą (VT) to think of one's own
įknúš'aga (VS) to be pregnant
įknúžaža (VR) to bathe oneself
įknúžužu (VR) to undress oneself
įknúza (VR) to dress oneself properly
įkóyakya (VT) to tie, harness, join it together
įkpá (N) tip, point
įkpákįda (VR) to wipe oneself
į́ksapya (VT) to annoy him/her

íkšukšuna (N) bean
iktómi (VS, N) 1) to be a liar; 2) trickster
iktų́skiya (PR, OM); **įtkų́skiya** (CTK) (VT) to finish, complete a task
iktų́yą yįgá (VI-N) to be a flame
iktų́ža (VS) to be drunk
ik'ú (N) chin
ik'úhį (N) hair under the chin of a buffalo
ik'ú háska (N) mountain goat (lit., long chin)
íkusana (N) mink
imą́ka gaksá (N) farming disk
imóȟtaga (VI) to bump, crash into it
imóȟtage (N) bumper
inázam; nazám (ADV) in the back of it
inázapadahą (ADV) from the back, from behind
ináži (VI) to stop
iní (VI) to do, go into a sweat lodge
iníbi (N) sweat lodge, sweat bath
ipáȟte (N) bridle
ípi (VS) to be full, sated
ipíya (VT) to sate, fill him/her/it
ipíyaga (N) belt
ipíyaga iją́šeye (N) belt buckle
ipí'įcíya (VR) to sate oneself
ispá (N) elbow
istó (N) arm
íš (PRO) he/she/it/they too, it is he/she/it/they; also
išną́na (PRO; VI-N) 1) single one, alone, by oneself; 2) to be alone (*mįšną́na* "I'm alone," *nįšną́na* "you're alone")
išną́n ų́ (VI, N) 1) to be alone; 2) bachelor
išną́ti (VI) to have menses (lit., to live alone)
ištá (N) eye
Ištágitų Tí (N) Indian Head (town)
ištáǧuǧa (VS) to be blind
ištáhį (N) eyelash
ištásaba (VS) to have black eyes (N) raccoon
ištáyabi (N) eyeglasses
ištáyabi sába (N) sunglasses
ištá gašpábi (N) blindfold
ištá ȟniȟní (VS) to have gummy eyes
ištá kmųkmų́za (VI) to blink repetitively
ištá kmų́za (VI) to blink
ištá kpá (VS) to be blind
ištá ogášpa (VT) to blindfold him/her
ištá ogíkma (N) mascara
ištéja (VS) to be bashful
iští (N) lower lip
ištíma (VI-N) to be asleep
ištípaȟte (N) Indian bridle
itáca (N) leader
ité (N) forehead
itkú (PR, OM); **įktú** (CTK) (VS) to be lit, in flames
itó (INTERJ) now, well
itógam (ADV) in the lead, in front, ahead
itúgasą (N) weasel
itúšį (VI) to lie, not to tell the truth
iwábamnaya (N) iron (i.e., for clothes)
iwáką (VI, N) 1) to be an expert; 2) expert
iwáštena (ADV) slowly, carefully
iwátape (N) horse used in buffalo hunting
iwátokšu; otókšu; tokšú (N) truck (e.g., pick-up truck)
iwátokšu tága (N) truck (e.g., trailer van)
iwą́knage (N) window, mirror
iwáyage (N) gunsight
iwą́žikte (N) first kill ceremony
iwikcémna šákpe (NUM) sixtieth
iwócape (N) long fork stick used to fork up puppy meat in the kettle dance
iwúga; iyúga (VT-N) to go to bed
iwúǧa; iyúǧa (VT-N) to ask it to him/her
íyą (N) stone
iyága (VI-Y) to run
iyáȟe; iyáȟe (N) mountain, hill
íyą oyáde (N) Stone nation
iyókšu (N) cartridge
iyúhibi (N) tobacco mixture used in ceremonies
iyúkcą (VI-Y) to think about him/her/it
iyúškį (VT-Y) to admire him/her
iyúšpe (N) key
iyúweǧa (VT) to cross something on the way there (N) crossing place
iyúžaža (N) soap
iyúžažamno (N) laundry soap
iyúga; iwúga (VT-N) to go to bed
iyúǧa; iwúǧa (VT-N) to ask him/her

įʼágam (ADV) over it
įʼágezaptą (NUM) fifteenth
įʼáni (N) ladder
įʼíjuna (N) cup
įʼútų (VT) to paint it
įʼútų įwókma (N) crayon

J

jé (PART) always, habitually
jéʼe (PART) agency, continuous action
jónana (QUANT) a small portion, a little
jukʼána (VS) to be small, narrow
júsina (VS) to be small
juwįna (N) sandpiper

K

ká (VT) to mean, indicate him/her/it
káda (VS) to be hot, feverish
kangíya (VR) to heat up one's own
kapéya (VI) to pass it, go beyond, to be more than
ką́ (N) gristle, muscle
Ką́ǧí Tóga (N) Crow person or nation
kąyútiba (VS) to have cramps; to suffer from epilepsy
keyá (N) snapping turtle
kibážį (VT) to be against him/her, jealous of him/her
kįkná (VI) to leave home
kiškána (N) spoon
kiškána tága (N) ladle
kišné (N) lover, boyfriend
kišnéya (VT) to love him/her/it
kiyą́na (ADV) close, near, approaching
kíza (VT) to fight him/her/it
knapá (VR) to put it in one's mouth
knaškíya (VS) to be insane, wild
knéba (VI) to vomit
kneknéǧa (VS) to be spotted
kní (VI) to return, to go home
knuhá (VPOS) to keep, have one's own
knúkʼeǧa (VR) to scratch oneself
knuksá (VPOS) to cut one's hair
knušnóga (VPOS) to take off one's own
knuštą́ (VPOS) to finish one's own; to finish it

knužáža (VPOS) to bathe one's own thing
kó (CONJ) also, and (ENCL) intensifier (irony, amazement; e.g., Hįįį aʼámna kó! "Oh! They are all mouldy too!")
kogípa (VT) to fear him/her/it
kókhįkna (VT) to make a clicking sound
koktóbawįǧe (N) thousand
košká̧ (N) young man (VS) to be a young man
koyákya (VT) to connect, fasten to it, hang it
kpakcá (VPOS) to comb one's hair
kpási (VPOS) to drive one's vehicle
ksahą́ (VS) to be broken
ksugíya (VT) to hurt because of him/her/it
ksuyá (VT) to hurt him/her/it
ktá (VS) to be heavy
kté (VT) to kill him/her/it
kténa (VT) to cheat, beat him/her (e.g., in a game)
kténasʼa (N) cheater
Ktusyą́ (N) Wolseley (town)
ktų́šya ų́ (VI) to be mentally ill
ktų́ža (VS) to be drunk
kudé (VT) to shoot it
kudína (ADV) low
kún (ADV) down
kušícu ~ kų́gisiktu (N) (his/her) grandmother
    mikúši "my grandmother"
    nikúši "your grandmother"
kušícu tága (N) his/her great-grandmother
kuwá (VT) to chase, to go after him/her/it
kuwága (VT) to court him/her
kʼį́ (VT) to carry it
kʼú (VT) to give it to him/her/it

L

Lakóta (N) Lakota person or nation

M

m (ENCL) imperative plural (female speaker)
magá (N) skunk
mağážu (VIMP) to be raining (N) rain
mağážu įkmúga (N) rainbow
mağážu waką́ (VIMP) to be a hot summer drizzling
mahén (POST) in, into, inside, inward, under

mahén hųskána (N) underclothes
mahén úbi (N) underwear
mahpíya (N) 1) sky, cloud; 2) heaven
mahpíyato (VIMP, N) 1) to be a blue sky; 2) blue sky; 3) Arapaho person or nation
mahpíya agícida (N) air force soldier
mah'ú (VT) to peel it
maká; mąká (N) earth, soil, dust
makáhasaba (N) coal
makámahen (N) basement, den
makáto (N) clay
makóce (N) land, territory, ground
makóce agícida (N) ground soldier
makóce wídaya (N) strait (lit., land-island like)
makóšija (N) badlands
maksá (VT) to cut off something with a knife or something sharp
makú (N) chest
makúša; cątkúša (N) robin
makú iyúskice (N) brassiere
maní (VS) to walk
manú (VT) to steal it
maskádo (VT) to pound metal (N) blacksmith
maskámna (VI) to earn money
mastúga (VS) to be rich, wealthy
maswícak'ubi ába (N) Treaty Day
mas'ápa (VT) to telephone him/her (N) telephone
mas'ápabi (N) telegraph
mas'íyapa (N) hammer
mas'íyapa tága (N) sledge hammer
mas'ówąyaga (N) bank
maškída (VT) to cut it
maštá (VIMP) to be a hot day
maštíja (N) rabbit, hare
maštíjatąga (N) jackrabbit
maštíja oyáde (N) Cree tribe
mató (N) black bear
Matóska (N) White Bear person or nation
mayá (N) ground, cliff, butte
mayátąga (N) mountain
mayáwašiju ~ mayášiju (N) little people, cave people (mythic being)
máza (N) iron; metal
mázagiyą (N) airplane

mázakada (N) hot metal
mázaska (N) money
mázaska éknąga (VT) to bet on it, put money on it
mázaska hągé (N) fifty cents
mázaska tíbi (N) bank
mázasni (N) cold metal
mázaša (N) penny
mázawada (N) train
máza'i (N) gun muzzle
máza'ocągu (N) train track
mąká; maká (N) earth, soil
mąkázi (N) sand
mąkíyutabi (N) kilometre
mąkóhnoga ~ makóhnoga (N) cave
mąkóškąšką (N) earthquake (short form for *mąkócoškąšką*)
mąs'ípahte (N) bridle and bit
Mikúši Makóce (N) Grandmother Earth
mína (N) knife
minátkes'a (N) drunkard (short form for *miníyatkes'a*)
miní (N) water
miní abápsųbi (N) baptism
miní agícida (N) navy soldier
miní iyáya (N) flood
miní it'á áya (VS) to be thirsty (lit., to be starting to die for water)
miní ot'á (VS) to drown
miníhaha (N) waterfall
minískuya (N) soda pop
miníšaša (N) wine
minítąga (N) lake
miníwaką (N) whiskey
miníyatką (VT-Y) to drink alcohol
miní'įbiǧa ~ miníbiǧa (N) beer
miyáde ~ mi'áde (N) my father
miyé (PRO) myself, it is I, I do
miyéh (PRO) myself specifically
miyéš (PRO) I as opposed to somebody else
miyéšį (PRO) it is not I
mįmá (VS) to be round
mįméya (ADV) round
mįméya wacíbi (N) round dance
míš (PRO) me too

mnaská (VS) to be flat
mnayą́ (VT, VI) 1) to collect it; 2) to be grouped
mnéza (VS) to be clear, pure, transparent
mnícağa (N) frozen water
mnihą́ (VS) to be strong
mnihé įc'íya (VR) to have courage in oneself
mníjahomni (N) windmill
mníkada (N) hot water
mnik'ábi (N) water well
mnísni (N) cold water
mniwája (N) sea, ocean
mnįp'ú (N) heron
mnóga (N) male buffalo
mnógedu (N) summer
mnogés'ą (ADV) throughout the summer, all summer
mnowága (N) water monster, said to create landslides (short form of *mniwáwąga*)
mocéğ'a (VS) to be greedy, cheeky, disrespectful
modą́ (VT) to bump against someone
mokpékna (ADV) direct
múhįkna (VI) to be a heavy sound (e.g., like a boom)

N

nagíȟma (VPOS) to hide one's own thing
nağí (N) spirit (i.e., unknown one)
nahą́nįštaš (PART) I wonder, I wish
nahą́ȟ (ADV) still, yet
naȟmá (VT) to hide him/her/it
naȟnóga (VT) to make a hole by kicking
naȟtága (VT) to kick him/her/it, to kick it to death
naȟ'ų́ (VT) 1) to hear, listen to him/her; 2) to obey him/her
naȟ'ų́šį (VS) to be deaf
nakmį́kmąbi (N) bicycle
Nakóda (N) Nakoda person or nation (VS) to be Nakoda
nakón- (PREF) related to the Nakoda
nakónįc'ina (VR) to behave like a Nakoda
nakón-iyabi ~ nakón-iya (N) Nakoda language
nakón-i'a (VI) to speak Nakoda
nakón-i'e (N) Nakoda word
nakón-wįcoȟ'ąge (N) Nakoda custom
nakón-wįco'i'e (N) Nakoda word
naksá (VT) to break it forcefully (e.g., with the foot or by pressure)
namú (VI) to make a loud sound with the foot
napá (VI) to flee, to retreat
napcá (VI) to swallow
napcó (N) upper arm
napcúwąga (NUM) nine
napcúwągana (NUM) only nine
napéšį (N) No Retreat Society
napsíja (VT) to kick something
nap'į́ (VT) to wear it on the neck
nasú (N) brain
naškóba (VT-Y) to bend it by body, foot pressure
natága (VT) to close it; a force closes it (e.g., wind)
nat'á (VT) to kick, to trample him/her/it to death
nazúda (VT) to wear it down
nážį (VI) to stand up
nąbát'a (VS) to have a numb hand
nąbáwąge įjínuba (N) middle finger
nąbáwąge įjíwažį (N) index finger
nąbáwąge įjíyamni (N) ring finger
nąbáwąhuge tága (N) thumb
nąbé (N) hand
nąbé catkána (N) left hand
nąbé gamúbi (N) hand drum
nąbé gaská (VI) to clasp one's hands together
nąbé škádabi (N) hand game
nąbíkpa (N) gloves
nąbímna (VS) to be delicious, sweet
nąbó'ųšna (N) thimble
nądáboğa (VS) to be bloated, swollen
nądáboğ'įc'iya (VS) to puff oneself up (e.g., frog)
nągáhą; nahą́ (ADV) now
nągáhąȟ; nągáȟ (ADV) right now, right away
nągú (CONJ) and (ADV) more, again
nąkáda (VI) to become hot (i.e., by itself, internal force)
nąpsíhu (N) finger
nąpsíhušage (N) fingernail
nąpsíhu hąwí akída (N) clock
nąšpá (VT) to open up forcefully with the foot
ną́įtkuya (VS) to start a fire, to light it up
né (DEM) this

néca (VS) to be this kind
nécedu (VS) to be like this (ADV) in this way
nécen (ADV) in this way
néci (ADV) around here
nedáhą (ADV) from here
néhą (ADV) at this time, now
nehą́kta (ADV) to be happening
nekšíco (N) his/her uncle (mother's brother)
    minékši "my uncle"
    ninékši "your uncle"
nén (ADV) here
nená (DEM) these here
newós (PRO) these two
néža (VI) to urinate (N) urine
nežémna (VS) to smell urine
ní (VI) to be alive
niǧá ~ niǧé (N) tripe, stomach
niǧé yazą́ (VS) to have a stomach ache
nína (ADV) really, very
niskó (ADV) this much
niyá (VI) to breathe
niyáhą ų́ (VI) to be living
niyáwašte (VI) to be in good health
niyé (PRO) yourself, it is you
niyéȟ (PRO) you yourself
niyéš (PRO) you as opposed to somebody else
niyéšį (PRO) it is not you, not you
nį́š (PRO) you too
no (ENCL) male declarative
nodé (N) throat
nodéhą (VS) to be greedy
nodį́t'a (VS) to be hungry, to starve
nówa (PRO) all these
nową́ (VI) to sing
nową́s'a (N) singer
núda (VS) red, scarlet
núǧe (N) ear
núǧe kpá (VS) to be deaf
nuní (VI) to be lost
núzahą (VI) to be fast
núba ~ nųm (NUM) two
núbabi (N) twins
núbagiya (ADV) two by two
nųbáȟ basísa (VT) to double stitch it

nų́mnana (NUM) only two
nųpį́; nųpín (PRO) both
nų́ške (INTERJ) uh! (hesitation marker)
nųwą́ (VI) to swim

O

obásisa (VT) to sew it on
obáwįǧe (NUM) hundred
ocábaza (N) pasture
ocágu (N) road, path, street
ocáguȟe (N) gravel road
ocágusaba (N) paved road
ocágutąga (N) highway
ocágu ceskámaza (N) highway patrol
océti (N) fireplace, hearth, stove, oven
océti awą́yaga (N) firekeeper
océti waką́ (N) microwave
óda (VS) to be many
ogáȟci (N) fringe
ogáȟniǧa (VT) to understand her/him/it
ogíciya (VI) to help each other
ogíciza (N) battle
ogíhi (VT, AUX) to be able to do it
ogíhišį (VI) to be weak
ogíjine (VT) to hunt for him/her
ogíjinoda (VT) to borrow it for someone else
ogíjiyaga (VT) to tell it for someone else
ogínoda (VT) to borrow it from someone
ogípi (VS) to be happy
ógiya (VT) to help him/her
ógiyabi (N) helper
ogíyaga (VT) to tell it to him/her
ógiyes'a (N) servant
oǧų́ǧa (VS) to be awake, waking up
óhą (ADV) among, in the middle, in it
ohą́ (VT) to wear footwear
ohą́ (VT) to cook it by boiling
ohídiga (VS) to be fearless, brave
ohídiga'įc'ina (VR) to figure one is fearless, brave
ohíya (VT) to win a game, a contest
ohóna (VT) to respect, honour him/her
oȟnáte (ADV) in between
oȟnóga (N) hole
oȟnóȟnoga (VS) to be full of holes

oh'áge (VS) to behave, act as such
oh'áko (VS) to be swift, fast
oká (ADV) even though
okáda (VIMP) to be hot inside
okíse (N) half
okmá (VT) to write, draw, paint it
okná (ADV) through, in
oknága (VR) 1) to tell for oneself; 2) confess oneself
oknága (VT) to put it away, in it
ókne (N) sleeve
ókneša (N) Royal Canadian Mounted Police
ókšą (ADV) around
okúwawašte; okúwašte (VS) to be tamed
omá (PRO) the other one
Omáha wacíbi (N) Omaha dance
omáka (N) year
omákateja (N) New Year's Day
omákawąži (ADV) annually
omáka'es'ą (ADV) throughout the year, all year
ománi (VI) to go for a walk
ómna (VT) to smell it (N) smell
omníjiye (N) meeting
omníjiye tága (N) conference
oná (N) prairie fire
onáhmą (N) secret
oné (VT) to look for it
oní (N) life
onįkte wací (VI-N) 1) to be meek, submissive; 2) to be a coward
onóda (VT) to borrow it
onówą (N) song
ópa (VT) to be part of it
opéšį (VT) to disqualify him/her
opétų (VT) to buy, purchase it
opí'įc'iya (VR) to behave, busy oneself
osąk-kta (VI) to be lonesome
osąkya; o'ósąkya (ADV) lonely, in a lonesome way
osmága (N) coulee
osní (VIMP) to be cold weather
Osní Wįcášta (N) Northern Nakoda group/ division
osnóhya (VT) to understand it
ošíjeja (VI) to be a storm

oškáda (N) playground
oškáde (N) picnic
ošódemna (VS) to smell like smoke
oštéga (VS) to be peculiar, odd, weird
ótana (ADV) straight, in a straight manner
otí (N) dwelling
otígadodo (N) broom
otí'įga; otíga (PART) it seems, apparently
otóką (ADV) different, differently, unusual
otúwe (N) city
otúweda (N) abandoned camp
ot'į apá (VIMP) to be a thunderclap
owá (QUANT) all
owácegiye ~ owácegiya (N) church
owácegiye tíbi (N) church
owáštena (ADV) slowly, carefully, with ease
owáštenagen (ADV) rather slowly
owáyaco (N) court of law
owáyak (ADV) nice, beautiful to look at
owáyawa (N) school
owáyawa otókšu (N) school bus
owáyušnoge (N) threshing machine
owáyužažabi (N) laundry
owá'okma ~ owó'okma (N) pencil
owąhįkna (VIMP) to be lightning (N) 1) electricity; 2) flashlight
owįcagaške (N) jail
owįcagaške awáyage (N) prison guard
owįcanebi (N) hunter
owįduka tíbi ~ owįduka (N) toilet
owįža (N) quilt, bedding sheet, blanket
owóde tíbi (N) restaurant
owókšubi (N) garden, planted area
owópetų (N) store
owópiye (N) cemetery
owúga (N) bed
oyáboda (VT) to shred it
oyáde (N) tribe, people, nation
oyága (VT-Y) to announce, tell it to him/her
oyák'ų ~ oyą́ku (N) socks, stockings
oyátaga (VS) to be stuck after being inserted, to get stuck while going out
oyúnwašte (VI) to taste good
ozį́kta ~ ozį́kta tága (N) tomato

ožúna (VI) to be full
o'énaži (N) town
o'éti (N) camping place, campsite
o'étibi (N) powwow
o'į́ (N) beads
o'į́knužaža (N) bathroom
o'óknage (N) fable, tale

P

pá (N) head
páda (VT) to butcher it
pağų́da (N) duck
pağų́dasaba (N) black duck
pahá (N) hair
pahá įbákca (N) hairbrush, comb
pahásapsaba (VS) to have black hair
paháskaskana; paháska (VS) to have white hair
pahá éyagu (VT) to scalp somebody
pahá gašnábi (N) haircut
pahá wamnúška (N) louse
pahį́ (N) porcupine
paȟní (N) snot, mucous
paȟtá (VT) to tie up
Pámnaska (N) Flathead person or nation
Panána (N) Arikara, Pawnee person or nation
Pásaba (N) Blackhead (personal name)
pasú (N) beak
pasú agástaga (N) turkey
Pasú Oȟnóga (N) Nez Perce person or nation
pašéja (N) dried-up skull
patkášina (N) slough turtle
pat'á (N) stupid person (lit., dead head)
payážą (VI) to have a headache
pá oȟnóȟnoga (VI) to be crazy (lit., a head full of holes)
pąğí (N) potato
pąšpážena (VS) to be soft, downy
pąžéna (VS) to be soft
pé (N) top of the head
péda (N) fire, matches
pedáğa (N) ember, charcoal
pedį́žąžą (N) oil lantern
peháğina (N) crane
péna (VS) to be sharp

penyúza (N) parhelion, sun dog
pésto (VS) to be a sharp point
péstona (VS) to be pointed
péšna (VS) to be bald
peží (N) hay
pežíȟoda (N) sage
pežíto (VI) to be grass green
pežíya amíknąk wací (N) grass dance
peží wįtkó (N) marijuana
pežúta éyagu ecúbi (N) medicine ceremony
pežúta tíbi (N) hospital, clinic
pežúta wįcášta (N) doctor
pigíciya (VI) to make one's bed
píȟpiğana (N) carrot
piȟyá (VI) to be a loud sound
piȟyáhą (VI) to be noisy
pináya (VT) to give thanks, to please him/her
piyá (VT) to bury him/her/it
piyá (VT) to make a bed
piyá (ADV) anew, again, in a different location
pi'écų (VT-N) to fix it
póğe (N) nose
psį́ (N) rice, wild rice
pšopšó (VI) to be baggy
ptą́ (N) otter
ptąyédu (N) fall
ptąyés'ą (ADV) throughout the fall, all fall
pté (N) buffalo cow, herd
ptecíjana (N) calf
ptecónica (N) dry buffalo meat
ptéğa (N) slough, lake
ptehá (N) buffalo hide
ptéjena (VS) to be short
ptemnóga (N) bull
ptewánu (N) cattle, domestic cow
ptewį́yena (N) cow
pudé (N) upper lip

S

sába (VS) to be black
sága (VS) to be dry, hard
sakím (ADV) together
Sakná (N) Metis, Frenchman
sakyábi (VT) to dry it

sakyé (N) cane
sám ~ sąm (POST) beyond, over (contraction of *sápa*)
są (VS) to be beige, faded
sąksája (N) dress
sąní (ADV) single, one side
sewímna (VI) to be a rancid smell
sicóna (ADV) barefoot
sicúha (N) foot sole
sihá (N) foot
Sihásaba (N) Blackfoot person or nation
siháškoba (N) club foot
sihú (N) bone of the lower leg
síja (VS) to be bad
sijáya (ADV) badly
síjecų (VT) to do something bad
siką́ (N) ankle
sikąsaba (N) blackleg disease
sipá (N) toes
sipášage (N) toenail
sipátąga (N) big toe
sit'át'a (VS) to have a numb foot
sįdé (N) tail
sįdégoskoza (N) mule deer
sįdésaba (N) blacktail deer
sįdéšana (N) red fox
skána (VS) to be white
skúya (VS) to be sweet
skúyemna (VI) to be a sweet smell
snągíya (VI) to grease, to anoint
sní (VS) to be cold
snohéna (N) snake
Snohéna Wįcášta (N) Shoshone person or nation
snokyá ~ snohyá; (VT) to know him/her/it
spą́ (VI) to be damp
stéya (ENCL) it seems like
stustá (VS) to be tired
stustáya (VT) to tire him/her/it
sú (N) seed, bullet, pellet
súda (VS) to be hard
susméja (N) dragonfly
susú (N) testicles
susú éyagu (VT) to castrate a male animal
susú éyagubi (N) castrated male
susú maksá (VI) to castrate a male animal
sųgágu (N) his/her younger brother
    misúga "my younger brother"
    nisúga "your younger brother"
sųkpé (N) muskrat
-s'a (ENCL) habitual
s'ámna (VS) to stink

Š

šá (VI) to be red
šagé (N) nail, hoof, claw
šagíya (VT) to redden it
Šahíya (N) Cree person or nation
Šahíya wašíju (N) Gros Ventres person or nation
Šahíyena (N) Cheyenne person or nation
Šahíyeskąbi (N) Piapot Cree person or nation
šah̃íyą (N) vagina
šaknóǧą (NUM) eight
šaknóǧąna (NUM) only seven
šákpe (NUM) six
šakpéȟ (ADV) six times
šákpena (NUM) only six
šašá (VS) to be fat
šašána (VS) to be orange
šašté (N) little finger
ša'įmna (VI) to be pink
šéba (N) dark coloured person
šéja (VS) to be dried
šic'éšicu (N) her male cousin
    mišíc'eši "my male cousin"
    nišíc'eši "your female cousin"
šic'étku (N) her brother-in-law
    mišíc'e "my brother-in-law"
    nišíc'e "your brother-in-law"
šiȟ'ą́ (N) beast
šijépągu (N) her sister-in-law
    mišíjepą "my sister-in-law"
    nišíjepą "your sister-in-law"
šijépąšicu (N) her female cousin
    mišíjepąši "my female cousin"
    nišíjepąši "your female cousin"
šikná (VI) to be mad, angry
šiná (N) blanket
šinágaȟci (N) shawl

šinásaba wįcáwaką (N) priest
šiyágo (N) boil
-šį (ENCL) negation
šįtú (VS) to be fat
škáda (VI) to play
škašká (VS) to be crooked, curved, wavy
šká (VI) to do, try, move, feel
škášį (VI) to be calm, still, quiet
škášį yįgá (VI-N) to sit still
škąšką́ (VS) to move by inner force, to shake
škóbá (VS) to be hollowed out
škóbena (VS) to be slightly crooked
škobyá (ADV) in a crooked, curved shape
škoškóbena (N) banana
šmá (VS) to be deep (e.g., water)
šmúwąga (VS) to be dripping
šnašnána (N) bells
šna'íyą; šnayą́ (ADV) clearly
šnušnúda (VS) to be slippery
šóda (N) smoke
šóga (VS) to be thick
šošéna (N) waterfall
špąyą́ (VT) 1) to cook, bake it; 2) to brand a horse, cow
Špe'óna (N) Mexican, Spaniard
štén (CONJ) if, when
štúnya (VT) to thaw, defrost it
štuštá (VS) to be salty, to have a salty flavor
štušténa (N) salt
šubé (N) guts, intestines
šų́; wíyaga šų́ (N) longest feathers on the wing
šų́ga (N) dog
šųgámna (VI) to smell like a dog
šųgána (N) old horse
šųgašána (N) red fox
šų́gatąga (N) horse
šų́gawį (N) female dog, bitch (*vulgar*)
šų́ga káda (N) hot dog
šųȟpéna (N) colt
šųkcíjana (N) puppy
šųkcíjana woháp̨i ecúbi (N) puppy ceremony
šųkcúk'ana (N) coyote
šųkhéyuke (N) sheep
šųkhíša (N) bay horse, red horse

šųkhį́to (N) blue horse
šųkhį́tokneška (N) straight-eyed horse, blue roan horse
šųkhótųtų (VS) 1) to be howling (e.g., wolf, coyote, dog); 2) to be neighing (e.g., horse)
šųkknékneǧa (N) pinto, spotted horse
šųkmánų (VI) to steal horses
šųkmnóga (N) stallion
šųknį́deska (N) Appaloosa horse
šųksába (N) black horse
šųksíhamaza (N) horseshoe
šųksį́deksa (N) bobtail horse
šųkskósko (N) mangy horse
šųkšká (N) white horse
šųkšóšona; šųkšóšo; šúšubina; šųkšúšu (N) mule, donkey
šųkšpáya (N) horse brand
šųktáwap'i (N) horse collar
šųktí (N) barn, stable
šųktógeja (N) wolf
šųktúske (N) stunt horse
šųkwáci (N) horse dance
šųkwágic'į (N) pack animal
šųkwíyena (N) mare
šųkwį́caȟtįyąną (N) old stallion
šųkzí (N) buckskin horse
šųk'áktagabi (N) horse race
šųk'ápeskana (N) palomino horse
šųk'íjapšįde (N) horse whip
šųk'į́kiya (VT) to gallop a horse
šųk'į́koyakya (VI) to harness a horse
šųk'ókuwasije (N) bronco

T

tá (N) ruminant, moose
tába (N) ball
tábapabi (N) baseball bat
tabéda (N) animal's back
tabéȟ'a hąwí (N) April
tabéȟ'a ~ tabáȟ'a (N) frog
tacá (N) body, carcass
tacá įknúžaža (VR) to bathe one's body
tacą́kįyutabi (N) foot (unit of measurement)
tacéwaknąga (N) flag

tacúba (N) marrow
tacúba ába (N) Friday
tadé (N) wind
tadéyąba; tadé'ąba (VIMP) to be a windy day
tadé omní tága (N) whirlwind
tagúšaša (N) buffalo berries
tahá (N) deer, moose, elk skin
taháçu (N) his/her brother-in-law
tahášicu (N) his/her male cousin
    mitáhąši "my male cousin"
    nitáhąši "your male cousin"
tahíha (N) breath, air
tahíšpa (N) awl
tahíšpajuk'ána (N) sewing needle
tahósoga (N) neck
tahú (N) neck, nape of the neck
tahȟáge (N) knee
tahȟágena (N) kneecap
táhȟca (N) deer
tahȟcámnoga (N) stag
tahȟcíjana (N) herd of deer
Tahȟé (N) Moose Mountain (place)
taká (N) deer, moose gristle
takónagu (N) his friend
    mitákona "my friend"
    nitákona "your friend"
takóžakpagu (N) his/her grandchild
    mitákoža "my grandchild"
    nitákoža "your grandchild"
takpéya (VT) to charge, run against, attack him/her/it
tamní (N) placenta
tanó (N) meat, flesh
tanóyukpąbi (N) ground beef, hamburger
tanó yúdabišį (N) Friday
tapnápsijabi (N) football
tapškáda (VI) to play baseball, to play ball
tapú; tapó (N) cheek
taspáhu (N) hawthorn bush
tasíde (N) ruminant tail
taspá (N) apple
taspá cogádu co'úbabi (N) apple pie
taspá ǧí (N) orange
taspá ǧí hįšmá (N) peach

taspá ǧí tóta (VI) lemon
taspá pestóstona (N) pear
tašáge (N) ruminant hooves
tašnáheja (N) striped gopher
tašnáheja akída hąwí (N) October
tatága (N) buffalo
tatágabina (N) buffalo herd
tatágašina (N) buffalo robe
tatága cągáha (N) buffalo corral, fence
tatága ohpáye (N) buffalo jump
tatógana (N) antelope
tatók'ana (N) butterfly
táwa (VS) to be one's, to own it
tawácį ecéduší (VS) to be stupid (lit., his mind is not right)
tawíju (N) his wife
    mitáwįju; mitáwį "my wife"
    nitáwįju; nitáwį "your wife"
tawíjutų (VT) to have a wife
tawóyude ~ wóyude (N) food
tayúza (VT-Y) to control him/her/it
tayúkašį (VT-N) to be reluctant to, dread it
tažúškatąga (N) horsefly
ta'ó (VT) to wound him/her/it
ta'óbi (N) wound
tága (VS) to be big, large
tągágu (N) her younger sister
    mitąga "my younger sister"
    nitąga "your younger sister"
tągán (ADV) outside
táguna (N) his older sister
    mitákena "my older sister"
    nitákena "your older sister"
tąkšícu (N) his younger sister
    mitákši "my younger sister"
    nitákši "your younger sister"
tąníjana (N) gnat, sand fly
tą'į (VS) to be visible
tą'íši (VS) to be lost, out of sight
téhą (ADV) long ago
téhąda (ADV) long ago, for a long time
téhąduwa; tehąda (ADV) a long distance, far
téhąn (ADV) far away
Téhąn Nakóda (N) Stoney Nakoda person or nation

tehápadahą; téhądahą (ADV) far from over there
teȟíga (VI) to be hard, difficult, critical
teȟína (VT) to love someone
teȟíšį (VI) 1) to be easy; 2) to be cheap
teȟíšįyą (ADV) easily
teȟíya (ADV) with difficulty
teȟíya k'ú (VT) to give someone a hard time
teȟpí (N) buckskin
teȟpíhąba (N) hide moccasins
teȟpí sąksája (N) buckskin dress
téjana (VS) to be young, new
temní (VS) to sweat
tí (VI) to live, dwell
tíbi (N) house, dwelling
tída; cída (N) home
tída kní (VI) to return home
tigáǧes'a (N) carpenter
tijáǧabi (N) sundance
timáhen (ADV) inside
timáhentahą (ADV) from indoors, from the inside
timágini (VT) to visit one's relative
timáni (VI) to visit
timnógu (N) her older brother
    mitímno "my older brother"
    nitímno "your older brother"
tín (ADV) inside a dwelling (often pronounced *cín*)
tiyám (ADV) towards home
tiyóba (N) door
tiyóbaska (N) police (lit., white door)
tiyóba įyúšpena (N) doorknob
tizí (N) belly
ti'ágam (N) roof
ti'įktu (N) arson, a house in flames
ti'óda (N) town, village
ti'ódatąga (N) city
ti'ókada (VIMP) to be a hot dwelling
ti'ókun (N) cellar, cold storage room
ti'óšijamna (VIMP) to be a smelly dwelling
ti'ósni (VIMP) to be a cold dwelling
ti'óšpaye (N) a group of relatives, an extended family
ti'úma (N) room
tįknámųmųna (N) partridge
típšina (N) wild turnip
típšinašaša (N) beet, beets
tó (VS) to be blue, green
tóga (N) enemy
togá (ADV) before, ahead of time (N) chief
togáda (ADV) ahead, front, in the future
togáhe (ADV) in the first place, the first
togáheȟ (ADV) the very first one
togáheya (ADV) the first one, in first place
togáȟ (ADV) ahead of time
togáȟtani (ADV) early evening
togám (ADV) in front, ahead
togápa (N) first-born child
tóȟtįyą (VS) to be purple
tokána (N) grey fox
toká (ADV) differently
tokáȟtįyą (ADV) quite differently
tokáyą (ADV) differently
tokšú (VT) to haul it
tósaba (VS) to be dark blue, navy blue
tosą (VS) to be light blue
tošá (VS) to be purple
totóna (VS) to be light blue
tugášina (N) 1) Grandfather; 2) Creator
tugášicu (N) his/her grandfather
    mitúgaši "my grandfather"
    nitúgaši "your grandfather"
tugášicu-tąga (N) his/her great-grandfather
tugígina (N) snail
tuȟmáǧa (N) bee
tuȟmáǧatąga (N) bumblebee
tuȟmáǧa cesní (N) honey (lit., bee feces)
tušú (N) tipi pole
tutá (VS) to be sour
tutú (VS) to be slobbering, have a messy behind
tų́ (VT) 1) to wear it, put it on; 2) to bear, deliver, give birth to him/her/it
tų́ (N) pus
tų́bi (VS) to be born
tųškácu (N) his/her nephew
    mitų́ška "my nephew"
    nitų́ška "your nephew"
tųwícu (N) his/her aunt (father's sister)
    mitų́wi "my aunt"
    nitų́wi "your aunt"

tužą́co (N) his niece (male speaker)
    mitų́žą "my niece"
    nitų́žą "your niece"
t'á (VS) to die, be dead
t'at'á (VS) to be numb, paralyzed

U, Ų

ú (VI) to come here
ubížade (N) barn swallow
ų́ (VI) to be
ų́ (VT-N) to wear it
ų́ca (VT) to imitate him/her/it
ųgíyeȟabi (PRO) us ourselves
ųgíyešį (PRO) it is not us
ųjí (N) Grandmother! (form of address)
ųjímąka (N) grandmother earth
ųká (VOC) Grandfather!
ųká (ENCL) counterfactual, it is supposed to happen but did not
ųkáš (PART) optative, I wish, if only
ųkcékiğa (N) magpie
ų́kšukšuna (N) beans
ų́kšuna (N) bullet
ų́na (VT) to wear it (e.g., as when a baby is wearing it)
ų́s (POST) using it, because of it
ųspé (VS) to learn on one's own, acquire a skill (N) axe
ųspékiya (VT) to teach him/her
ų́š (PART) I wish, if only
ų́ši (VS) to be pitiful
ų́šiga (VS) to be poor, pitiful
ų́šigiya (ADV) pitifully, humbly
ų́šina (VT) to pity him/her
ųwą́šį (ADV) still
ųzé (N) buttocks
ųzį́kpakįda (N) toilet paper
ųzį́kpakįda (VR) to wipe one's butt
ųzóȟnoga (N) anus, rectum
ųzóžuha (N) pants

W

wá (N) snow
wabámnaya (VI) to iron clothes
wábaha (N) eagle staff
wabáȟta (N) sacred bundle
wacápa (VI) to stab
wacáğa (N) sweetgrass
wacégiya (VI) to pray
wacégiyabi (N) prayer
wací (VI) to dance (N) dance
wacíbi (N) dance
wacís'a (N) dancer
wacį́ (N) mind, plan, goodwill (VI-N) to feel like doing it
wacį́giya (VPOS) to depend on one's own
wacį́ya (VT) to depend on it
wacó'ųba (VI) to bake
wáda (N) canoe
wádagiyą(ya) (N) airplane
wadópa (VI) to paddle
Wadópena; Wadópana (N) Band of Nakoda called the 'Paddlers'
wagágana (N) old woman, lady
wagíc'į (VI) to pack things
wagíyą (N) thunderbird
wagíyą ȟubáhu máza (N) iron wing thunderbird
wağį́ (N) grizzly bear
wahába (N) snowshoe (English calque)
wahą́bi (N) soup, broth
wahíkiyabi (N) 1) yuwipi ceremony, tie up ceremony; 2) radio
wahíyoknąga (N) bottle, glass
wáhįhą (VIMP) to snow
wahį́kpe (N) arrow, flint
wahógų (VI) to give advice, dare
wahóȟpi (N) nest
wahóȟpiya (N) rookery
wahóȟpi agą́n-yąga (VI-N) to nest
wahúkeza (N) spear
waȟcá (N) flower
waȟcánebi (N) decoration
waȟé'ağa (N) mole
waȟpé (N) leaf, tea
waȟpécąni (N) kinnikinnick
waȟpéȟpena (N) flower (with leaves)
waȟpé-ce'aga (N) peppermint
waȟpécağa; waȟpé acáğa (N) iced tea
waȟpé céğa (N) tea pot

waȟpé ǧí wí (N) September
waȟpé wóšma hąwí (N) June
waȟpé tága (N) cabbage
waȟténaši (VI) to hate, dislike him/her/it (e.g., taste, task, person)
waȟ'ákšija (N) bear, grizzly bear
waká (VS) to be holy, mysterious, powerful
wakák'į (N) battery
wakásija (N) bad-spirited being; (VS) to be evil spirited
wakátąga (N) 1) Great Spirit; 2) God, Holy Spirit
wakátąga cįhíktu (N) Jesus
wakáya (ADV) in a holy way
wakíbaži (N) grudge
wakmúhaza (N) corn
wakmúhazaskuya (N) sweetcorn
wakmúha (N) gourd rattle
wakpá (N) river
waktá (VI) to be expecting, alert, on the lookout, aware of
waktá ų (VI) to be anticipating it, anxious, alert
waktáši (ADV) carelessly
waktáya (ADV) in anticipation
wakté wacíbi (N) scalp or victory dance
wak'į (N) backpack
wak'ígitų (VI) to carry things on the back
wak'į táwa (VI-N) to be saddled
wamánųs'a (VI) to be a thief (N) robber
wamákamani (N) bear
wamákaška (N) creature, animal
wamní (N) eagle
wamní įpíyaga wací (N) eagle belt dance
wamnónija (N) orphan
wamnónija hąwí (N) March (because orphans often died at the end of winter)
wamnúška (N) ant, bug, insect
wamnúškaša (N) flea
wamnúška hįšmášmą (N) caterpillar
wamnúška mnaská (N) bed bug
wamnúška pašáša (N) red ant
wamnúška sapsábina (N) cricket
wamnúška-wíyą (N) ladybug (calque from English)
waná (ADV) already, now
wanágaš (ADV) long ago
wanáǧi (N) spirit (i.e., of someone else)
wanáǧi núba ~ waǧínųba (N) homosexual (lit., two spirits)
wanáǧi wacíbi (N) northern lights (lit., the spirits are dancing)
wanáȟ'ųšį (VI) to disobey
wanéyas'ą (ADV) throughout the winter, all winter
waníta (VS) to be vigorous
waníyedu (N) winter
waníja (VS) to be gone, to be dead
wanúȟ (ADV) maybe
wapá (VI) to bark
wapáda (VI) to butcher meat
wapáha (N) cap, hat, bonnet
wapíwacį (VS) to be clean
wasáza (VS) to be ill-tempered
wasképana (VI) to be a white person (N)
waskúya (N) berries
wasnókya (CTK); **wasnóhya** (PR, OM) (VI) to be clever, knowledgeable
wasnókya įc'ína; wasnóhya įc'ína (VR) to consider oneself as knowledgeable
wasnókyeši (VI) to be stupid (lit., he does not know things)
wasú (N) hail
wasú hįhá (VIMP) to be hailing
wašáša (N) berries
wašáša wí (N) July
Wašíju (N) 1) minor spirit, deity; 2) Caucasian (VS) to be Caucasian
Wašíjusaba (N) Black man, African
Wašíjusaba wíyą (N) Black woman, African
wašíju tíbi (N) framed house
wašínįc'ina (VR) to behave like a white person
wašíkna (VI) to be bereaved
wašmú (N) melting snow
wašná (N) 1) dried goods, pemmican; 2) fat, grease, lard
wašpáyą (VI) to cook
wašpáyes'a (N) cook, chef
wašpá'įc'iya (VR) to cook for oneself
wašté (VS) to be good, nice, nice-looking
waštégina (VT) to enjoy, be pleased with it
waštéjaga (VS) to be kind, good-natured

waštémna (VS) to smell good
wašténa (VT) to like him/her/it
wašʼáke (ADV) unbearably
watápe (VT) to hunt buffalo; (N) elderly man
watéȟina (VI) to be stingy
watéjana (VS) to be sort of young
watókana (VS) to be wild, untamed
wayáco wįcá (N) judge (male)
wayáco wíyą (N) judge (female)
wayáhoda (N) oats (lit., the thing one chokes on)
wayáwa (VI-Y) to read
wayáwa tíbi (N) school
wayáwa-wįcakiye (N) school teacher
wayúpi (VI-Y) to be good at it
wayúžaža (VT-Y) to wash by scrubbing
Wazíȟe (N) Cypress Hills (place)
wazíya (N) Santa Claus
wazíyam (N) north
Wazíyam wįcášta (N) Inuit person or nation
waʼáhope ~ wóʼahope (VI) to show respect for something
waʼákinija; wakínija (VI) to debate, argue
waʼákni (VI) to bring back home
waʼáʼiʼa (VI) to gossip
waʼáʼiʼabi (N) gossip
waʼécų (VI-N) to hex, to do things against people
waʼíçaȟye (N) farmer
waʼókma (N) credit
waʼókmabi waká (N) email
waʼóyabi (N) paper, letter
waʼóyabi tága (N) book
waʼúcana (N) monkey
waʼúspekiya, waʼúspe (N) teacher
waʼúspewįcakiya (N) male teacher
waʼúspewįyąkiya (N) female teacher
waʼúšina (VI) to pity people, to be kind to people
wągá (INTERJ) as if (it was true), irreality marker
wága (AUX) repetitive
wągán (ADV) above
wągádahą (ADV) from above
wągáduwa (ADV) way above, way up there
wągíciknagabi (VI) to see each other
wája (ADV) once, one time
wąyága (VT-Y) to see him/her/it

wąyákʼi (VT) to go and check on him/her/it
wąží (NUM, ART) 1) one; 2) a, an
wąžíkšina (ADV) one by one
wąžína (NUM) only one
wąʼíçʼiknaga (VR) to see oneself
wé (N) blood
wédu (N) spring
weȟáȟa (VS) to bleed constantly, to have a hemorrhage
wésije (VS, N) to have a blood poisoning; blood poisoning
wéskuya (N) diabetes
Wé wįcášta (N) Blood person or nation
wí (N) sun, moon
wicáguǧa (N) road builder
wída (N) island
wídagiya (N) small island
wíhinąpa (N) east
wikcémna (NUM) ten
wikcémnana (NUM) only ten
wištó; įkcé wištó (N) common tent
wiwí (N) swamp, marsh
wiwína (VI) to be swampy
wíyaga (N) feather
wíyaga wapáha (N) feather hat
wíyaga wapáha sįdé yuké (N) war bonnet with trailer
wiyákpa (VS) to be shiny, to shine
wiyáska (N) sand
wiyéknašį (ADV) very, a lot
wiyódahą (ADV) noon, midday, afternoon
wiyódahąm (N) south
wiyóhąbam (N) east
wiyóȟpeyam (N) west
wiyópeya (VT) to sell it
wiyóti; wiʼóti (N) tipi, dwelling
wiyóʼesʼa (ADV) throughout the afternoon, all afternoon
wíyukjašį (VI-Y) to be bold, brave
wíbazuką (N) saskatoon berries
Wíbazuką wakpá (N) Saskatoon (place)
wįcá (N) man, human (in compounds) (VS) to be a man
wįcábaǧe (N) announcer
wįcágasoda (VT) to massacre people

wįcáȟniȟni (N) smallpox
wįcáȟpi (N) star
wįcáȟpi éstenaȟ (N) Venus
wįcáȟpi iyúšna (N) big dipper
wįcáȟtįyąna; wįcáȟtįyą (N) old man
wįcákta (VI) to become manly
wįcákte (N) killer
wįcák'u (VI) to give things to people
wįcák'ubi (N) give-away ceremony
wįcánuȟnugena (N) pumpkin
wįcášta(bi) (N) person, man (SG), people (PL)
Wįcášta Hąska (N) Tall Man (personal name)
wįcášta tága (N) giant
wįcášta wįcáȟpi (N) star people
wįcáteja (N) new, young man
wįcáwaką (N) Holy man
wįcáwodes'a (N) cannibal, man-eater
wįcáyawabi (N) census
wįcą́ (N) raccoon
wįcíjana (N) girl
wįcíšta yazą́ hąwí (N) March
wįcógądu (ADV) midwinter
wįcógądu hąwí (N) December
wįcógądu sųgágu hąwí (N) November
wįcóh'ąge (N) way of life, custom, tradition
wįcóni (N) human life, human ways, spirit; ghost
wįcóni wašté (VS) to be in good health
wįcóyazą (N) illness
wįcóyazą tíbi (N) hospital
wįcó'i'e; wįcó'i'abi (N) language, word
wíc'į (N) leather
wíc'į hųská (N) chaps
wída (VI) to crawl
wíduka (VS) to urinate, defecate, to relieve oneself
wíhamna (VI) to seek a vision, to dream
wįjáka (VI) to be honest, to tell the truth
wįjákiya (ADV) truthfully, honestly
wįkni (N) fat, grease, lard, gas, oil
wįkniskana (N) lard
wįkni pedį́žąžą (N) oil lantern
wįkóške (N, VS) adolescent girl, to be an adolescent girl
wįkta (VI) to become womanly
wįkúwa (VI) to chase, bother, flirt with a woman

witéȟi hąwí (N) January
wįtka (N) egg
wįkta šagíyabi (N) Easter
wįtkó (VS) 1) to be contrary; 2) to be crazy
wįtkógaǧa (VI) to clown
wįtkógaǧe wacíbi; wįtkógaǧa wacíbi (N) clown dance
Wįtkógawį (N) Crazy Woman (personal name)
wįtkótkoga (VI) to be somehow crazy
wįtkótkoga i'á (VI) to talk backwards, as in a clown dance ceremony
wįtkótkoyaken (N) in a crazy manner, crazily
wįwázija (N) widow
wįwín'ų (VI) to crawl all over
wíyą (VS, N) to be a woman; woman
wįyą́ša (N) penny
wįyą́teja (N) 1) new, young woman; 2) cranberries
wįyą́wašoga (N) nickel
wíyena (N) 1) female animal; 2) doe
wíyįkta (VI) to turn effeminate
wįyúkcą (VI-Y) to think
wíyų (VT) to use it
wo (ENCL) singular male imperative
wócegiya (N) church service
wócegiya óȟ'ą ų́ (VI) to be Christian
wócegiya wįcášta (N) minister
wócegiye (N) religion
wócį (VT) to beg for something
wócįs'a (N) beggar
wóda (VI) to eat
wódabi (N) feast
wóga; wóǧa (N) grasshopper
wogákana (N) pretty woman
wógidą (VS) to get honours
wógijišpi (VT) to pick berries for him/her
wogíksuya wódabi (N) Memorial feast
wóguǧa (VS) to be beautiful, attractive
wóhą (VI) to cook by boiling
wohéna (N) cook
wóhįste (N) plume, down feathers
wóknaga (VI-POS) to tell one's own story, to discuss it
wóknagabi (N) story
woksá (VI) to break one's words, to betray

wókšu (VI) to sow, to plant
wókšus'a (N) farmer, agriculturist
wók'u (VT) to feed someone, something
wóne (VI) to look for (unspecific)
wópetu (VI) to buy (N) merchant
wópina (N) gratitude, thanks, gratefulness
wópina k'ú (VT) to give gratitude
wopíyabi (N) burial
wópiyena (N) medicine bundle
wóšma (VS) to be dense, tightly packed
wóšpi (VT) to pick berries
wótijağa (N) medicine lodge, sun dance
wótijağa anówąbi (N) quarterly singing
woťá (VI) to die in a distance
wówaȟtani (N) sin
wówaši (N) job, work, occupation, working place
wówįcak'u (N) rations
wówįȟ'aga (VS) to be funny
wóyapte (N) table scraps
wóyude; tawóyude (N) food
wožábi (N) gravy, stew
wó'ahope (VI) to respect, show respect for
wo'íye (N) cloth offering
wó'ošija (N) rattlesnake

Y

yá (VI-Y) to go away from here
yahóda (VI-Y) to choke, gag on it
yaȟéba (VT) to drink it all
yaȟnéja (VT) to tear it with the teeth
yaȟtága (VT-Y) to bite him/her/it
yaȟúgabi (N) peanut
yajúsina (VT) to belittle him/her
yaksá (VT-Y) to bite off
yámni (NUM) three
yámnigiya (ADV) three by three
yámnina (NUM) only three
yamnúğa (VT-Y) to crush with the teeth
yapá (VI) to put in his/her/its mouth
yapcá (VI-Y) to swallow
yašpá (VT-Y) to break, crack open with the teeth (e.g., a peanut)
yašpúya (VS) to be itchy
yatá (VI-Y) to chew it

yatká (VT-Y) to drink
yaťá (VT) to kill by biting, to kill by inhaling or ingesting poison
yazą́ (VS) to be sick
ya'íškada (VT-Y) to tease, play tricks on him/her
ya'óniya (VT) to congratulate, honour him/her/it
yągá; yįgá (VI-N) to be seated on (AUX) to remain doing, do continuously
yubéhą (VT-Y) to twist it
yucába (VI-Y) to be trotting
yucápcabadugen (ADV) to be sort of trotting along
yucéya (VT-Y) to cause to cry
yúda (VT-Y) to eat something
yudáyą (VT) to repair something broken, ameliorate it
yuwóguga (VT) to decorate it
yuhá (VT-Y) to have it, carry it
yuhókšu (VT-Y) to wreck, dismantle it
yuȟcína (VT-Y) to tear it (e.g., cloth)
yuȟíja (VT-Y) to wake him/her
yuȟná (VI-Y) to make a rattling sound
yuȟnéja (VT-Y) to tear it with the hand
yuȟnóga (VT) to make a hole in it with an instrument, or with the hand
yukába (VT-Y) to catch a rapid or flying object with the hand
yuką́ (VI) to exist
yuksá (VT) to cut off with a tool (e.g., scissors)
yupíya (VS) to be valuable (ADV) skillfully, in a good manner
yusíja (VT-Y) 1) to wake him/her up by shaking; 2) to destroy it
yusíjabi (N) damage
yusmága (N) crease
yusní (VT-Y) to milk a cow; to squeeze the liquid out
yús náyuza (VT-Y) to hold, clinch, grasp on it
yuškóba (VT-Y) to bend it by hand
yušná (VT-Y) to ring a bell
yušnóhą (VI-Y) to drag, slide it
yušnóšnoga (VT) to dismantle
yušpá (VT-Y) to open up
yušpí (VT-Y) to pick berries
yuštą́ (VT-Y) to let it go, to loosen it
yųš'íyeya (VT-Y) to frighten him/her/it

yutóką (VT-Y) to make it differently, to change it manually, to disguise it
yut'á (VT-Y) to kill by strangulation
yut'íza (VT) to tight it up by stretching
yuwáką (VT) to bless him/her, to impose hands on him/her
yuwákąbi (N) blessings
yuwášteya (ADV) in a tasteful manner
yuwášte (VT-Y) to give it a good taste
yuwídana (ADV) a small amount
yúza (VT-Y) to catch, hold, apprehend him/her/it
yuzíja (VT-Y) to stretch it manually
yužáža (VT-Y) to wash by scrubbing (e.g., clothes)
yužága (VT-Y) to mistreat, pick on him/her/it
yužį́ (VI-Y) to squint
yužúžu (VT-Y) to take it apart, to strip him/her/it off
yužúžu wacíbi (N) stripper
yužúžu wíyą (N) female stripper
yu'į́ktų (VT) to turn it on (e.g., light)

Z

záptą (NUM) five
záptąȟ (ADV) five times
záptąna (NUM) only five
zezéya (ADV) hanging down
zí (VS) to be brown, dark yellow, tan
zibéna (VS) to be thin
zitkána (N) bird
zitkánato (N) bluebird
zizíbena (N) cloth, ribbon, fabric
zizíbena cuwį́knąga (N) T-shirt
zizímnąna (VS) to be thin
zizína (N) gold
zuyá (VI) to go on the war path
zuyés'a (N) warrior
zuyés'a tíbi (N) warrior lodge society

Ž

žé (DEM) that there
žéca (VS) to be of a certain kind
žécedu (VS) to be like that (ADV) in that way, thus
žécedušį (ADV) in an incorrect way
žécen (ADV) in that way; then, so
žecéš (ADV) only that
žéci (ADV) around there, over there
žéciya (ADV) over there, over that way
žécų (VI) to do that
žedáhą; žedą́hą (ADV) from there, from it (VS) to be from there
žehá (ADV) just then, at a certain point in the past
žehą́du (ADV) at that time
žehą́duga (ADV) about that time
žehą́ga (N) end of a story
žehą́geȟi (ADV) only that far off
žehą́naga (CONJ) and so now
žén (ADV) there
žená (DEM) those there
ženą́ga (VS) to be enough
žewós (PRO, DEM) those two
žeyá (VI) to say that
žé'ųs (ADV) that is why
žó (VI) to whistle
žubína (N) pile